NOTABLE SOUTHERN FAMILIES

VOLUME I

COMPILED BY
ZELLA ARMSTRONG

JANAWAY PUBLISHING, INC.
Santa Maria, California

Notice

In many older books, foxing (or discoloration) occurs and, in some instances, print lightens with wear and age. Reprinted books, such as this, often duplicate these flaws, notwithstanding efforts to reduce or eliminate them. The pages of this reprint have been digitally enhanced and, where possible, the flaws eliminated in order to provide clarity of content and a pleasant reading experience.

Notable Southern Families. Volume I

Copyright © 1918, by Zella Armstrong

Originally published
Chattanooga, Tennessee
1918

Reprinted by:

Janaway Publishing, Inc.
732 Kelsey Ct.
Santa Maria, California 93454
(805) 925-1038
www.janawaygenealogy.com

2015

ISBN: 978-1-59641-362-7

Made in the United States of America

CONTENTS

ARMSTRONG
BANNING
BLOUNT
BROWNLOW
CALHOUN
DEADERICK
GAINES
HOWARD
KEY
LUTTRELL
LYLE

McADOO
McGHEE
McMILLAN
PHINIZY
POLK
SEVIER
SHIELDS
STONE
TURNLEY
VanDYKE

Copyright, 1918, by Zella Armstrong

FOREWORD

The Southern States were settled by three great waves of emigration, —Cavalier, Scotch-Irish and Huguenot. These types retain their characteristics to this day, perhaps, largely, because groups of relatives, friends or neighbors settled in one section and gave a dominant tinge in creed, and church, and custom. The sons and daughters of these families married, and creed and custom grew stronger from year to year. Thus the Scotch-Irish, a people of Scotch origin, though living in Ireland for many years before the American emigration, settled in certain parts of Virginia, North and South Carolina, and what is now East Tennessee, in great numbers and impressed their Presbyterian faith upon their posterity.

In the chapters of this book examples will be given of each of these groups—Cavalier, Scotch-Irish and Huguenot.

The early history of these well known Southern families is here presented, being published, at least in collected form, for the first time. The compiler takes no credit for authorship, as genealogy is not a science of invention. The facts, however, are clearly stated, and in the case of each family each line may be brought down to the present day from the earliest settler in America.

The Colonial, Revolutionary, 1812 and War Between the States record of each family is set forth succinctly. No space has been given to tradition, though many traditions in the families mentioned are interesting and doubtless could be followed up and proved. Many histories have been consulted and many family documents studied, only reliable records being used.

Though the chief endeavor of these chapters is to show the Colonial or Revolutionary settler and his posterity, a brief line of his progenitors is given in some cases, as the origin of name and family is always interesting.

NOTABLE SOUTHERN FAMILIES

Hundreds of histories, court records and family documents have been examined in the preparation of this volume, and the following family authorities have been consulted:

Robert A. J. Armstrong, Mrs. Martha Turnley Armstrong, Mrs. Penelope J. Allen (who prepared the Deadrick and VanDyke data), Pearson Banning (who prepared the Banning data), Mrs. Virginia E. McNaught (who prepared the Gaines data), Mrs. Louise Sevier Giddings, Mrs. J. F. Alexander, S. G. Heiskell, Calvin M. McClung (who prepared the McGhee data), John A. Kelly, the late Parmenas Taylor Turnley, John Bell Brownlow (who prepared the Brownlow data), the late Oscar K. Lyle, and many others.

Notable Southern Families

ARMSTRONG

The family of Armstrong derives its name from the following circumstance: An ancient King of Scotland, had his horse killed under him in battle. Fairbairn, his armor-bearer immediately grasped the King by the thigh and set him upon another horse. For the assistance at such a critical moment the King rewarded him with lands on the border, and to perpetuate the memory of so important a service, as well as the extraordinary manner in which it was performed, the King gave him the appelation Armstrong and assigned him for a crest an armed hand and arm grasping a leg in armor. This is the left hand.

The hero of the exploit, "Siward, the Armstrong," Earl of Northumberland, first of the name and ancestor of the renowned Border family of Armstrong, was one of these stalwart figures who will never pass away from the pages of history and tradition. In his physical strength and prowess, wit and wisdom, loftiness of character, defiance of danger and death, he was remarkable. He was undoubtedly a Christian, for he built the minster of York, but he reminds us of those old heroes of the Edda, from whom his ancestors were said to have descended. He acquired honor for England by his successful conduct in the only foreign enterprise undertaken during the reign of Edward the Confessor. (Johannes Brinston, Saxe Gramatieur, George Stephens). Duncan, King of Scotland, was a prince of gentle disposition, and lacked the genius requisite for governing so turbulent a country as Scotland, and one so infested by the intrigues and animosities of the great Macbeth. Siward embraced, by Edward's orders, the protection of the royal distressed family. He marched an army into Scotland and having defeated Macbeth in battle, restored Malcolm, Duncan's son, to the throne of his ancestors. This service, added to his former connection with the royal family of Scotland, brought great accession to the authority of Siward in the North.

Soon after his return from this campaign he was attacked by a fatal disorder. As he felt his end approaching he said to his attendants, "Lift me up that I may die on my legs like a soldier, not couching like a cow. Dress me with my coat of mail, cover my head with my helmet, put my shield on my left arm and my battle axe in my right hand that I may die under arms."

Ingulf's record of his death reads as follows:

"In the year of our Lord 1056, Siward the brave earl of Northumberland, departed this life and was buried in the cloister of the monastery of Saint Mary, which he had built without the walls of the city of York."

Siward was a Dane and he was much beloved by the Northumbrians, who were chiefly of a Danish extraction.

Siward married twice. His son by the first wife, called Young Siward in "Macbeth", was killed by Macbeth in the battle of Dunssinmore. Siward married for his second wife Aelfled, daughter of Alfred Earl of Northumberland and through her, acquired that title and great authority The Northumbrians were of Danish extraction and rejoiced at being ruled by the great Earl who was of Danish blood. His son by Aelfled, succeeded to the title and his daughter by Aelfled, married David I, King of Scotland.

Here is a list of the different forms of Siward's name. In the Irish records he was called the Strong, in the Terwinney records he was called Fayborn and the Armstrong; in old manuscripts brought over by Armstrongs to North Carolina from Londonberry, Ireland, in 1711, he was called the Strong.

In the old records the names most frequently given to the Armstrongs are Rolland, Geoffry and Robert, all showing the ancient Norman extraction. Robert is the name most frequently used in every branch of the family to this day.

From Siward the Strong Arm the Armstrong clan is descended. The ancient border family grew and flourished and though, in the years, and centuries that followed they roamed afar, even as Siward himself roamed from his native land, they retained the spirit of Siward and were always bold, courageous, war like and high principled.

Their adventures in the history of the Border are many and interesting. They fought in every war and after their emigration to America they participated in every war undertaken by the United States, from Indian fighting before the Revolution to the present time.

In the fifteenth century, Thomas Armstrong, fifth Lord of Maingerton, had four sons, of whom the eldest, Alexander Armstrong was the sixth Lord. He had seven sons. Thomas the eldest succeeded and was Seventh Lord Maingerton, but the second son was called John Armstrong, of Gilnockie. All the Armstrongs in Ireland in the seventeenth century are descended from him, and all the American Armstrongs, who trace through the Scotch-Irish clan. He was Robin Hood of the Border, and the stories of his exploits run through all Scottish literature. Sir Walter Scott makes frequent reference to him.

ARMSTRONG

All descendants whose names are recorded in the following pages are eligible to the Societies of the Colonies, Revolution, Mexican War, 1812 and the War between the States. It is an interesting fact that in the War between the States, in which the Armstrongs of the Southern Clan fought on each side of the great conflict, that one Regiment of Tennesseans was made up largely of Armstrongs and their kin, and that every officer was an Armstrong by name. Siward the Strong Arm therefore must be sleeping peacefully in his tomb after his eight centuries to think that his descendants continue the game.

To return however, to Siward's immediate posterity. In the time of James the First of England, great bodies of land in Province of Ulster, Ireland, were forfeit to the crown in consequence of the rebellion of Tyrone and Tirconnell and these lands were offered to the Scotch and English people for settlement.

Thousands of the Border Scots, including many Armstrongs, old Siward's descendants, accepted the offer and went to the new land. It was estimated in 1638 that there were forty thousand Scotchmen in Ulster.

These are the people who became known subsequently as the Scotch-Irish, though they had in most instances not a drop of Irish blood. A hundred years or more they lived in Ulster and then early in seventeen hundred an emigration to America began.

ROBERT ARMSTRONG THE FIRST

Robert Armstrong emigrated from the Province of Ulster, County Antrim, Ireland, to America in 1735, bringing with him his wife, Alice Calhoun Armstrong, his four year old son Robert Armstrong, the Second, and an older son, John Armstrong. Robert Armstrong the First was born in Ireland, Province of Ulster, County Antrim, about 1700. He married about 1728 Alice Calhoun (born in Ulster, County Antrim, about 1705). She was of the family that produced Patrick Calhoun and John C. Calhoun. She was a sister of James Calhoun, the emigrant of the Calhoun family and an aunt of Patrick Calhoun.

The Calhouns emigrated from Ireland at almost the same time with the Armstrongs going first to the same location in Pennsylvania selected by the Armstrongs, and from there moving South to Abbeyville District, South Carolina, an example closely followed by the Armstrongs. The connection between the families was close for several generations and when John C. Calhoun was Secretary of State he appointed to office in Tennessee his cousins, Robert Armstrong, the Third, and Robert Armstrong Houston, as will be noted later. The Calhoun family is given in another chapter of this book.

NOTABLE SOUTHERN FAMILIES

Robert Armstrong the First, who came to Pennsylvania in 1735, landed in Philadelphia, went into one of the interior counties on the Susquehannah River, and resided there for some years. From Pennsylvania, some time previous to 1760, the family went to Abbeyville District South Carolina, now Anderson County, where Alice Calhoun Armstrong's Calhoun kinsmen had preceded them by a short time.

Robert Armstrong, the First, died in Abbeyville District, South Carolina, about the year 1775, being close to his seventy-fifth year. Alice Calhoun Armstrong is not mentioned again in the family record and the date and place of her death are not known. Her older sons, John Armstrong and Robert Armstrong, the Second, were born in Ireland. Her younger children were born in Pennsylvania.

All the Armstrongs and their connections were Presbyterians and it is noted that a sister of Robert Armstrong, the First, whose first name is not given married ——————— Holmes, a Protestant preacher. It is recorded in the family Bible, that Robert Armstrong and his son Robert Armstrong, "were of patriotic spirit and most resolutely withstood, in the Carolinas, the aggressions and cruelties of the Tories."

The children of Robert Armstrong, the First, and Alice Calhoun Armstrong were nine, namely:

(1) John Armstrong.
(2) Robert Armstrong.
(3) James Armstrong.
(4) Benjamin Armstrong.
(5) Kate Armstrong.
(6) Hannah Armstrong.
(7) A daughter, name not known.
(8) Alice Armstrong.
(9) A daughter, name not known.

(1) John Armstrong born in Ireland about 1729 married and settled in Georgia. A large family comes through him.

(2) Robert Armstrong, the Second, born in Ireland in 1731 married Margaret Cunningham in 1767. Died in 1796. A sketch of him follows:

(3) James Armstrong married and settled in Louisiana.

(4) Benjamin Armstrong, married and settled in Tennessee.

(5) Kate Armstrong, married ——————Stuart (sometimes spelled Stewart) and settled in South Carolina.

(6) Hannah Armstrong married ——————— Summers and settled in Kentucky.

(7) ——————— Armstrong, married James Donaldson and settled in North Carolina.

8

ARMSTRONG

(8) Alice Armstrong, (named for her mother, Alice Calhoun) married ——————— Houston, and settled in South Carolina and later in Tennessee. A large family comes through her. She had several children, among others, Robert Armstrong Houston, born in Abbeyville District, South Carolina 1765, died April 2, 1834, who was appointed by Secretary of War John C. Calhoun, to the position of United States Commissioner in the Indian Treaty at the same time that Robert Armstrong, the Third, was appointed United States Surveyor. This was for the Indian Treaty of 1819.

Robert Armstrong Houston, married Margaret Davis (or Dallas) and had four daughters and at least two sons, Alice, Amelia, Malinda, Rutelia, James and Horace Houston. Of the daughters, each one, by a coincidence, comes into the Armstrong Family again, either by her own marriage or by the marriage of a descendant.

Alice Houston, the daughter of Robert Houston, married James McMillan and had: Robert McMillan (who married twice and had by his first wife, Martha Isbell, two children: Alice McMillan who is not married and James Benjamin McMillan who married Cynthia Cunningham and had William Cunningham McMillan, Alice McMillan, Rutelia Isbell McMillan, Mary McMillan, and Kitty B. McMillan; and had by his second wife, Missouri Isbell, two children: Robert Houston McMillan, Second, who married Sarah Gray and left Robert Houston McMillan, Third, who died young, Allen Gray McMillan and Catherine McMillan; and Fannie McMillan who married J. F. Wikle, and left Robert McMillan Wikle and Jesse Wikle); Alice McMillan (who married Major Gaines McMillan as his second wife and had no children); and James White McMillan (who married Laura Hendrick and had Julia Hardin McMillan, Amelia Alice McMillan, Annie L. McMillan, Mary Lurina McMillan, William Hendrick McMillan, Nannie Missouri McMillan, James White McMillan, Second, Luke Hampton McMillan, Laura Houston McMillan, Frances Louise McMillan and Frank Alexander McMillan).

Amelia Houston, second daughter of Robert Houston and his wife Margaret Davis or Dallas Houston married her cousin, Drury Paine Armstrong and is mentioned later.

Malinda Houston, third daughter of Robert Houston and his wife, Margaret Davis or Dallas married a ——————— McNutt.

Rutelia Houston, fourth daughter of Robert Houston and his wife Margaret Davis or Dallas Houston, married James Isbell (see Howard Family) and had Margaret Isbell (who married Major Joseph Hardie, but had no children); Fannie Isbell (who married William Boynton and had William Boynton, Second, and Dwight Boynton); Houston Isbell (who never married); Thomas Livingston Isbell (who married Mattie J. Norris and had Rutelia Houston

Isbell, who married W. H. Lane and has one child, Rutelia Isbell Lane); and Alice Isbell (who married her cousin William Park Armstrong and had William Park Armstrong, Second, who married Rebekah Purvis and has children and lives at Princeton, New Jersey; Houston Armstrong, who married Mina Lamar and lives in Selma, Alabama; Margaret Hardie Armstrong, who married Ainslee Power Ardaugh and lives in Orcilla, Canada, and Ann E. Armstrong, who married Thomas Stoo Johnson and lives in New Orleans).

James Houston, the elder son of Robert Houston and his wife, Margaret Davis or Dallas Houston married——————————.

Horace Houston, the Second son of Robert Houston and his wife Margaret Davis or Dallas Houston married ——————.

(9) ————Armstrong, married ————— Henry and settled in West Tennessee.

This completes the list of the children of Robert Armstrong the First. Some of the foregoing information was obtained from papers left by his grandson, the late Drury Paine Armstrong, all being of very great value. In the single instance of the Calhoun information are his notes misleading. He mentions Alice Calhoun as a sister of "the emigrant Patrick Calhoun", whereas the emigrant Calhoun was named James; also Alice Calhoun was a generation older than Patrick who was a son of James, the emigrant, and who had no sister by the name of Alice. It is therefore, very evident that Drury Paine Armstrong in his notes meant to say that Alice Calhoun was a sister of the emigrant James Calhoun.

ROBERT ARMSTRONG, THE SECOND

Robert Armstrong, the Second, son of Robert Armstrong the First and Alice Calhoun Armstrong, was born in Ireland, in County Antrim, Province of Ulster, in 1731. When he was four years old he emigrated to America with his father and mother and at least one older brother, John Armstrong, in the year 1735, and settled with them in an interior County of Pennsylvania on the Susquehanna River. The party had landed in Philadelphia. Some time previous to the year 1760, the exact date not being given, they followed the Calhouns to Abbeyville District South Carolina, where the Calhouns had established a settlement.

In August of 1767 being thirty-six years old, Robert Armstrong, the Second married Margaret Cunningham, whose mother was a McKamy or McCamy and whose father resided about sixty miles above Charleston, S. C., on the Little River.

ARMSTRONG

Robert Armstrong the Second served in the Revolution, and probably before that time, in the Colonial Army. It is of him that the Family Bible speaks in the quotation already given:, "He was of patriotic spirit." He was prominent in the military affairs of the state (South Carolina) for many years. In Heitman's Historical Records, Page 66, Robert Armstrong's name appears as First Lieutenant of the First South Carolina Regiment. This was the regiment made famous by such officers as Colonel Charles Pinckney and Major (afterwards General) Francis Marion.

In the year 1784, with his wife and children, Robert Armstrong the Second, moved from South Carolina to the waters of the Holston, to what is now Washington County, Tennessee. There he lived for three years. In the spring of 1787 he moved again and this time for the last time. He settled on a place five miles east of the present site of Knoxville, Knox County, Tennessee. On this plantation eleven years later, February 28, 1798, he died, leaving his widow, Margaret Cunningham Armstrong who survived him forty years. He is buried in the old family cemetery. His grave though unmarked is the oldest in the lot and a somewhat newer mound beside it is that of Margaret Cunningham Armstrong. Major Shed Armstrong (Ethelred W. Armstrong) remembered being present, a boy of ten, when his grand-mother, Margaret Cunningham Armstrong was buried in this grave beside her husband, who had predeceased her forty years. This establishes the location of the two graves.

Margaret Cunningham Armstrong whose father————Cunningham "resided about sixty miles above Charleston on the Little River and whose mother was a McKamy," was a person of strong and splendid character. She lived to see all her children grown and performing valuable service to the world and to see many of her grandchildren grow up. She had red hair. She died June 3, 1873 being ninety-two years of age. This would establish her birth in the year 1745 and would make her fourteen years her husband's junior. At the date of her marriage 1767, she would have been twenty-two, while Robert Armstrong was already thirty-six. In some of the records she is given as being ninety-seven at the time of her death.

The Cunninghams had removed from Augusta County, Virginia, in 17——to their home on the Little River where they were established in August 1767, the date of Margaret's marriage. (A family of McKamy settled in Virginia in the Lexington District, before the Revolution. A McKamy, Francis McKamy was a native of Ulster and emigrated to America like so many of the Ulstermen in the early part of the eighteenth century. He was the first Presbyterian minister in America. He helped to organize the first Presbyterian Church and planted the germs of the Presbyterian Church in America).

NOTABLE SOUTHERN FAMILIES

Robert Armstrong, the Second, and his wife Margaret Cunningham Armstrong had seven children, four sons and three daughters, namely:

(1) Robert Armstrong, the Third.
(2) Moses Armstrong.
(3) Aaron Armstrong.
(4) John Armstrong.
(5) Mariah Armstrong.
(6) Margaret Armstrong.
(7) Elizabeth Armstrong.

(1) Robert Armstrong, the Third, born 1774, married 1798 Elizabeth Wear. A sketch of him follows:

(2) Moses Armstrong, born August 3, 1787, married Amelia Morrow. His descendants live on the East bank of the Holston River, one mile from the place where his father settled at the Armstrong Ferry. His children were: Lucy (who married William Goddard); Martha (who married James Kennedy); John D. (who married Cynthia Campbell); James Newton Armstrong (who married first Amelia Armstrong and second May Turbeyville); Moses Houston Armstrong (who married Mary Jane Gibson); Aaron Armstrong, (known as Tip, who married Nancy Bell); Margaret Armstrong (who married first Jack Davis and second Jesse Nicodemus); Elizabeth Armstrong, (who married Jack Campbell); Robert Armstrong (who married Polly Fisher); and Alexander Armstrong (who married Patsey Merryman).

(3) Aaron Armstrong, born August 3, 1787, a twin to Moses Armstrong, married Elizabeth Bounds and settled in Tennessee on his father's homestead. His children were Moses Armstrong, the Second (who married Elizabeth J. McMillan) Frank B. Armstrong (who married Eliza White); John W. Armstrong, who married Eliza McMillan); Ethelred W. Armstrong (known as Shed, who married Mattie Carter); James M. Armstrong (who married Pricey Monday); Eliza Armstrong (who married Richard Campbell); Wallace Armstrong (who married Emma Effort); Margaret Armstrong (who married Alfred Ault); Betsy Armstrong (who married Andrew McMillan); Amelia Armstrong (who married her cousin James Newton Armstrong as his first wife); and Martha Armstrong (who married William Kennedy).

(4) John Armstrong born 1777, married 1800 Nancy Weir, a distant kinswoman of Elizabeth Wear, whom his brother Robert Armstrong married, and settled in Indiana. His children were Ambrose Newton Armstrong, married first Nancy Weir and married second Ellen Curry; Alfred Weir Armstrong (who married first Margaret Fulkerson and married second Jane Washfield and married third,

ARMSTRONG

Jane Willett); Pleasant Armstrong, (who was killed by Indians): John C. Armstrong (who married first ——————Spofford and second ——————Webster); Margaret Armstrong (who married John Stonewall); Nancy Armstrong (who married Wilson Smith, but had no children); Martha Armstrong (who married Joseph Landes); Lethia Armstrong (who married Felix Landes); Amanda L. Armstrong (who married Joshua McDonald); Alvira Jane Armstrong (who married Reverand J. P. May); Mary Emmeline Armstrong (who married Thomas McNamee); Robert Edwin Armstrong.

(5) Martha Armstrong, born 1783 married James Churchwell Luttrell (see Luttrell Family) and had six children namely: James Churchwell Luttrell, Fourth; Annie Luttrell who married Joseph Shields Luttrell, Robert Armstrong Luttrell, died young, and Fannie Luttrell, died young.

Of the foregoing: James Luttrell the Second, married Eliza Bell and had six children, (1) James Churchwell Luttrell, Third, (who married Josephine Brooks, (see McMillan Family) and had James Churchwell Luttrell, Fourth, Annie Luttrell who married Joseph Shields and had Josephine Shields who married Leonard Murphey; Libbie Luttrell married Benjamin F. Moore and has Margaret Moore and Benjamin F. Moore, Second; Fannie Luttrell, married—————— Powers; Samuel Bell Luttrell, Jr., who died unmarried; Ernest Luttrell; and Sophy Luttrell married Harry Harmon, Second, and has Harry Harmon, Third); (2) Samuel Bell Luttrell (who married Margaret McClung Swan and had Samuel Bell Luttrell, who died young; Margaret Luttrell, married William E. Sullins and has Samuel Sullins and David Sullins; Jennie Luttrell, married Charles M. Mitchell and has Margaret and Mary Mitchell; Mary Luttrell married Dr. Thomas ap R. Jones and Charles Luttrell died unmarried); (3) Elizabeth Saunders Luttrell (who married Dr. William Morrow and had nine children, James Morrow, Frank Murfree Morrow, Lillie Morrow, Emma Morrow, Sallie Hooper Morrow, Libbie Luttrell Morrow, Ada Murfree Morrow, Walter S. Morrow and Margaret Bell Morrow. Of the foregoing: James Luttrell Morrow married Jane Ewing and their children are: Irene Ewing who married Dr. Essler Hoss, a descendant of John Sevier, Elizabeth Morrow, who married Arthur Timmons, William Morrow, Third, Jane Morrow and Orville left one son William Leigh Morrow, who married Dolly Post. Lillie Morrow married Judge James M. Anderson and has one daughter, Emma Morrow Anderson who married Harold B. Whiteman. Emma Morrow married John B. Atchison and has Thomas Ayres Atcheson, Lillian Morrow Atcheson and Emma Morrow Atcheson. Sallie Hooper Morrow married F. Ludlow Chrystie and has Elizabeth Ludlow Chrystie, Thomas Walter Chrystie and Frances Nicholson

NOTABLE SOUTHERN FAMILIES

Chrystie. Libbie Luttrell Morrow is not married, Ada Murfree Morrow married D. F. Reeves and has Joseph S. Reeves and Daniel F. Carter Reeves, Second, Walter S. Morrow is not married. Margaret Bell Morrow married Clarence B. Simpson and has Isabel Simpson and John Morow Simpson, (4) Martha Armstrong Luttrell, second daughter of James Churchwell Luttrell and Eliza Bell Luttrell married Stokeley Donelson Mitchell and had three children: Mabel W. Mitchell, William M. Mitchell and Libbie Luttrell Mitchell, who married John McMillan Moulden and has John McMillan Moulden, jr., and Margaret Luttrell Moulden. (5) Eliza Bell Luttrell, daughter of James Churchwell Luttrell and Eliza Bell Luttrell married Jesse H. Thomas and had Jesse H. Thomas, jr., and James Luttrell Thomas. (6) Mary M. Luttrell, daughter of James Churchwell Luttrell and Eliza Bell Luttrell married Charles E. Griffith and had four children: Charles E. Griffith, jr., Sallie M. Griffith, Lillian Bell Griffith and a child that died young.

Margaret Luttrell married Matthew Ambrose Gaines, son of Ambrose Gaines (see Gaines Family) and had five children namely: Matthew M. Gaines, Martha Gaines, who married Richard Bearden, Mary Gaines, who married ———————Bearden, Ambrose Gaines, Third, who married Mary Winston Townes and has six children: (1) George Gaines, married and has Ethel Smith Gaines and Katherine Woodville Gaines; (2) Margaret Gaines, married Garland Buffington; (3) Etta Gaines, who married H. B. Hogan; (4) Blanche Gaines, who married F. J. Hoyle; (5) Mary Townes Gaines, who married Reuben S. Payne, and (6) Ambrose Gaines, fourth who married Edith Lucie Jenks and has Margaret Gaines, Ambrose Gaines, Fifth, Edith Gaines, and Mary Townes Gaines, James Luttrell Gaines, (son of Matthew Ambrose Gaines and Margaret Luttrell Gaines) married Belle Porter. He was a gallant officer in the Confederate Army. He had five children namely: Ambrose Porter Gaines, Matthew Gaines, Lillian Gaines, who died young, and James Luttrell Gaines, Second.

Martha Luttrell daughter of James Churchwell Luttrell and Martha Armstrong Luttrell married Richard Bearden.

Amanda Luttrell, daughter of James Churchwell Luttrell and Martha Armstrong Luttrell married Reverend George Horn and had three children, Sarah Horn, married James Newman, James Horn, unmarried, and William Horn, married Kate Kelso.

(6) Margaret Armstrong married John Bounds and supposedly married Thomas Lovelady for her second husband, they moved to Oregon and all trace of the family is lost.

(7) Elizabeth Armstrong married William McKamy and had Robert McKamy who married Jemima Park; Barton McKamy married,———————Robbins; John Armstrong McKamy (who married

ARMSTRONG

Margaret Bradley); Peggy McKamy (not married); and William C. McKamy the Second (who married Polly Parks.)
This completes the List of children of Robert Armstrong, Second, and Margaret Cunningham Armstrong.

ROBERT ARMSTRONG, THE THIRD

Robert Armstrong, the Third, son of Robert Armstrong the Second and Margaret Cunningham Armstrong, was born in Abbeyville District South Carolina, December 13, 1774.

When he was ten years old he accompanied his father and mother on their trip to the then unsettled territory which is now Tennessee. This adventure was undertaken in 1784. Their first location in Tennessee was only temporary and three years later they moved to a place near Knoxville, upon which members of the family still reside.

Robert Armstrong the Third, as the family Bible says of his father and grandfather was of "patriotic spirit." When he was eighteen years of age, in 1792 he served a term of three months under Captain Hugh Beard and was stationed near Nashville. He was one of the "gallant thirty-eight" who in September 1793 defended Knoxville against fifteen hundred Indians, being then a lad of not quite nineteen. He was also one of the detachment of eight or ten who by order of Colonel White and under Captain Gillespie, after lying in the pass to defend Knoxville, went over to Buncombe County, North Carolina, scouting for Indians, after the burning of Carter's Station. He also served in the United States Regular Army in a Cavalry Company under Captain Nathanial Evans in the winter of 1793. And not content with service while he was still a young man, Robert Armstrong was a member of Captain Davis' Company of local militia in 1828 when he reached the age of forty-nine.

October 19, 1798, Robert Armstrong, Third, married Elizabeth Wear, born 1780, died 1820, daughter of the distinguished Tennessee pioneer, Colonel Samuel Wear. Robert and Elizabeth Wear Armstrong established themselves on a plantation one mile north of his father's home on the West bank of the Holston River. Their old homestead is now in existence on this old plantation.

Robert Armstrong was an expert surveyor and was surveyor for Knox County for forty years. In 1819 his cousin, John C. Calhoun, then Secretary of War, appointed him United States Surveyor in the famous Cherokee Treaty of 1819. Robert Armstrong Houston (his first cousin) was at the same time appointed United States Commissioner for the same Treaty by John C. Calhoun.

Elizabeth Wear Armstrong, died February 13, 1820. After the

death of his first wife, Robert Armstrong married Charlotte Perry by whom he had no children.

Robert and Elizabeth Wear Armstrong had twelve children, five sons and seven daughters namely:

Drury Paine Armstrong.
Addison Wear Armstrong.
Robert Horace Armstrong.
James Houston Armstrong.
Samuel Thompson Armstrong.
Maria Armstrong.
Rutelia Armstrong.
Charlotte Armstrong.
Dialthea Perry Armstrong.
Malinda Armstrong.
Margaret Cunningham Armstrong.
BetseyArmstrong.

It is said that Robert Armstrong returned from a journey in connection with his appointment as United States Surveyor October 19, 1819, to find his wife dangerously ill and three of his children dead. They were: Robert Horace Armstrong, Samuel Thompson Armstrong, and a new born child, Betsey. The death of his wife Elizabeth Wear followed this tragic event in a few months, April 5, 1820.

Robert Armstrong the Third, died February 13, 1849.

COLONEL SAMUEL WEAR AND THE WEARS

The father of Elizabeth Wear who married Robert Armstrong the Third, was Colonel Samuel Wear. The first Wear whom we know definitely is Robert Wear, the father of Samuel. The family came from Ulster Province, Ireland, and was Scotch-Irish. Robert Wear's wife was Rebecca.

The Wears reached Augusta County, Virginia, by way of Pennsylvania and Frederick County, Virginia, like many other emigrants. The name Wear was originally de Vere which betrays the Norman origin and it can be traced in that form for hundreds of years. It is variously spelled in early histories Weir, Wier, Wear, etc., and this variation causes confusion, but Robert Wear, ancestor of the Virginia-Tennessee family and his son Samuel Wear spelled their name Wear and both were men of education and have left written proof of this spelling, though Ramsey's Annals and other volumes in giving Colonel Wear full credit for his important service in the Revolution and early history of Tennessee spell his name Weir. He was Clerk of the State

ARMSTRONG

of Franklin, a signer of the Constitution of Tennessee and Clerk of the County of Sevier and signed his name literally hundreds of times.

In April 1719 a Robert Weir was one of the settlers in Nutfield, near Haverhill, Massachusetts, but in New Hampshire, under the leadership of James McKeen. It is possible that this Robert Weir was the father of Robert, whom we afterwards have located in Augusta County, Virginia.

The settlement of Nutfield was thought to be in Massachusetts, but the General Court of May, 1719, decided it was in New Hampshire. James Gregg and Robert Wear, in behalf of the Scotch Irish at Nutfield, asked the Governor and Court assembled at Portsmouth, N. H., for a township ten miles square. They and others obtained a deed from Colonel John Wheelwright. Londonberry, N. H., was then incorporated June, 1722. Robert Wear's name appears on petition. The town in December, 1719, voted to grant a lot to each of the first comers "which is the number of twenty." Robert Wear is one of these.

To Robert Wear and his wife, Martha, a daughter, Elizabeth, was born in 1723.

Bolton gives the settlers of Londonderry, N. H., in 1722, and among the names are several of interest to people reading this volume, for instance, Robert Armstrong, James, John and Robert Doak, Robert Wear, etc.

Robert Weir, or Wear, probably this same Robert, was Commissioner in Antrim County, Antrim, Ireland, in 1717.

In 1752 a deed is recorded to Robert Wear and John Cunningham, of eight hundred and thirty-three acres in Borden's Tract, Augusta County, Virginia, and in 1754 Borden's executors deeded two hundred and forty acres to Robert Wear. So we have the family of Robert Wear and his wife Rebecca settled in Augusta County close to the year 1750. There their children were born, including Samuel Wear, who was destined to become a distinguished pioneer of the new state of Tennessee, John Wear and probably other children whose names have not been preserved. Robert Wear was still living in the year 1789.

Samuel Wear was born in Augusta County, Virginia about the year 1753. In 1777 he was appointed Ensign of the Augusta County Militia.

In the year 1778, in Augusta County, Virginia, Samuel Wear married Mary, sometimes called Polly Thompson, daughter of William Thompson and his wife Elizabeth Lyle Thompson. (see Lyle Family).

The birth of Elizabeth Wear, the eldest daughter, named evidently for her maternal grandmother, Elizabeth Lyle Thompson, occured October 4, 1780. A list of other children of Samuel Wear is given in the Lyle record and it is interesting to observe that Samuel

NOTABLE SOUTHERN FAMILIES

Wear named his next daughter for his mother, Rebecca, and his first son for his father, Robert Wear. It is also not uninteresting to notice that Elizabeth Wear's birth took place when Colonel Samuel Wear was already on his way to that famous ground, King's Mountain. He probably did not know that he had a daughter until he was one of the successful Captains of that famous engagement.

Leaving Augusta County, Virginia, perhaps in the same year of his marriage, 1778, Samuel Wear followed the tide of emigration setting in toward the new country, which is now Tennessee.

John Sevier and Samuel Wear knew each other in Virginia and undoubtedly Samuel Wear's removal to Tennessee was influenced by Sevier's enthusiasm. Their careers are singularly similar. They were born in the same neighborhood within a few years of each other. They grew up to know each other well. They both entered the Militia early, both married young, probably school girl sweethearts, both entered into a second marriage, later in Tennessee. They moved to the Mountains about the same time. Both served at King's Mountain with rank and honor, both served in innumerable Indian campaigns, both were instrumental in the formation of the State of Franklin, were in fact, its leading spirits, both served in the early story of Tennessee, Territory and State, and occupied high offices, both were in the War of 1812 with rank and honor and finally died at nearly the same time after each had named a son for the other. They were through all this companionship intimate and confidential friends and after the fashion of the South the children of Samuel Wear and the grand--children were taught to call the Governor Uncle John. To this day many of the descendants in writing to the author of this manuscript have insisted that we are descended from the Seviers because we have always called Governor Sevier "Uncle John."

Though we do not know the exact date that Samuel Wear moved to the new country it was certainly between his marriage in 1778 and the Battle of Kings Mountain, October 7, 1780, when he was already a member of the new community and a man of property and position. He was selected as one of the Captains, either at John Sevier's request, which is probable, or by election.

Lyman C. Draper in Kings Mountain and Its Heroes, page 424 says:

"Samuel Wear was another of Sevier's Captains at Kings Mountain. He was an active participant in the Franklin Republic movement; led a party in 1793 against Tallahassee, killing sixteen Indians and taking four prisoners. In 1793 and 1794 he was a member of the Convention that formed the Constitution of Tennessee and served many years as Clerk of Sevier County Court; and lived to a good old age. He was fully six feet in height, dark complexioned, and possessed much energy of character."

In "Wear's Cove," protected by towering mountains and refreshed by pure chalybeate water, Samuel Wear built his home and raised his family. It is an instance of the dangers that beset him, that he and his two young sons were fired upon by a party of thirty savages. Again on June 19, 1793, a band of Indians entered "Wear's Cove", cut down the growing corn, stole one horse, killed ten and destroyed the mill. Samuel Wear, with a party of friends pursued these marauders and at Tallahassee a battle raged which resulted in the death of sixteen Indians and the capture of four Indian prisoners.

In 1784 Samuel Wear began his political history, for in that year he was elected "deputy to the Convention to deliberate upon public affairs." The convention met at Jonesboro, August 23, 1794. At that convention the first which was held in what is now Tennessee, was born the State of Franklin.

Samuel Wear was thus a member of the first Legislative body ever assembled in Tennessee, the first Franklin Convention.

When the State of Franklin had become a fact, its Governor, John Sevier, in June, 1785, appointed Samuel Wear Clerk of the County Court of the County of Sevier, and Colonel of the Regiment. In the summer of 1786 he was one of the commissioners appointed to negotiate a treaty with the Indians. This conference between savages and Commissioners lasted four days and ended August 3, at Coyton.

With Samuel Wear and the other commissioners at Chota Ford 1786 for this treaty were Old Tassel and Hanging Maw. The land claimed by the settlers in this treaty was the island in the Tennessee at the mouth of Holston and from the head of the Island to the dividing ridge between Holston, Little River and the Tennessee, sold to them by North Carolina.

After the rise and fall of Franklin, of which Samuel Wear was a leading spirit, an election was held in December 1793, according to the proclamation of Governor Blount. This resulted in Samuel Wear becoming a member of the first assembly of the Territory of Tennessee (representing the County of Jefferson) which was called to order in Knoxville in February 1794. He was one of the Committee of five appointed by this assembly to draft an address to Congress. In this address the people demanded a Declaration of war against the Creeks and Cherokees.

THE CHILDREN OF ROBERT ARMSTRONG THE THIRD

(1) Drury Paine Armstrong, born 1799, married 1823, died 1856. Married his cousin, Amelia Houston, daughter of Robert Armstrong Houston and Margaret Dallas Houston. His children were: Robert Houston Armstrong (who married Louisa Franklin and had Robert Franklin Armstrong, who married twice; first, ,Celia Houston and second Annie Wetzel and had no children; Adelia Armstrong who married J. Edwin Lutz and had Louise Lutz who married Dr. Victor Holloway and Edwin Lutz, married Edith Atkin; and Elizabeth Rogers Armstrong, who married James P. McMillin, second son of James P. McMillin and Nannie Cravens McMillin and had Robert Armstrong McMillin, who died young, James P. McMillin, third, who married Margaret Angeline Hayes, and Laura McMillin, who married Thomas H. Wagner, and has Mary Elizabeth and Anne McMillin Wagner); Marcellus Murat Armstrong (called Whack, who married Elizabeth C. McGhee, and had Drury Paine Armstrong, second, died unmarried; Joseph McGhee Armstrong married Mary L. Hampton; Leonidas Bruce Armstrong, second, married first Pauline Fearn and married second Margaret Bradford; and Amelia Armstrong, married J. H. Bankston); Leonidas Bruce Armstrong, first (who died unmarried); and Adelia Armstrong (who married William Calvert Hill and had George Armstrong Hill, who married Georgia Ann Wallis and has children and Amelia C. Hill who married Clement C. Douglass and has children.)

(2) Addison Wear Armstrong, born 1801, died 1873. A sketch of him follows.

(3) Mariah Armstrong, born 1803, married first 1821, married second 1851, died 1885. Married first John Brooks and had children. Married second James MacMillan. By her second marriage she had no children. By her first marriage she had John Newton Brooks (who married Eliza J. McMillan and had William A. Brooks and Mariah Brooks); Drury Armstrong Brooks (who married first Mary Jane Anderson, married second Lizzie Shoemate); Robert Brooks, (who died in Mexico in 1874); and Moses Brooks (who married Eliza Salmon and had Agnes Brooks, Moses, Marie Brooks and Isabell T. Brooks).

(4) Rutelia Armstrong, born 1806, married 1828, died 1862. Married Thomas Gillespie Craighead and had Elizabeth J. Craighead (who married Thomas K. Rawlings and had Edward A. K. Rawlings and Margaret Rawlings); Mary Ann Craighead (who married David O. Hoge and had William Edgar Hoge, Sarah R. Hoge and Lena Hoge); Mary Clark Craighead (who married Alex-

ander K. Alley and had Marcellus Murat Alley.) William Alexander Craighead, who married Eliza Cox Doss and had Jack Doss Craighead, who died young, William Alexander Craighead, second, who died young, Thomas Gillespie Craighead, second, James R. Craighead, Charles C. Craighead, Libbie Kate Craighead); Adelia Craighead (who married Edwin F. Redfield and had Hal Linwood Redfield, who married Marguerite Austin and has Evelyn Redfield, and Maude E. Redfield, who married Allen L. Pitts and has Allen Linwod Pitts.)

(5) Charlotte Perry Armstrong, born 1807, married first 1825, married second, 1829, died 1854. Married first Samuel Armstrong, by whom she had no children. Married second, Henry Baldwin and had Robert Elsner Baldwin, Euel Erasmus Baldwin, Armstrong Wear Baldwin, Addison T. Baldwin, Susan Elizabeth Baldwin, Moses Marcellus Baldwin, and James Henry Baldwin, most of whom married and had children.

(6) Robert Horace Armstrong, born 1809, died 1819.

(7) Margaret Cunningham Armstrong, born 1811, married 1832, Samuel Hannibal Love, died 1856, and had Elizabeth Wear Love (who married O. H. Caldwell); William Armstrong Love (who married Lou Luttrell); Drury Paine Love (who married, first, Jesse McMillan and second Anna Green); Emma Love (who married Samuel Webb); Rutelia Love, (who married Andrew L. McCampbell); John Armstrong Love (who married first Martha McCampbell, and second, Ellen Reatherford) and Hannibal Jasper Love, second.

(8) Dialthea Perry Armstrong, born 1814, married 1831, died ———. Married Pleasant M. Love and had Robert Love Armstrong; Nancy Jane Love; Bridgett Love; James Love; Samuel Love; Hannibal Jasper Love.

(9) James Houston Armstrong, born 1815, married 1839, died 1872. Married Anne E. Park, of Knoxville (daughter of William Park and Jennie Armstrong Park, who was not a close kinswoman, but was a descendant of "Trooper" Armstrong of Revolutionary fame), and had children: Frank Armstrong (who married Lazinka E. Martin and had Mary Armstrong who married Howard Ijams); Robert Armstrong (who never married); William Park Armstrong (who married his cousin, Alice Isbell, daughter of James Isbell and Rutelia Houston Isbell and a descendant of Robert Armstrong, the first, and Alice Calhoun Armstrong, and had William Park Armstrong, second, who married Rebekah Purvis and has Rebekah Purvis Armstrong, William Park Armstrong, third, George Purvis Armstrong, Ann Elizabeth Armstrong, and Jane Crozier Armstrong; Houston Churchwell Armstrong married Mina Lamar and has Houston Churchwell Armstrong, second, Alice Isbell Armstrong and Mina Cary Armstrong; Marga-

ret Armstrong, who married Ainslee Power Ardagh and has Margaret Ardagh, Ainslee Power Ardagh, Jr., Alice Ardagh, Kathleen Ardaugh, Edith Ardaugh; and Annie E. Armstrong, who married Thomas Stoo Johnson and lives in New Orleans.

(10) Malinda Armstrong, born 1817, married 1840, died 1884. Married Samuel Morrow and had: Robert Morrow (who was in the United States army and was not married); Samuel Morrow (who never married); Anna Hale Morrow (who married James Addison Anderson); Mary E. Morrow (who married Captain William P. Chamberlain as his first wife, but died without issue); and Amelia Isabella Morrow (who married Captain Hiram Sanborn Chamberlain, brother of her sister's husband, and had Minnie M. Chamberlain who married Henry Overton Ewing and has Margaret, Rosalind and Winnifred Ewing, Morrow Chamberlain who married May Douglass and has Douglass, Louise and Nan Chamberlain; Louise Chamberlain, who married Richard A. Clifford and has Charlotte Clifford; Susan Willie Chamberlain, who married a Hoskins and has no children, and Hiram Sanborn Chamberlain, second, who married Emily Wright and has Hiram Sanborn Chamberlin, third.)

(11) Samuel Thompson Armstrong, born 1818, died 1819.

(12) Betsy Armstrong, born 1819, did not live.

Addison Wear Armstrong, born 1801, married 1825, died 1873, was the second son of Robert Armstrong, the third, and Elizabeth Wear Armstrong. He was born at his father's homestead on the Holston River.

He became an expert surveyor as so many members of his family were and practically inherited the place of County Surveyor, of Knox County, Tennessee, which was held for forty years by his father. His grandfather, Samuel Wear, had also been a Surveyor, the profession espoused by George Washington.

Addison Wear Armstrong married Nancy Jane McMillan, daughter of John McMillan and Jane Meek, and a descendant of Alexander McMillan, Revolutionary soldier. (See that family.)

He held a number of public offices and was for twelve years Justice of the Peace. He was County Surveyor for twelve years and owing to his accurate knowledge of the surrounding country as well as to his well-known fairness and his reputation for justice in all things he was called upon to settle many land disputes, many disputants preferring to leave the matter to Addison Armstrong's decision instead of going to law.

He was an elder in the Presbyterian church at Spring Place from the time of its organization near his home until his death in 1873.

He was an enrolling officer during the occupancy of East Tennessee by the Confederate Army.

ARMSTRONG

He was polite and affable to all and extremely modest in disposition. He died on his plantation May 22nd, 1873, and is buried in Spring Place Cemetery a few miles from his home.

Addison Wear Armstrong and Nancy Jane MacMillan Armstrong had three sons and three daughters, Elizabeth Jane Armstrong; John MacMillan Armstrong; James Monroe Armstrong; Margaret Evelyn Armstrong; Amelia Armstrong; Robert Addison Armstrong (R. A. J. Armstrong.)

Elizabeth Jane Armstrong, born 1826, married 1850, died 1899. She married Shannon Anderson and had Isaac Howard Anderson (who married Fannie McNabb and has Shannon Anderson, second, Claiborne Anderson, Howard Anderson and Edward Anderson).Minnie Anderson (who married Henry Gauffon and has Elizabeth Gauffon and Henry Gauffon, Second); Mary Anderson (who married her cousin, William Brooks and has Lucile, Helen, Newton and Agnes Brooks). Alice Anderson (who married Andrew Gamble and has Emma Gamble); James Addison Armstrong (who married Anna Hale Morrow and has no children); Nannie Anderson (who married Dr. Samuel Love Tillery) and Evelyn Anderson (who married James H. Crawford and has no children.)

John MacMillan Armstrong, born 1828. A sketch of him follows.

James Monroe Armstrong, born 1831, died 1840.

Margaret Evelyn Armstrong, born 1833, married 1856, died 1908. Married Patrick Henry Watkins and had Anna (who married James W. Berry and Lula (who married Thomas N. Doyle.)

Amelia Armstrong, born 1838, married 1881. Married Jacob Kizer and had no children.

Robert Addison Armstrong, born 1844, married 1873, married Anne Buffat. Robert Armstrong added a "J" to his name as there were many Robert Armstrongs in Knox County. He has been known therefore all his mature life as Robert A. J. Armstrong. He has been County Surveyor for many years and has held other positions of public esteem. He has inherited the confidence his neighbors accorded his father and grandfather and in consequence has been frequently appealed to to settle land disputes, his extraordinary knowledge of the lands in Knox County and the surrounding territory making his opinion authoritative in practically every instance, the surveying and engineering of this section having been in the hands of these three men, Robert Armstrong, Third, Addison Wear Armstrong and Robert A. J. Armstrong for something more than a century. Like his forbears he is a Presbyterian and an elder in his church.

He married Anne Buffat of an old French family resident in Knox County and they have had six children, Wear Francis Armstrong (who married Louisa J. Posey, became a physician and was achieving eminence in his profession when he died young leaving two daughters, Louisa Posey and Sarah Francis), Robert Armstrong(who married Marie Ferguson and has Wanda Marie Armstrong), Addison MacMillan Armstrong (who married Augusta Wohlwend and has Charles Wilburn Armstrong and Robert Addison Armstrong); and three daughters, Clyde Evelyn Armstrong, Sylvie Elizabeth Armstrong and Grace Anna Armstrong, neither of whom is married.

John MacMillan Armstrong, son of Addison Wear Armstrong and Nancy Jane MacMillan Armstrong was born November 30th, 1828, in the homestead of his parents, Knox County, Tennessee. He graduated from Maryville College, Tennessee, June, 1848. He went to Abbeville, District, S. C., where he lived for five years. Returning to Knox County he resided there for five years and in 1858 he moved to the then small village of Chattanooga where he engaged in business and established his permanent home. At the breaking out of the War Between the States he immediately offered his service to the Confederate States and assisted in organizing a Battery of Light Artillery which became known as Lookout Battery, Robert L. Barry commanding, afterwards called Barry's Battery, Colonel Williams Regiment of Artillery, Confederate States Army. He was a Lieutenant and was a gallant and able officer greatly loved by officers and men. He was present with the Battery at its first service in defense of Chattanooga when the town was shelled by Union troops in June, 1862, when Lookout Battery responded to the fire, and afterwards in all its engagements until he was promoted to Major and Ordnance Officer in 1863. He engaged in many battles and continued in the service until after the last battle at Spanish Fort and was parolled with General Joseph E. Johnston's command at Meridian in 1865, having returned to his battery (after his detail as Ordnance Officer), just before the close of the war.

December 19th, 1867, he married Martha J. Turnley, daughter of Judge and Mrs. Mathew J. Turnley, of Jacksonville, Ala., a descendant of Colonial and Revolutionary families on both sides of her house. (See Howard and Turnley Families). John MacMillan Armstrong returned to Chattanooga after the war and re-entered business. He died February 28th, 1897, leaving a son and daughter, Turnley F. Armstrong, who died unmarried and Zella Armstrong.

BANNING FAMILY

The name Banning is of great antiquity. It is probably of Danish origin, applying in very early times to a class called "Hero Worshippers." It signifies a Home or Dwelling. Reference to it is found in the Scot and Bard Songs, the earliest ballads on record, where it says, "Becca Ruled the Banning." This Becca was no doubt the Hero, or Ruler, of the Banning Clan of Vikings.

The distinctive Anglo-Saxon termination "ing" has always marked the name and in general it has suffered very slight changes throughout its many hundred years of existence and travel into different countries. Whatever changes have occurred are due to misspelling or to the natural accomodation to the language. The name appears with the Ruling Families of Holland, from which country it went to Westphalia, Scotland, England, Ireland and America. They have eventually taken a leading part in the countries settled in.

We find Robert Banning living in Burbage, Wiltshire, England, in 1539, and again, as an old man, in 1565. His son, John Banning, was also found in Burbage, in 1565.

His son, John Banning, we find in 1613. John, the next generation, of Burbage and Magdalene College, Oxford Register, B. A. 1630—M. A. 1634—Subsidary Roll 1642. His son, Stephen, had a wife, Mary. He died 1688; they had Stephen, known of in 1714. He had John, of Mitton Wilts, who married Elizabeth Noyes of Wooten River Wilts, heiress of Noyes, in 1694, and died in 1716. They had six children, Elizabeth, Mary Frances, John, Martha and Susan. Their son John Banning was born in 1705 in Mitton, married Mary Ayres (Eyers) in 1744, widow of H. Ayres, sole heiress of John Griffin, and had three children. He died 1772; she in 1805, both buried at Mitton. They had John, Thomas and Elizabeth Banning.

Two English Coats of Arms and four Holland Coats of Arms have been granted the family at different periods.

In Talbot County, Maryland, and adjacent parts in Delaware, as well as near Lyme, Connecticut, Bannings settled about 1650-60. Edward Banning located in Talbot County about that time. He is supposed to have been a cousin of John Banning who located at Lyme, Connecticut, and brother of the father of James, John and Richard Banning of Talbot County, Maryland. James Banning, just referred to, had a son, Jeremiah Banning, who was a sea captain for many years. On one of his voyages to England he brought back with him various things from relatives whom he had been visiting.

NOTABLE SOUTHERN FAMILIES

Among them was a "sampler" that had been given him by Mary Ayres (Banning,) the wife of a cousin of his father. This "Sampler" is today in existence and is evidence that this line belongs to the early English line first referred to. The facts sewed into the "Sampler" verify the date of marriage of John Banning to Mary Ayres and it also had Mary Ayres' name worked into it. Edward, and the father of James, John and Richard Banning were sons of Stephen Banning and uncles of John Banning, who married Mary Ayres.

James Banning of Talbot County, Maryland, married Jane Spencer and had three children, Jeremiah, Henry and Anthony Banning. Following his death his widow married Nicholas Goldsborough, who made these boys his heirs.

Jeremiah Banning, born March 25, 1733, in Talbot County, Maryland lived at "The Isthmus" near Easton, Maryland, where he died in 1798. He was a sea captain and shipper for twenty years. He had a most eventful life, retired wealthy and became a man of the greatest influence locally. His home was one of the very finest of the times. He was very intimate with Washington, and was elected to represent Talbot County in the Ratification of the "Federal Government of the United States." He was a Colonel in the Revolution, Magistrate, Collector of the Port of Oxford, and held many other positions of honor and trust. To quote an early reference,"The Isthmus," the home of Jeremiah Banning, was the scene of great hospitality during the early period preceding the Revolution. Here Washington, Lafayette, William Morris, the financier, and others of fame during that period, held nightly gatherings.

"The rooms of this noble old mansion could tell tales of State and Society interest. The owner was a man of daring mind and adventurous tendencies, which later on got him into trouble over smuggling to this country of (Zakery) Hood and other piratical people. The Isthmus was one of the finest houses of that early period and the youth and beauty of Maryland gathered there during the early days." Jeremiah Banning's children were: Robert, Freeborn and Clementina.

Henry, brother of Jeremiah Banning, was born 1736, in Talbot County, Maryland, and held many public appointments. He died in 1817. Issue, Anthony, Wesley, Jane and Thomas.

Anthony, the other brother of Jeremiah Banning, was born 1740, in Talbot County, Maryland. He married Anna, the daughter of James and Anna (Murray) Calder. He died February 27, 1787, in Chestertown, Maryland. Issue, Anthony, Katherine and Annie.

Robert Banning was born in 1776. He married first a Miss Thomas, descended from the Oldham family. Their children were Jeremiah, Robert, Alexander, Maria, Katherine F. and Susan. He was married a second time to Mary Macky and of this marriage there

BANNING

were two children, Matilda and Mary Elizabeth Banning. He died in 1845, at Miles River Neck, Talbot County, Maryland. Was Collector of Port of Oxford and Member of House of Delegates, Captain, et cetera.

Freeborn Banning was born May 24, 1777, in Talbot County, Maryland. Married a second time Sarah Geddes, on November 14, 1814, in Talbot County, daughter of Captain Henry Geddes and Margaret Latimer Geddes. He entered the Navy and June 1, 1799, was made Lieutenant, resigned from the Navy in 1802. He died in 1826, and his wife May 19, 1855, both in Talbot County, Maryland. Issue, Emily, Samuel and Henry Geddes Banning.

Clementina Banning married a Mr. Hopkins.

Anthony Banning, born April 2, 1768, at Royal Oak, Maryland, had four children, Emma, Annie, Caroline and James C. Banning.

Anthony Banning, son of James Banning, was born May 13, 1768, in Talbot County, Maryland. He married Sarah Murphy (Pierce) June 30, 1791, in Connellsville, Pennsylvania. About 1812 he went to Ohio, becoming one of the founders of Mount Vernon, Ohio. He was a Methodist minister and a very successful business man and leader in public affairs. Appointed Judge in 1827. He was drowned February 4, 1844. His wife died June 4, 1844, both deaths taking place in Mount Vernon. Issue, Sarah, Jacob Murphy, Rachel, James Smith, Elizabeth, Mary, Priscilla and Anthony.

Katherine Banning, born July 6, 1770, in Chestertown, Maryland; married Benjamin Chew, Jr., son of Chief Justice Chew, of Germantown, December 11, 1788, at "The Isthmus."

Henry Geddes Banning, born March 8, 1816, in Talbot County, Maryland. Married Emilie Eschenburg, April 7, 1847. She was born April 8, 1825, in Buenos Aires. Lived in Wilmingon, Delaware, where he was one of the leading bankers and citizens for many years. There he died March 12, 1906. Issue, James Latimer and John Henry Banning.

James Latimer Banning, born April 8, 1848, in Wilmington, Delaware. Married Emma Harris, June 3, 1879, daughter of Alexander and Maria Spencer Harris. He died April 8, 1914, Wilmington, Delaware. Issue, Henry Geddes and James Latimer Banning.

Henry Geddes Banning, born June 28, 1880, in Easton, Maryland, died unmarried, January 15, 1914 Wilmington, Delaware.

James Latimer Banning, born January 13, 1882, at Easton, Maryland. He lives unmarried, in Wilmington, Delaware.

James Smith Banning, born June 11, 1800, in Connellsville, Pennsylvania, married March 12, 1822 to Eliza, daughter of James Blackstone, in Connellsville. In 1812 they moved to Mount Vernon, Ohio, where he died May 22, 1867, and she September 29, 1878.

Issue, Anna, Sarah Davidson, James Blackstone, Anthony Rogers, Priscilla, William Davidson, Henry Blackstone, Elizabeth Blackstone, Thomas Davidson and Mary Blackstone.

Anna Banning, born 1824, in Mount Vernon, Ohio. Died young.

Sarah Davidson Banning, born 1826 and died in 1881, at Mount Vernon. Unmarried.

James Blackstone Banning, born April 5, 1825, died August 28, 1897, at Mount Vernon. No issue.

Anthony Rogers Banning, born August, 1831, Mount Vernon. No issue. Was a director on the Baltimore and Ohio Railroad for years. The town of Banning, Pennsylvania, was founded by him. There he died, September 10, 1905.

Priscilla Banning, born January 5, 1829, Mount Vernon, Ohio. Married John D. Thompson, of Dublin, Ireland. February 18, 1864. No issue.

William Davidson Banning, born July 29, 1830, Mount Vernon, Ohio. Married Mary Lake. Issue, Eliza, Priscilla, Mary Lake, Anna Lake, Lake and William Davidson Banning.

Henry Blackstone Banning, born November 10, 1836, in Mount Vernon, Ohio. Was Brigadier General and Congressman. He married Julia, daughter of Timothy Kirby, of Cincinnati, Ohio, September 9, 1868. He died December 10, 1881, in Cincinnati, Ohio. Issue, Kirby, Harry Byron, Ella Kirby and Clinton Kirby Banning.

Elizabeth Blackstone Banning, born August 21, 1837, Mount Vernon, Ohio. Married William Burr Brown, October 14, 1862, in Mount Vernon, Ohio. Issue, Bessie, James and William Brown.

Thomas Davidson Banning, born in 1840, Mount Vernon, Ohio. Died at Mount Vernon, November 21, 1913, and was unmarried.

Mary Blackstone Banning, born July 11, 1843, Mount Vernon, Ohio. Married Frank William Watkins, December 12, 1875, Mount Vernon, Ohio. She died July 27, 1911, Springfield, Massachusetts. He died October 29, 1914, Los Angeles, California. Issue, Lila Banning Watkins.

Lila Banning Watkins, born February 28, 1878, Mount Vernon, Ohio. Married Pierson Worrall Banning (descended from the John Banning line, immediately following this line) May 16, 1913, in Los Angeles. William Dean Howell's mother was a sister of the father of Frank William Watkins, while a sister of Frank Williams Watkins was the mother of Vaughn and Paul Kester. William Watkins, an uncle of Frank William Watkins, the famous miniature painter of London, England, once painted the eye of Queen Victoria on a piece of ivory no larger than his thumb nail.

John Banning, brother of James Banning, whose line precedes

BANNING

this, was probably born in Talbot County, Maryland. He had the following children: John, Benoni, Asa and James Banning, the latter went to Edgartown, Massachusetts.

Benoni Banning lived for a long time on a point of land on the Tred Avon River, Talbot County, Maryland, now known as "Benoni's Point." He later went to Virginia, and was in the Battle of Kings Mountain. His brother, John Banning, was a Captain in the Virginia Militia. Benoni Banning had the following children: Elizabeth, who married William Fullwood, and had seven children: W. B. Pulaski, a descendant of hers now lives at Pulaski, Tennessee; John Banning and Clark Banning.

John Banning, born March 23, 1764, in Talbot County, Maryland. He married Elizabeth, daughter of Henry and Martha Black, October 24, 1797. From Maryland they moved to Rockbridge County, Virginia, where he became a leader in local matters. He died March 5, 1833, in Rockbridge County. Issue, William, Henry, Salina, John, Martha, Asa, Ephraim and Mary Banning.

Ephraim Banning, born June 2, 1811, in Rockbridge County, Virginia. In 1824 he went to Wheeling, remaining ten years. From there he went to McDonough County, Illinois, settling near the present town of Bushnell. He returned to Wheeling and married Mary Potter, January 26, 1836. Their children were William Frederick, John and James Henry Banning. She died and he married secondly Louisa Caroline Walker, May 12, 1842, in McDounough County, Illinois. She was born near Columbia, Adair County, Kentucky, daughter of Joseph Gilmer Walker and Martha Scott. Her father and brothers were lawyers and public men. Judge Pinkney H. Walker, a brother, was for twenty years on the Supreme Bench of Illinois. They moved to Brookfield, Missouri, where he died November 8, 1878, and she August 10, 1887. He was a leader in civic matters, holding several public offices. Issue, Joseph Gilmer, Pinkney Asa, Elizabeth Mary, Ephraim, Thomas Allen, Cyrus Walker, Hubert Ashley, Cynthia Ellen and Martha Bell Banning.

Joseph Gilmer Banning, born March 8, 1843, in McDonough County, Illinois. Married Letitia Ann Miller, November 3, 1870, in Linn County, Missouri. He died May 9, 1908, in Brookfield, Missouri. Issue, Ephraim Pinkney, Margaret Ellen, Letitia Louise, Thomas Gilmer and Caroline Agnes Banning.

Pinkney Asa Banning, born July 22, 1845, in McDonough County, Illinois. He died in Nashville, Tennessee, unmarried.

Elizabeth Mary Banning, born January 31, 1847, in McDonough County, Illinois, married Charles Vertrees, September, 1881. She died June 17, 1902. They had two children, both died young.

Ephraim Banning, born July 21, 1849, in McDonough County,

NOTABLE SOUTHERN FAMILIES

Illinois. Married Lucretia Thalia Lindsley October 22, 1878, in Onarga, Illinois. She was born June 5, 1853, in Medina, New York, and was the daughter of Thales Lindsley and Caroline Lucretia Pierson. She died February 5, 1887, in Chicago. They had three sons, Pierson Worrall, Walker and Ephraim Banning. September 5, 1889 he married Emilie Bartlett Jenne, in Elgin, Illinois. No issue. He was a man of great prominence in the legal profession, a leader in civic work and of the highest standing in the community. He died December 2, 1907, in Chicago.

Pierson Worrall Banning, born September 13, 1879, in Chicago. Married Lila Banning Watkins, (of the James Banning line, already given) May 16, 1913, in Los Angeles, California.

Walker Banning, born February 9, 1882, in Chicago. Married Clara Louise Wahrer, July 30, 1902, in Chicago. He was an attorney; died January 19, 1918. Issue, Clara Louise and Walker Banning.

Ephraim Banning, III, born August 7, 1885, in Chicago, Illinois. Married Beatrice White Smith, June 22, 1909, in Chicago. He is an attorney. Issue, Emilie Jenne, Ephriam IV. and Thalia Banning.

Thomas Allen Banning, born January 16, 1851, in McDonough County, Illinois, married Sarah Jane Hubbard, December 21, 1875. She was born in Bowling Green, Kentucky, July 23, 1854. He is an attorney of prominence in Chicago. Their winter home is in Alabama. Issue, Samuel Walker, Edith, Helen Ruth, Thomas Allen, Jr., Sarah Louise and Dorothea-Esther Banning.

Cyrus Walker Banning, born January 4, 1853, in McDonough County, Illinois. Married Nancy Ellen Miller, April 18, 1878. Issue, Bertha Lucile, Jennie Malvern, Thomas Ephraim, Alma Louise, Cyrus Walker, Hubert Charles and Wayne Elson Banning.

Hubert Ashley Banning, born June 7, 1855, in Douglas County, Kansas, married Viola H. Suydam, November 23, 1881, in New York City. He died January 3, 1916, in New York. He was an attorney. Issue, Hubert Temple Banning.

Hubert Temple Banning, born October 24, 1882, in New York City. Married Olga Kurzrock, daughter of Ernest August Fredrich Kurzrock and Theresa Alvina (Wolf) Kurzrock, of Berlin, Germany, September 17, 1909, in Bavaria. He is one of the three or four greatest linguists of the present generation, and is living in New York at the present time. Issue, Hildegard Banning, born November 19, 1913, in Ayas Pasha, Constantinople, Turkey.

Cynthia Ellen Banning, born March 6, 1858, in Douglas County, Kansas. Married Hiram Almanson Smith, November 16, 1882, in Chicago, Illinois. Issue, Cynthia Ellen, Alice Marion and Hiram Almanson Smith.

Martha Bell Banning, born June 12, 1860, in Pettis County

BANNING

Missouri. Married George Augustus Lawton, September 6, 1887, in Chicago. He died August 7, 1915, in Daphne, Alabama. Issue, Sophia Louise, Helen Margaret, Grace, George Augustus, William Ephraim, Walter Banning and Ruth Lawton.

The Banning COAT-OF-ARMS is described as follows: Argent, two bars sable, each charged with as many escallops or. CREST: On a mount vert an ostrich argent, in the beak a key or. MOTTO: Fidus et Audax ("Faithful and Bold"). The coat-of-arms was granted in 1588.

BLOUNT FAMILY

The Blount family has been pronounced the oldest in North Carolina and this means of course in Tennessee also. No family, according to Governor Henry T. Clark, genealogist and historian, came to the Province earlier than James Blount, who settled in Chowan, North Carolina in 1664. He was a younger son of Sir Walter Blount, of Sodington, Worcestshire, England, and was a Captain in Life Guards of Charles II.

In England the family can be carried back for many generations, to and through the conquest into Normandy and then for many years. So the Blounts can truly boast of being an "old family". With William the Conqueror three young Blounds, sons of Blound the Lord of Guisnes went to England. From two of them the English family sprang and in the succeeding years changed the family name less than most of the conquering Normans, for it now appears almost as written then.

JAMES BLOUNT THE EMIGRANT

When James Blount, younger son of Sir Walter Blount, of Sodington, came to the Province of North Carolina, he is said to have been accompanied or followed by a brother who settled on Taw or Pamlico River. Their adherence to the royal cause probably accounted for their emigration.

James Blount the emigrant, son of Sir Walter Blount, is said to have emigrated to America in 1664, though the settlement of Chowan is given as in 1669. He settled on a tract of land there which remained in the posession of his family until the death of his descendant, Clement Hall Blount in 1842. James Blount was a member of the Governor's Council and was one of the Burgesses of Chowan. He married and left one son, John Blount.

John Blount, son of the Emigrant, was born in 1669. He died in 1725. He married and left ten children, six daughters and four sons. Three of the six daughters married and left children, the Worleys, Midgets, Manns, and other North Carolina families come through these daughters. The sons were: John Blount, Second, Thomas Blount, James Blount, and Joseph Blount.

John Blount, Second, married and left three sons and two daughters, namely, James Blount, Wilson Blount, Frederick Blount, Elizabeth Blount, and Mary Blount. Of these: James Blount married Ann Hall and left three children, namely; Clement Hall Blount,

Governor William Blount
Tennessee's Only Territorial Governor

BLOUNT

who died in 1842 unmarried, Sarah Blount left no issue and Frederick Blount, who married Rachel Bryan, a widow, born Heritage, and left children: Frederick S. Blount (who moved to Alabama and became the ancestor of a large family) Alexander Clement Blount and Heritage Wistar Blount of Lenoir County. Wilson Blount, son of John Blount, Second, seems not to have married. Frederick Blount, son of John Blount, Second, married and had a daughter, Mary Blount, who married William Sheperd of Newberne, North Carolina, and left children: Anne Sheperd (who married her cousin, Ebenezer Pettigrew) William B. Sheperd, Charles B. Sheperd, James B. Sheperd and a daughter ——————— Sheperd (who married John H. Bryan. The recurring B in the names of Mary Blount Sheperd's sons tempts one to think that she gave each of them Blount for a middle name. Elizabeth Blount, daughter of John Blount, Second, married J. B. Beasley. Mary Blount daughter of John Blount, Second, married Charles Pettigrew, first Bishop of North Carolina, and left children: Ebenezer Pettigrew (Member of Congress, who married his cousin Anne Sheperd and left children: William S. Pettigrew, General James Johnston Pettigrew, Charles I. Pettigrew and two daughters).

Thomas Blount, the son of John Blount, First, was born in 1709. He married and left one daughter, Winnifred Blount, who married Whitmed Hill, of Martin, North Carolina. They left numerous descendants.

James Blount, the son of John Blount, First, (and grandson of James Blount the Emigrant) was born in 1710. He married and left two daughters, Nancy Blount and Betsy Blount. Nancy Blount married Dempsey Connor (son of Dempsey Connor and Mary Pendleton Connor, great grand daughter of Governor Archdale) and left one daughter, Frances Clark Pollock Connor, who married firstly, her cousin Joseph Blount, Third and married secondly William Hill. Betsey Blount married Jeremiah Vail.

Joseph Blount, son of John Blount, First, was born in 1715 and died in 1777. He married firstly Sarah Durant, a descendant of George Durant, the first known English settler in North Carolina. They had one child, a daughter, Sarah Blount, who married William Littlejohn. Joseph Blount married, secondly, Elizabeth Scarborough, by whom he had two sons: Lemuel Edwards Blount, who was drowned and Joseph Blount, Second, who married first Lydia Bonner and had two children, John Bonner Blount (who married Mary Mutter and had Thomas Blount and others) Mary Blount (who married William T. Muse and left children, one of them, William T. Muse, an officer in the United States and Confederate States Navies). Joseph Blount, Second, married for his second wife Ann Gray, daughter of William Gray of Bertie County and left children: Joseph Blount, Third, born 1785, (who married his cousin, Frances Clark Pollock Connor and left one son, Joseph Blount, Fourth, who died unmarried); Frances Lee Blount, (who married Henderson Standin, left one son, William H. Standin); Sarah Elizabeth Blount, (who married but left no children). Elizabeth Ann Blount married John Cheshire and left children); Eleanor Gray Blount (married John Cox and left one daughter, Ann B. P. Cox, who married William J. Epps, of Halifax, North Carolina.

THOMAS BLOUNT THE EMIGRANT.

Thomas Blount, said to have been a third son of Sir Walter Blount, of Sodington, Worcestshire, England, also crossed to America in 1664. He settled in North Carolina on the Taw or Pamlico River in 1673, no record being given of the intervening years. He married though we do not know whom, and had six sons, namely: Thomas Blount, Second, John, James, Benjamin, Jacob and Esau, the latter being twins. It is said that the great Tuscarora Chief King Blount who was devoted to the white people in the Indian wars had his name in honor of one of these six Blounts, having formed a deep attachment for him. Five of these six sons have left no record obtainable.

The eldest, Thomas Blount, Second, married Ann Reading, (given sometimes as Elizabeth Reading), and left four sons, Reading, James, John, and Jacob Blount. All left descendants, but the last named, Jacob Blount, through his sons, gave the name its prestige in the Southern States for two of his six sons became Governor of Tennessee, and by the similarity of their names have probably caused more confusion in the minds of amateur students of the State's history than any other two citizens. William, the first son of Jacob, became Territorial Governor of Tennessee in 1790, and Willie, the sixth son, was elected Governor in 1809.

Jacob Blount, born 1726, died 1729, fourth son of Thomas Blount and Ann Reading, was in the battle of Alamance in 1771, was a member of the provincial Congress and an officer in the Revolutionary War. He married, first (1748) Barbara Gray, and second a widow, Mrs. Hannah Baker, nee Salter, and third Mrs. Mary Adams, by whom he had no children. He was the father of twelve children: William, Ann, John Gray Blount, Louisa, who married Richard Blackledge; Reading, who married Lucy Harvey; Thomas, who married, but died without issue; Jacob married ————Collins; Barbara; Willie, who will be mentioned later, Sharpe, who married Penelope Little and two others probably died young.

BLOUNT

TENNESSEE'S ONLY TERRITORIAL GOVERNOR

William Blount, first child of Jacob Blount by his wife, Barbara was born in Craven County, North Carolina, in 1749. He married Miss Mary Grainger, of Wilmington. He was elected a member of in legislature in 1783 and was elected to the Continential Congress in 1782-83-86-87. He sat in the convention that formed the constitution of the United States in 1787. Immediately upon the cession of what is now Tennessee by North Carolina, to the Federal Government President Washington appointed William Blount Territorial Governor. This was, by the way, a somewhat important position for he was appointed "Governor of the Territories of the United States South of the Ohio."

He was elected Senator- from the State of Tennessee when the territory became a state and he was expelled from the Senate, for alleged treasonable practices in endeavoring to incite the Indians to hostilities against Spain.

Despite this action of the Federal Senate he was admired and loved in Tennessee and immediately after his expulsion, the member from Knox resigned his seat in the Tennessee House of Representatives that William Blount might be elected to it and become its speaker. This vindication by his own friends must have been a pleasant thing for William Blount. Governor Willie Blount in 1835 wrote a full vindication of Senator William Blount, and placed the papers in the hands of Dr. J. G. M. Ramsey. These, together with other valuable papers, were burned when the home was burned during the war. Mr. Lyman C. Draper made an exact copy of this paper, which copy is now in the State Historical Society of Wisconsin at Madison, Wisconsin.

The house in which Governor Blount lived while in Knoxville is still standing just as it was when it was the Governor's mansion. His grave in the yard of the First Presbyterian church, of which he was a member, is marked with a large marble slab and a similar stone covers the remains of his wife.

No man except John Sevier was ever so much beloved by the people of Tennessee as was Governor William Blount. In bearing he was of Chesterfieldian grace. His personal magnetism was wonderful.

He was a member of the Convention which adopted the Constitution of the United States, over which Washington presided. He was honored with the personal friendship and confidence of Washington, who appointed him Governor of the Territory South of the Ohio River. He and his wife, who was Mary Grainger, daughter of Colonel Caleb Grainger, lie in the old church yard in Knoxville, which city they helped to found and where, while he was Governor, they dispensed, for that age, a regal hospitality The Governor's mansion was the rendezvous for society, wit and politics and the Governor himself with his charming, courtly manners, with his beautiful wife, made the center upon which all social life of the place and period turned. The University of Tennessee was founded then and was first known as Blount College, afterwards, East Tennessee University, and now the University of Tennessee. In his honor a county and a town were named Blount County and Blountville; while Grainger County and Maryville were named for his wife who was Mary Grainger.

William Blount died in 1800 in Knoxville. It is believed that only his death prevented his election to the office of Governor of the State, (he had been Governor of the Territory) as a vindication, so great were the love and admiration for him throughout the State of Tennessee.

William and Mary Blount left children, namely: Ann Blount, Mary Louisa Blount, William Grainger Blount, Richard Blackledge Blount, Barbara Blount and Eliza Blount. Of these Ann Blount married firstly, Henry Irwin Toole, Second, of Edgecomb, North Carolina, and had children, Henry Irwin Toole, Third, (born 1810, died 1850, married Margaret Telfair) and Mary Eliza Toole (born 1812, who married Dr. Joseph Lawrence) and married secondly, Weeks Hadley, of Edgecomb by whom she had several children. Mary Louisa Blount married Pleasant M. Miller, and left several children, one of whom, Barbara Miller, married William H. Stephens. William Grainger Blount, son of Governor William Blount and Mary Grainger Blount was a member of Congress from Tennessee. He never married. Richard Blackledge Blount married and left children. Barbara Blount, daughter of Governor William Blount and Mary Grainger Blount, married General Edmund Pendleton Gaines as his second wife and left one son, Edmund Pendleton Gaines, Second, who never married. Eliza Blount, daughter of Governor William Blount and Mary Grainger Blount married Dr. Edwin Wiatt and left children.

John Gray Blount, second son of Jacob Blount and his wife, Ann Reading Blount, was a companion of Daniel Boone but settled in Washington, North Carolina. He married Mary Harvey, daughter of Colonel Miles Harvey and left children namely: Thomas Harvey Blount, John Gray Blount, Second, Polly Ann Blount, William Augustus Blount, Lucy Olivia Blount and Baker Blount.

Reading Blount, third son of Jacob Blount and Ann R. Blount, was born 1757. He was a Major in the War of the Revolution. He died in 1807. He married Lucy Harvey, a daughter of Colonel Miles Harvey and a sister of his brother, John Gray's wife (who was Mary Harvey). They left five children namely: Polly, Louisa, Willie, Caroline Jones Blount and one son, Reading Blount, Second, who married and left a son, Reading Blount, Third.

Thomas Blount, fourth son of Jacob Blount and Ann Reading Blount was born in 1759 and died in 1812. He was an officer in the War of the Revolution, a Major in Colonel Buncombe's Regiment. He married first Patsy Baker and second, Mary Sumner, daughter of General Jethro Sumner. He left no issue.

Jacob Blount, second son of Jacob Blount and Ann Reading Blount was born in 1760 He married firstly his cousin, Ann Collins, daughter of Josiah Collins and had children. He married secondly Mrs. Augustus Harvey, a widow, but had no children by this marriage.

GOVERNOR WILLIE BLOUNT

Willie Blount, the ninth child of Jacob Blount was the first child by his second wife, Mrs. Hannah Salter Baker. He was born in 1768 and was twenty years younger than his distinguished brother the Colonial Governor. The similarity of his name with that of his elder brother causes confusion to the casual student of Tennessee history. Though it was spelled Willie it was pronounced Wylie and was probably a family name in his mother's line.

His first political position was Secretary to his brother then Governor William Blount and he evidently made the most of his opportunities for at twenty eight he was a Judge of the Supreme Court of Tennessee and at forty was elected Governor. He served as Governor six years, (1809 to 1815) in an exciting period of history. During the War of 1812 he tendered to the United States, two thousand five hundred volunteers, and it is from them that the State gained its name, the Volunteer. He pledged his personal credit to equip three regiments which went to General Andrew Jackson at New Orleans. He was active in the Creek War also, raising almost as many volunteers and three hundred thousand dollars which for that period was a tremendous sum of money. He died at the residence of Wylie Johnston near Nashville in 1835 and is buried at Clarksville.

He married Lucinda Baker, daughter of John Baker and his wife Anne Norfleet Baker. They had two daughters, one of whom married Dr. J. T. Dabney and the other a ———Dortch. A son of the latter, Willie Blount Dortch, married a daughter of Governor Aaron V. Brown.

The monument in Clarksville erected by the State to the memory of Governor Willie Blount gives his birth place and his brother's as

NOTABLE SOUTHERN FAMILIES

Bertie County, North Carolina, but the Historian, John H. Wheeler credits Blount Hill in Pitt County as their birthplace.

Sharp Blount was the tenth child of Jacob Blount and the second by the second wife, Mrs. Hannah (Salter) Baker Blount. He was born in 1771 and died in 1810. He married Penlope Little, daughter of Colonel George Little and had children: William Little Blount, Jacob Blount, and George Little Blount. Of these, only the last left children.

Few family names are more identified with North Carolina and Tennessee. Heitman's Historical Register gives six Blounts as officers in the Revolution and every one is given as a resident of North Carolina, showing that the Blount family in America is practically all from this one North Carolina-Tennessee line, or at least, that during the period of the Revolution there were no other Blounts in America.

The following names are in the Register:

Jacob Blount, Paymaster, North Carolina Militia.
Jesse Blount, Commissary, Eighth North Carolina Regiment.
James Blount, Captain Second North Carolina Regiment.
Reading Blount, Captain Third North Carolina Regiment.
William Blount, Paymaster, Third North Carolina Regiment.
Thomas Blount, Lieutenant, Fifth North Carolina Regiment.

BROWNLOW FAMILY

All the people of the name Brownlow in the United States are descended from James and Kate Brownlow, who emigrated to the United States about 1745, from the County of Antrim, North Ireland. They were both school teachers and members of the Presbyterian Church. James taught the boys and his wife the girls. James was a classical scholar and taught Latin and Greek. He taught at Lexington, Rockbridge County, Virginia, and among his pupils there was the boy Sam Houston, the Hero of San Jacinto, Governor of Tennessee, President of Texas and United States Senator from that State after annexation and in 1861 Governor of Texas and the only Governor of the eleven seceded States who opposed the secession of his State. After teaching several years at Lexington, the Brownlows removed to Abingdon, Southwestern Virginia, where they followed the same occupation of school-teaching and here one of James Brownlow's pupils was the afterward famous orator and Senator, William C. Preston, of South Carolina. Both of these distinguished men ever retained a grateful recollection of their faithful teacher, two of whose sons, Alexander and Isaac, fought under General Jackson at the battle of the Horseshoe, the most important of the many battles Jackson fought with the Indians, and which led to his command at the battle of New Orleans. Two others of them, Samuel and William, died Naval Officers. Of the latter Commodore Charles Stewart, "Old Ironsides," under whom he served as a Lieutenant, said: "He was one of the bravest men I have ever known."

James and Kate Brownlow had seven children, six sons and a daughter, namely:

(1) Alexander Brownlow.
(2) Isaac Brownlow.
(3) Samuel L. Brownlow.
(4) William. L. Brownlow.
(5) John Brownlow.
(6) Margaret Brownlow.
(7) Joseph A. Brownlow.

(1) Alexander Brownlow is honorably mentioned in the history of the War of 1812-15 as a Lieutenant in the regular Army in command of Fort Bowyer on the Mississippi. He so distinguished himself in defending this Fort from an attack by the British that he was

promoted to Captain and, like his brothers, William and Samuel of the Navy, he was retained for gallant and meritorious service after the war ended, when the regular Military and Naval Service was reduced by Congress. He died in the service and his remains are in the Cemetery at New Orleans. Among the descendants of Captain Alexander Brownlow is the wife of Honorable Andrieus A. Jones, United State Senator from New Mexico. Senator Jones is a native of West Tennessee.

(2) Isaac Brownlow, great-grand-father of Honorable Louis Brownlow, one of the Commissioners of the District of Columbia, was an inferior officer under General Jackson and bore his dispatches from the Creek War to Huntsville, swimming the Tennessee River on horseback. His numerous descendants in 1861 enlisted in the Confederate Army.

Among the descendants of Isaac Brownlow are Honorable Louis Brownlow, one of the Commissioners of the District of Columbia, and the late John F. Brownlow, Mayor, and a leading citizen of Columbia, Tennessee. Poetry is not associated with warlike qualities, but if the poems written and published in the newspapers of the period by Lieutenant William L. Brownlow and Isaac Brownlow, Captain of Scouts, under Jackson, were collected they would make a small volume.

(3) Samuel L. Brownlow, was a wagon master under General Jackson, and was in the battle of the Horseshoe.

(4) William L. Brownlow, who served as a Lieutenant under Commodore Charles Stewart died a Captain in the Navy and his remains repose in the Navy Yard at Norfolk, Virginia.

(5) John Brownlow was an inferior officer in the Navy and died at sea.

(6) The only daughter, Margaret, married a Scotchman, John McClelland. A son of theirs, Isaac Brownlow McClelland was for about thirty years Clerk and Master of the Chancery Court at Somerville, West Tennessee, and an elder in the Presbyterian Church. A grandson, Lawrence Sparks, was for many years Pastor of a Presbyterian Church at Pittsburg, Pennsylvania. All the descendants of John McClelland and Margaret Brownlow were Presbyterians in religion and were Confederates in the War Between the States.

(7) Joseph A. Brownlow married Catherine Gannaway. His first military service was as a private in the War of 1812. Later he was given a Lieutenant's commission. His son, William Ganaway Brownlow, is the most distinguished of the name. He was born in Wythe County, Virginia, August 29, 1805.

After ten years as a traveling minister (Circuit Rider) of the Methodist Episcopal Church from 1826 to 1836 he located, that is ceased to be in charge of a congregation, and entered Journalistic work. He became editor and publisher of a newspaper in the interest of the Whig party. For years before the Civil War his Newspaper had the largest circulation of any Journal south of the Ohio or Potomac Rivers unless George D. Prentice's Louisville Journal be excepted. People took it for its editorials as it was without Associated Press Dispatches. That after the War Between the States he became Governor of Tennessee and United States Senator is well known; but the incidents of his early life, which contributed to the production of so remarkable a character, and subsequent incidents of his career are not so well known.

Brownlow believed in blood and was himself the offspring of that sturdy race from the North of Ireland which has given to our country three-fourths of its Presidents and its leading statesmen, editors, merchants and soldiers—the race of Jackson, Monroe, Harrison Polk, Taylor, Pierce, Buchanan, John C. Calhoun, the Prestons, Blairs, Breckinridges, Moreheads, Stewarts, Porters, Greeleys and many others who might be named, prominent in all the walks of American life. His mother's maiden name was Catherine Gannaway, daughter of William Gannaway and his wife, Elizabeth Wright, who were natives of Augusta County, Virginia, and large slave-owners. They were a family distinguished for moral worth, good sense and Christian piety. The father of William Gannaway Brownlow was a Presbyterian. He died when his son was ten years of age. His mother was a Methodist and he joined her church.

A nephew of the late Governor Brownlow was the Honorable Walter Preston Brownlow, who died in 1910 while a Member of Congress in the fourteenth year of his service. Walter Preston Brownlow at the time of his death had had appropriated for his District more money than had previously been appropriated for the whole state of Tennessee. This included more than two millions for the National Soldiers Home at Johnson City, public buildings at Bristol, Johnson City and Greeneville, a Fish Hatchery, the only one in Tennessee, in Unicoi County, and he had the burial place of Andrew Johnson made a National Cemetery. When he secured an appropriation of $35,000 for this purpose Congress had only made appropriation to mark or beautify the burial grounds of three Presidents.

It is in the military Service of the country that the Brownlows have been especially zealous. Joseph A. Brownlow was third Lieutenant in the Fourth Regiment, Tennessee Militia, in the War of 1812.

James Patton Brownlow, youngest son of Governor William G. Brownlow, was Colonel of the first Tennessee Cavalry Volunteers, U. S. Army, in the Civil War. After having been shot through both legs and four horses shot under him he was promoted to Brigadier General when only twenty-three years of age.

As to the service of General James P. Brownlow, I quote the following letter addressed to Andrew Johnson, Military Governor, by the distinguished soldier who died as Commander-in-chief of the United States Army:

Nashville, Tennessee, May 21, 1863.

"Governor:

"Having been informed that Lieutenant Colonel Brownlow of the First East Tennessee Cavalry is spoken of for Colonel of one of the new regiments to be raised in your state, I desire to recommend him as eminently qualified and deserving. I have rarely seen a cavalry officer who excited my admiration in so high a degree. He is energetic, daring and skillful. Success with him and his gallant command is the invariable rule.

"I am, Governor,

"Very respectfully your obedient servant,

"J. M. SCHOFIELD, Major General."

His Excellency, Andrew Johnson,
Governor of Tennessee.

General William H. Jackson and the late Rev. Dr. D. C. Kelley, the latter the youngest and one of the most distinguished of General Forrest's subordinate commanders, testified that the most intrepid fighters Forrest's command ever encountered was the First East Tennessee Cavalry under the command of Colonel James P. Brownlow.

The only other son of Governor Brownlow, Colonel John Bell Brownlow, now residing at Knoxville, was Commander of the Ninth Regiment Tennessee Volunteer Cavalry, U. S. A., in the Civil War. His regiment, under his command, was one-third of the Federal troops numbering about 1,300 men, which on the fourth of September, 1864, completely surprised and attacked the Confederate brigade of General John H. Morgan at Greenville, Tennessee. In this engagement General Morgan was killed and about eighty of his men killed and wounded. The Federal force, about 1,300, was comprised in equal numbers of the Ninth Tennessee, Thirteenth Tennessee and Tenth Michigan. Only three men were killed on the Federal side; two of Colonel Brownlow's regiment and one of the Tenth Michigan, commanded by Major Newell. Eighteen men were wounded on the Federal side, twelve of whom were of Colonel Brownlow's command. Two pieces of the Confederate artillery were captured in the fight and this was done by a charge led by Colonel Brownlow. One of these guns was sent as a present to Andrew Johnson, then Military Governor of Tennessee.

BROWNLOW

The reason for the complete victory for the Federal troops on this occasion was that the Confederates, before daylight, were completely surprised, their pickets having been captured asleep. Only a few weeks later the Confederates surprised this Federal Brigade and as completely surprised and defeated it as it had been surprised and defeated.

William Gannaway Brownlow married Eliza O'Brien who was a descendant of the Gaines family (See Gaines).

The children of Governor William Gannaway Brownlow and his wife, Eliza O'Brien Brownlow are: Susan Brownlow, Colonel John Bell Brownlow, General James P. Brownlow, Mary Brownlow, Fannie Brownlow, Annie Brownlow and Caledonia Temple Brownlow.

Of the foregoing:

Susan Brownlow married first Dr. James H. Sawyers and had one child, Lillie, (who married Rev. Samuel D. Long, President of Martha Washington College, Abingdon, Virginia, and married Dr. Daniel T. Boynton as her second husband, and had four children: Lucile Boynton (who married Clarence A. Benscoter and has Daniel Boynton Benscoter); Edmee Boynton (who married Louis D. Huntoon); Ilia Boynton (who married Franklin Pierce Swindler and has Franklin Pierce Swindler, Jr., and Jean Swindler); Dr. Emerson Boynton (who married ——————————— and has Daniel E. Boynton, Lewis D. Boynton and Charles G. Boynton).

Colonel John Bell Brownlow married Fanny Fouche and had three children; William Gannaway Brownlow); second (who married for his first wife Miss Gertrude Mattingly of Washington City, and has Fannie Fouche Brownlow, who married Len G. Broughton, jr., and married for his second wife, Isabel Sevier Williams); John Fouche Brownlow (who married Miss Helen Clark, of Washington City, and has John F. Brownlow, Jr., and Helen Clark Brownlow); and Jennie Brownlow (who married Edward J. Ashe and has Jane Brownlow Ashe.

General James P. Brownlow married Belle Cliffe and had no children.

Mary Brownlow married Henry M. Aiken and had Fannie B. Aiken (who married Frank Carnahan and has Elizabeth Carnahan); William Brownlow Aiken, Horace Aiken, Halmer Aiken, Frank Aiken, Eliza Brownlow Aiken and Henry M. Aiken, Jr.

Fannie Brownlow married George G. Latta and had Georgia Latta; William Brownlow Latta, Ernest Latta, and Vivian Latta.

Annie Brownlow married William F. Patrick and had William Brownlow Patrick.

Caledonia Temple Brownlow married John C. Hale and had John Boynton Hale.

NOTABLE SOUTHERN FAMILIES

Nancy Brownlow, daughter of Joseph A. Brownlow and Catherine Ganaway Brownlow, married John S. Martin, who was born in Virginia in 1795. He removed to Salem, Illinois, in 1845 and died in 1865. From 1825 to 1845 he was Clerk of the County and Circuit Courts of Scott County, Virginia. On removing to Illinois he emancipated several slaves. His first wife was a Morrison. Their son, James Stewart Martin was Colonel of the 111th Illinois Infantry and Brevet Brigadier General of Volunteers, elected as a Republican to Congress in 1872 defeating Judge Silas Bryan, father of Honorable William J. Bryan.

John S. Martin's second wife was Nancy Brownlow, who died in 1846, leaving several children. Their third child, Nancy Rogers Martin, married Samuel Bradford, of Illinois. They had two children, John S. Bradford and Mary Bell Bradford, who died young. John S. Bradford is now President of the Bank of Greenville, and has two children, one of whom, Edgar Bradford, is now with the United States Army in France.

Robert Martin, the fourth child of Nancy Brownlow Martin and John S. Martin, was a Captain in the Union Army in the War Between the States. He married Alice Scott, of Salem, Illinois. They have three children, Dora Martin, Charles Martin and John Martin, and four grandchildren, of whom the oldest, Louis Martin, is in France.

Catherine Martin, the fifth child of Nancy Brownlow Martin and John S. Martin, married C. R. Bennett, of Greenville, Illinois. They had two children, Louis E. Bennett and Charles Courtney Bennett. Courtney Bennett died unmarried.

Louis E. Bennett is a Lieutenant Colonel in the Regular Army of the United States. He served in the Spanish-American War since when he has been in the Regular Army. For two months he was in command of a rgiment in France on the fighting line. He was then transferred to an important position and is now Commander of the Organization of Central Training No. 1, Heavy Artillery. He has several thousand officers and men under his training.

Colonel Bennett married Josephine Tippin, of Greenville, Illinois. They have no children.

Thompson G. Martin, son of Nancy Brownlow Martin and John S. Martin, was a soldier in the Union Army in the War Between the States and was in twenty-one battles. He married Jennie Wrenn, of Salem, Illinois, and had four children, namely: Winifred Martin, Nellie Martin, Edna Martin, and Harry Martin and seven grandchildren, the eldest of whom, Lawrence Martin, is in France.

Benjamin Estell Martin, the sixth child of Nancy Brownlow Martin and John S. Martin, was also in the Union Army in the War Between the States, but was so young he could only enlist as a drummer boy. He married Florida Cunningham, of Salem, Illinois. They had several children, among them, Mary Martin, Bertha Martin, Nancy Martin, Estelle Martin and John Martin.

Matilda Martin, the seventh child of Nancy Brownlow Martin and John S. Martin, married John Gibson, of Alma, Illionis. They have three children, Joseph Gibson, John Gibson and Jane Gibson. Matilda Martin Gibson died while in the Philippines on a pleasure trip. Their daughter, Jane Gibson, married Frank Phillips and resides in Oklahoma.

CALHOUN

The origin of the family and name of Calhoun can be traced for seven hundred years to a younger son of King Conock of Ireland. The name Conock became Colquohoun, Colquhoun, Colhoun and finally Calhoun as the American family spell it now. In Great Britain it is pronounced as if spelled Ca'houn.

Umphredies, the great ancestor of the family who obtained the Barony of Calquohoun in Dumbartonshire, lived in time of Alexander the II of Scotland. His son, Robert lived in the reign of David and was ordered by that monarch to take the Castle of Dumbarton. He sent his answer to the king in three simple words "Si Je Puis!" (If I can.) and that was the motto granted by the king in memory of the exploit when he had succeeded in taking the fortified castle. He did succeed by a strategy. He organized a magnificent hunt and when his clansmen and followers were all out the defenders of the Castle swept out also to join the gay throng and at a signal, Sir Robert Calhoun's men ran back to the castle and captured it without a blow. King David gave the clever huntsman a crest with a stag's head and the three significant words "If I can" for a motto.

After Robert, came Sir Humphrey (which of course is a revival of Umphredies) and after him was John. A second Sir John was followed by several James and Patricks, one following the other, one of whom obtained an estate near Glasgow. Then came Sir James who married Mary Falconer. They had among other children Patrick Calhoun, and he had a son, James Calhoun, who is the Founder of the Family in America.

Of the founding of the family in America, John Ewing Calhoun's brief account is authoritive. He says:

"In 1733 James Calhoun emigrated from the County of Donegal, Ireland, with his wife, Catherine Montgomery. They brought over with them four sons, and one daughter, James, Ezekial, William and Patrick and Catherine. Catherine was married to a Mr. Noble, who left two sons, Alexander and James Noble. The former was the father of the late Governor Noble.

"The family came first to Pennsylvania; we next find them on the waters of the Kanawha, probably within the limits of the present Wythe County, Virginia. After Braddock's defeat they were driven by the Indians, and arrived at Calhoun's Settlement in February, 1756. Their settlement was again broken up in 1760.

"They were overtaken by the Indians about a mile below Patterson's Brigade on Long Cane, and after a desperate engagement, a large portion of the settlers were killed, among them James Calhoun, the eldest son.

"The father of James, the emigrant, was Patrick Calhoun, whose father was James, and so on alternating with these two names for several generations." (From the Memoirs of John Ewing Calhoun.)

The encounter with the Indians on Long Cane, Granville county, took place February 1, 1760, as they were preparing to move for safety to Augusta. Twenty-three members of the little party, including Mrs. James Calhoun, (Catherine Montgomery), and her son, James were massacred. Patrick Calhoun, one of the surviving Calhoun brothers erected stones to mark the site of this massacre, upon one of which appears the following inscription:

> Pat k. Calhoun, Esq.,
> In Memory of Mrs.
> Catherine Calhoun
> Aged 76 years Who
> With 22 Others Was
> Here Murdered By
> The Indians The
> First of Feb. 1760.

James Calhoun, the Emigrant, who was born in Ireland about 1680, had evidently died some years before the Massacre. His wife, Catherine Montgomery Calhoun, who was seventy-six years old in 1760 was born in Ireland in 1684.

Despite tribulation the party persisted and succeeded in establishing the Calhoun Settlement in Abbeville District.

The Calhouns having emigrated to America in 1733, there followed very shortly (1735) their sister, Alice Calhoun, and her husband, Robert Armstrong. They also came first to Pennsylvania and like the Calhouns decided upon a more Southern clime, but they did not follow the wave of emigration which had set out from Pennsylvania to Virginia, but instead went directly to the Calhoun Settlement in Abbeville District, South Carolina. This was after and just subsequent to the massacre, 1760.

Robert Armstrong and Alice Calhoun Armstrong are the progenitors of the large Tennessee Armstrong family, for their son, Robert, who married Margaret Cunningham, moved to Tennessee, and is numbered among the pioneers of the Volunteer State. His body lies beside his wife's on the place which he settled several miles above Knoxville.

The family connection was close for several generations and John C. Calhoun, when Secretary of War, appointed his cousins, Robert

NOTABLE SOUTHERN FAMILIES

Armstrong and Robert Armstrong Houston, both of Tennessee, United States Surveyor and United States Commissioner in the Cherokee Treaty of 1819.

The children of James Calhoun, the Emigrant and his wife, Catherine Montgomery Calhoun were:

I James Calhoun, Second.
II William Calhoun.
III John Calhoun.
LV Catherine Calhoun.
V Ezekiel Calhoun.
VI Patrick Calhoun.

I JAMES CALHOUN

James Calhoun, the Second, eldest son of James Calhoun, the Emigrant and his wife Catherine Montgomery Calhoun, was born in Donegal County Ireland about 1716. He was killed in the Indian Massacle at Long Cane Creek, February 1, 1760.

II WILLIAM CALHOUN

William Calhoun, the second son of James Calhoun, the Emigrant and Catherine Montgomery Calhoun was born in Ireland in Donegal County Ireland, about 1718. He was in the Massacre and suffered more than the other brothers for one of his children was killed and two daughters were captured by Indians and held in captivity for many years. He was a Justice of the Peace for Granville County and later for Ninety-Six District South Carolina under the Provisional Government. He married Agnes Long, October 18, 1749. They had eleven children:

(1) Joseph Calhoun.
(2) Catherine Calhoun.
(3) Anne Calhoun.
(4) Mary Calhoun.
(5) Patrick Calhoun.
(6) Rachel Calhoun.
(7) Esther Calhoun.
(8) William Calhoun, Second.
(9) Ezekiel Calhoun.
(10) Agnes Calhoun.
(11) Alexander Calhoun.

(1) Joseph Calhoun, son of William Calhoun and Agnes Long Calhoun was born October 22, 1750. He was a member of the

CALHOUN

Legislature of South Carolina, was a Colonel of Militia and in 1807 was elected to Congress where he served until 1811, when he was succeeded by his cousin John Caldwell Calhoun. He died April 14, 1917.

He married first his cousin Catherine Calhoun and married, second Martha or Patsey Moseley, daughter of William Moseley, of Virginia. His children by his first wife, Catherine Calhoun Calhoun, were: Ann Calhoun (who married William Perrin); Joseph Calhoun, Second; Catherine Calhoun (who died unmarried) Mary Calhoun (who died unmarried); and by his second wife, Martha or Patsey Moseley Calhoun, Eliza Calhoun (who married James Holt); John Ewing Calhoun (who married Miss Speed); Martha Calhoun (who married John Speed); Samuel Calhoun (who died unmarried) and William Calhoun (died unmarried, was a captain in the Seminole War).

Of the foregoing: Joseph Calhoun, Second, was born July 22 1787. He was educated by Dr. Moses Waddell, was commisioned in the United States Army and attained the rank of Captain. Was in the Richmond Theatre the night of the Great Fire, December 26, 1811 and was badly wounded in the Battle of Lundy's Lane. He married Frances Darricourt. They had nine children: Rebecca Calhoun (who died young); Thomas Smith Calhoun (who died young); Joseph Selden Calhoun (who died young); Louisa Calhoun (who died young); Eliza Calhoun (who furnished much of the early records here quoted); Elizabeth Mary Calhoun (who died unmarried); Frances Josette Calhoun (who married Dr. J. W. Marshall); Ann Calhoun (who died young); and Joseph Calhoun (who married Mary E. Sayre and had Mary Elizabeth Calhoun, died young; Harriet Louise Calhoun, married H. N. VanDeVander; Lilla Frances Calhoun, married R. Morgan; William Sayre Calhoun, married V. B. Loomis; Joseph Selden Calhoun; Marie Estelle Calhoun; and John Joseph Calhoun.

John Ewing Calhoun married Miss——————Speed and had Elizabeth Calhoun (who married James LeRoy); Martha Calhoun (who married George Brown); Margaret Calhoun; and John Ewing Calhoun.

(4) Mary Calhoun, daughter of William Calhoun and Agnes Long Calhoun was born November 1, 1757. She was captured and carried away by Indians in the Long Cane Massacre and was never heard of again. She probably died in the hands of the Indians.

(5) Patrick Calhoun, son of William Calhoun and Agnes Long Calhoun, was born February 18th 1760. He was killed by Indians June 26, 1776, while he was serving as an Ensign in Captain James McCall's Expedition to the Cherokee Country. He was only sixteen years old.

NOTABLE SOUTHERN FAMILIES

(6) Rachael Calhoun, daughter of William Calhoun and Agnes Long Calhoun, was born September 19, 1762. She married Patrick Norris.

(7) Esther Calhoun, daughter of William Calhoun and Agnes Long Calhoun, was born September 30, 1765. She married William Love.,

(8) William Calhoun, Second, son of William Calhoun and Agnes Long Calhoun was born April 5, 1768. He married Rebecca Tenneyhill. Their children were: Ezekiel Calhoun; Catherine Calhoun; Rachel Calhoun (who married Handly Harris); William F. Calhoun; James Montgomery Calhoun; Joseph Calhoun; Rebecca Calhoun; Sarah Calhoun; and Mary Elizabeth Calhoun (who married Nathan Massey).

Of the foregoing children of William Calhoun, Second: Ezekiel Calhoun married Lucy Wellborn and had Carolina Calhoun (who married John S. Williams); Georgia Calhoun; Virginia Calhoun (who married Oliver Coussins); Indiana Calhoun; Edward Calhoun; Pickens Calhoun; Missouri Calhoun (who married Dr. Martin); and Florida Calhoun (who married her sister Missouri's widower, Dr. Martin).

James Montgomery Calhoun married Emma Elizabeth Dabney and had William Lowndes Calhoun (who married Mary Oliver and Emma Carolina Calhoun, married Silas Connelly; James Montgomery Calhoun, Second, who married a Templeton; Mary Calhoun; William Dabney Calhoun; William Lowndes Calhoun, Second; and Nettie Aline Calhoun); Emma Calhoun; Anna Calhoun (who married Dr. DuBose); Chattanooga Calhoun; Rebecca Calhoun (who married J. H. Matthews); James V. Calhoun; Patrick H. Calhoun (who married firstly Frances S. Fuller and had Charles Augustus Calhoun and married secondly Ida Cole and had Rosa Calhoun); Hannah Calhoun; and John Dabney Calhoun).

Joseph Calhoun married Ann Cross and lived in Mobile, Ala. They had William Joseph Calhoun (who married Margaret Alexander and had John Carroll Calhoun; William Joseph Calhoun; Edward Jones Calhoun; Gaines Calhoun; and Margaret Alexander Calhoun); Amanda Abbeville Calhoun; Ella Ann Calhoun (who married William Hunter Harlan); James Butler Calhoun (who married Fanny Barham); Isabella Cross Calhoun; John Carroll Calhoun; Frank Howard Calhoun; Aline S. Calhoun (who married———McDougald); and Lida Rebecca Calhoun.

(9) Ezekiel Calhoun, son of William Calhoun and Agnes Long Calhoun, was born November 27, 1770. He married Frances Hamilton, daughter of Major Andrew Hamilton. Their children were William Calhoun (who died unmarried); Joseph Calhoun (who

CALHOUN

died unmarried); Harriet Calhoun (who married Thomas Davis, of Washington, D C.); Jane Hamilton Calhoun (who married Dr Webb Simonds and had a son Andrew Simonds, who married his cousin, Sarah Calhoun Martin); Ephriam Calhoun; Catherine Calhoun (who married Dr. John W. Parker, of Columbia, South Carolina); and Andrew Calhoun.

Of the foregoing children of Ezekiel Calhoun:

Ephriam Calhoun married Charlotte Moseley, of Abbeville District, and had Motte Calhoun (who married Sallie Goodwin and had William Goodwin Calhoun, Roland R. Calhoun and Augusta Calhoun); Eliza Calhoun (who married Dr. John H. Logan the historian); Augusta Calhoun (who married Peter Goodwin); Franklin Ramsay Calhoun (who married Annie E. Turpin and had Augusta Calhoun, Dr. Alfred Turpin Calhoun, Annie Calhoun, married William David Link, of Erie, Pennsylvania; Daniel Calhoun, and Charlotte Moseley Calhoun, married W. T. Bates); Charles Moseley Calhoun (who married Emily Nelson and had Robert Edger Calhoun, (married Mamie Ziegler), Ida Chicora Calhoun, Daniel Du Pre Calhoun, Eliza Elliott Calhoun, John Franklin Calhoun, Charles Ramsay Calhoun, Motte McG. Calhoun, Waring Parker Calhoun, Nina Nelson Calhoun, and Fanny Emma Calhoun (who married Daniel Dupre).

Andrew Calhoun married Susan Wellborn, of Georgia, and had Martha Frances Calhoun, (who married Dr. Divine); Ann Elizabeth Calhoun (who married William Caldwell); Abner Wellborn Calhoun (who married Louise King Phinizy, see Phinizy Family, and had Dr. Ferdinand Phinizy Calhoun, who married Marion Peel and has Ferdinand Phinizy Calhoun, Jr., Lawson Peel Calhoun and Marion Peel Calhoun; Susan Wellborn Calhoun, who married Junius Oglesby and has no children; Andrew Wellborn Calhoun, who married Mary Trigg, of Chattanooga, and has James Trigg Calhoun, Abner Wellborn Calhoun and Louise Phinizy Calhoun; and Harriet Calhoun who married Stuart Witham and has Stuart Witham, Jr).

(10) Agnes Calhoun, daughter of William Calhoun and Agnes Long Calhoun his wife, was born August 29, 1773. She married General Hutton.

(11) Alexander Calhoun, son of William Calhoun and Agnes Long Calhoun was born December 21, 1776. He married Kitty Johnson and had one child, Kitty Calhoun (who married Edward Tillman).

III JOHN CALHOUN

John Calhoun, son of James Calhoun, the Emigrant and Catherine Montgomery Calhoun was born in Ireland about 1720. He married and had two children.

IV CATHERINE CALHOUN

Catherine Calhoun, the only daughter of James Calhoun, the Emigrant and his wife Catherine Montgomery Calhoun was born in Ireland about 1718. She married John Noble in Ireland, (and therefore was evidently not with her parents when they emigrated to America in 1732). She had three children, the eldest of whom Alexander Noble was born at sea as his father and mother came to America. Catherine Calhoun Noble became a widow early in life and made her home with her brothers' families. She and her children escaped the Massacre at Long Cane Creek and settled with other members of the family in Abbeville District. Her children were, Alexander Noble, James Noble, and a daughter whose name is not given.

(1) Alexander Noble married his first cousin, Catherine Noble the daughter of Ezekiel Calhoun and Jean or Jane Ewing Calhoun. They had a son, Patrick Noble, who became Governor of South Carolina.
(2) James Noble.
(3) ——————Noble, a daughter.

V EZEKIEL CALHOUN

Ezekiel Calhoun, son of James Calhoun, the Emigrant and Catherine Montgomery Calhoun, was born in Donegal County, Ireland 1720. He was with his family in all the Indian Persecutions. He married Jane or Jean Ewing some years previous to 1759 for in that year September 3, his will is dated and in it he makes mention of his wife Jean and his seven children:

(1) John Ewing Colhoun.
(2) Patrick Calhoun.
(3) Ezekiel Calhoun, Second.
(4) Mary Calhoun, married ———— Carr.
(5) Rebecca Calhoun (who married Andrew Pickens).
(6) Catherine Calhoun (who married her cousin, Alexander Noble).
(7) Jean or Jane Calhoun, (who married John Steadman).

(1) John Ewing Calhoun, son of Ezekiel Calhoun, and Jean or Jane Ewing Calhoun, was born about 1750. He joined Captain Charles Drayton's Company of Militia for Revolutionary Service and he signed his name to the roll of that Company "John Ewing Col-

CALHOUN

houn" and continued so to write his name until his death as his descendants did after him. He died October the 2, 1802. He married Floride Bonneau, daughter of Samuel Bonneau. Their children were Benjamin Colhoun (who died young) Floride Bonneau Colhoun (who married her cousin John Caldwell Calhoun); John Ewing Colhoun, Second; James Edward Colhoun; (who married Maria Simpkins, but left no children) and William Sheridan Colhoun (who died young).

Of the foregoing children of John Ewing Colhoun: John Ewing Colhoun married Martha Maria David and had John Ewing Colhoun (who died young); Martha Maria Colhoun (who died young); William Ransom Colhoun; Susan Colhoun; John Ewing Colhoun; Florence Colhoun (who died young); Warren Davis Colhoun (who died young); Henry Davis Colhoun; Edward Boiseau Colhoun (who married Sarah C. Norwood. He served in Lucas' Battalion of Artillery in the War Between the States and was a captain. He married Sarah C. Norwood. Their children were: Martha Colhoun; Sarah Louise Colhoun (who married Allen McShoen of Richmond, Va.); Floride Bonneau Colhoun; Willie Norwood Colhoun.

VI PATRICK CALHOUN

Patrick Calhoun, son of James Calhoun, the Emigrant and his wife Catherine Montgomery Calhoun was born in Donegal County, Ireland, in June 1727. He was seven years old when his parents emigrated to America. Patrick was with his people in all their troubles of settling the new home and was a leading spirit in the family as well as in the community. Having survived the terrible Massacre he erected some years later the monument to his mother and the twenty-two victims at Long Cane Creek He was appointed by the provincial Government Commander of a body of Rangers.

He was Justice of the Peace for Granville County and later for Ninety-Six District, South Carolina under the Provincial Government.

At an election on the 7th and 8th of March 1769 Patrick Calhoun was elected to the Commons House of Assembly from Prince William's Parish. He served until the next election in October 1772 and was the first representative from the Up-Country. He was sent as a Deputy to the First Congress (January to November 1775) from Ninety-Six District and was re-elected to the Second Provincial Congress (November 1775 to March 1776.) and was a member of the First General Assembly (1776) of the State of South Carolina. He thereafter served in almost every Assembly until his death. He died February 15, 1796, being in his sixty-ninth year.

Patrick Calhoun was married twice. His first wife, a Miss Craighead, daughter of Reverand Alexander Craighead, left no children. His second wife was Martha Caldwell by whom he had five children:

(1) JAMES CALHOUN
(2) CATHERINE CALHOUN (married Rev. Moses Waddell and had only one child who died young.
(3) WILLIAM CALHOUN.
(4) JOHN CALDWELL CALHOUN.
(5) PATRICK CALHOUN, Second.

(1) James Calhoun, son of Patrick Calhoun and Martha Caldwell Calhoun, married May 4th, 1802, Sarah Caldwell Martin, daughter of Dr. James Martin, Surgeon of the 3rd, South Carolina Continental Line. Their Children were: Patrick Calhoun, died young; James Martin Calhoun; John Alfred Calhoun; Caroline, died young; William Henry Calhoun; Benjamin Calhoun, died young; Sarah Calhoun; George MsDuffie Calhoun, died young.

Of the foregoing:

James Martin Calhoun, married Susan Pickens and had Susan Wilkison Calhoun(who married Alexander Noble, a descendant of Catherine Calhoun who married John Noble); Andrew Calhoun (who married Frances E. Lee and had Susan Wilkinson Calhoun, Rebecca Lee Calhoun, Julia Fishburn Calhoun, James Martin Calhoun, Second, Harriet Eliza Calhoun, Sarah Pickens Calhoun, and Ellen Lee Calhoun.)Sarah Lee Calhoun married William T. Wade; James F. Calhoun (who married Florence Oliver Lee for his first wife and Emma R. Lee for his second wife had by his first wife Mary Louisa Calhoun, Martin Lee Calhoun, Marion Pickens Calhoun and Florence Oliver Calhoun; and had by the second wife: Martha Eleanor Calhoun, James Francis Calhoun, Andrew Pickens Calhoun and Julia Emma Calhoun); and John C. Calhoun (who married Mary Graham and had Annie Graham Calhoun, and Mary Kennon Calhoun).

John Alfred Calhoun married Sarah Morvin Norwood and had JAMES CALDWELL CALHOUN (who married Blandina M. Kirtland and had Isaac Kirtland Calhoun, James Caldwell Calhoun, John Alfred Calhoun, Second (who married Mat North Colcock), Lucy Calhoun, and Tredwell Ayers Calhoun.) MARY NORWOOD CALHOUN (who married General William Lomax) AURELIA CALHOUN (who married Alexander R. Rucker); SARAH MARTIN CALHOUN (who married Andrew Simonds, son of Jane Hamilton Calhoun and Dr. Joseph Webb Simonds);

CALHOUN

WILLIAMSON NORWOOD CALHOUN (who married Virginia Caroline Bowman, daughter of Reverend Peyton Green Bowman and had Sarah Norwood Calhoun, James Caldwell Calhoun Marie Bowman Calhoun, who married R. H. Baker, and Virginia Calhoun); CAROLINE CALHOUN CALHOUN (who married George Erskine Heard); JOHN ALFRED CALHOUN (who died unmarried); ORVILLE TATUM CALHOUN (who married Sallie P. Gilbert and had Gilbert Calhoun); ANNA SUSAN CALHOUN (who married William A. Ancrum); WILLIAM PATRICK CALHOUN (who married Gladys Boykin); TENNENT LOMAX CALHOUN; and KATE CALHOUN (who married Alonzo H. O'Farrell.)

WILLIAM HENRY CALHOUN married Jane Orr and had FLORENCE C. CALHOUN (who married John T. Tankersley of Mississippi); JAMES LAWRENCE CALHOUN; MARTHA J. CALHOUN; J. CHRISTOPHER CALHOUN; SARAH CAROLINE CALHOUN (who married L. T. Taylor of Mississippi); JOHN CALDWELL CALHOUN (who died unmarried); and WILLIAM HENRY CALHOUN (who married Susan Reed for his first wife, by whom he hod no children and married Clifford Winston for his second wife by whom he had Fanny Calhoun).

(3) WILLIAM CALHOUN, the second son of PATRICK CALHOUN and his wife, Martha Caldwell Calhoun, married Catherine Jenna de Graffenreid. Their children were: TESCHARNER CALHOUN (who died unmarried) PATRICK CALHOUN (who died unmarried); MARY CALHOUN (who died unmarried); JANE CALHOUN (who died unmarried); LUCRETIA ANN CALHOUN (who married first Dr. Henry Townes of Greeneville and second Dr. Tescharner de Graffenreid of Alabama); THOMAS CALHOUN; MARTHA CATHERINE CALHOUN (who married Armistead Burt); JAMES LAWRENCE CALHOUN; SARAH CALHOUN (who married Ezekiel Pickens Noble, a descendant of Catherine Calhoun who married John Noble); EUGENIA CALHOUN (who marrier Dr. Edwin Parker); and GEORGE McDUFFIE CALHOUN.

Of the foregoing THOMAS CALHOUN married Margaret Meek and had William Calhoun (who married Mary Bailey) James Calhoun; Henry Townes Calhoun, Jane Calhoun (married Henry Harper); Elizabeth Calhoun (married Rr. Robert Harper,) and Margaret Meek Calhoun.

JAMES LAWRENCE CALHOUN married for his first wife Mary Hunter and for his second wife Jane Verdier and had by his first wife CATHERINE L. CALHOUN, (who married George Jones of Alabama); EUGENIA CALHOUN (who married

NOTABLE SOUTHERN FAMILIES

James Duncan); and THOMAS CALHOUN (who married Miss ———Blakeford) and had by the second wife: Sallie Calhoun (who married John G. Winter), and JAMES LAWRENCE CALHOUN, Second(who married Miss Moore).

GEORGE McDUFFIE CALHOUN, married Julia Goodwin of Columbia. Their children were A. BURT CALHOUN (who died young);ROBERT C. CALHOUN (who died young); JOHN CALHOUN (who died young); GEORGE CALHOUN (who married in Texas); and JULIA CALHOUN.

JOHN CALDWELL CALHOUN

JOHN CALDWELL CALHOUN, the son of PATRICK and Martha Caldwell Calhoun, was born March 18, 1782. He entered Yale in 1802 and graduated two years later; he studied law at the Litchfield Law School of Conneticut in 1805-06 and was admitted to the Bar in 1807 and elected to the House of Representatives of his native state the same year. The next year he was appointed to the staff of Governor Drayton. In 1810 he was elected to Congress and was re-elected in 1812, 1814, and 1816. In 1817 he was selected as Secretary of War by President Monroe and served until 1825, at which date he was inaugurated Vice-President. In 1828 he was again elected Vice-President and from that office he resigned in 1832 in order to serve as Senator from South Carolina, succeeding Robert Young Hayne, the recently elected Governor of that State. He took his seat in the Senate in 1833, was re-elected in 1834 ind in 1840; he resigned in 1842, but served until the next year. In 1844 he was a candidate for the Presidency, but withdrew and was appointed Secretary of State by President Tyler for a year. From that office he was again elected to the Senate succeeding Judge Daniel Elliott Huger, who had resigned that Calhoun might be returned to that body. He Died in Washington, March 31, 1850, having reached the age of sixty-eight.

On January 8, 1811, he was married to his cousin, FLORIDE COLHOUN, the daughter of JOHN EWING COLHOUN and the granddaughter of EZEKIAL CALHOUN.

JOHN CALDWELL CALHOUN, the First, and his wife Floride Calhoun Calhoun had eight children, namely: ANDREW PICKENS CALHOUN; ANNA MARIA CALHOUN, married Thomas G. Clemson; PATRICK CALHOUN, died unmarried; JOHN CALDWELL CALHOUN, the Second; MARTHA CORNELIA CALHOUN; JAMES CALHOUN, died unmarried; WILLIAM LOWNDES CALHOUN.

CALHOUN

Of the foregoing:

ANDREW PICKENS CALHOUN married first Miss Chappell who left no children, and married second, Margaret Green, daughter of Duff Green and a descendant of Mildred Washington aunt and godmother to President George Washington, by whom he had: DUFF GREEN CALHOUN (who married Elizabeth Beaseley, of Texas, and had Andrew Calhoun, who married his cousin Floride Lee a grand daughter of Anna Maria Calhoun, Clemson.) JOHN CALDWELL CALHOUN, (born July 9th 1843 served in the Confederate Army from Fort Sumter to the surrender, entering the service when he was only eighteen. He served as faithfully in the interest of the South after the surrender. He makes his home in New York. He married Linnie Adams, a grand niece of Vice President Richard M. Johnson and has four children: James Edward Calhoun, Captain in the United States Army, David Calhoun (who married Olga Dininy and has John Caldwell Calhoun) John Caldwell Calhoun and Julia Johnson Calhoun (who married Baron E. deNagell of Holland of the Diplomatic Service of that Country); MARGARET MARIA CALHOUN; ANDREW PICKENS CALHOUN (who died unmarried) and PATRICK CALHOUN (who makes his present home in Cleveland, Ohio, though he has lived in many other cities, Dalton, Georgia, Atlanta, Baltimore, Pittsburgh, St. Louis and San Francisco. He married Sarah Porter Williams and has six children, namely: Martha Calhoun; Margaret Green Calhoun, (who married Scott Foster and has a son); Patrick Calhoun, serving in the United States Army, George Williams Calhoun, serving in the United States Army, Andrew Calhoun, serving in the United States Army, and ─────── Calhoun serving in the United States Army). James Edward Calhoun (who died unmarried; and Mary Lucretia Calhoun, (who died young).

JOHN CALDWELL CALHOUN (son of Vice President JOHN CALDWELL CALHOUN) married first Anzie Adams, by whom he had no children and married second, Kate Kirby Putnam by whom he had JOHN CALDWELL CALHOUN, and BENJAMIN PUTNAM CALHOUN (who married Julia Peterman).

WILLIAM LOWNDES CALHOUN (who married first, Margaret Cloud by whom he had no children and married, second, his brother's widow, Mrs. Kate Kirby Calhoun, by whom he had a son, William Lowndes Calhoun, Second.)

(5) PATRICK CALHOUN, son of PATRICK CALHOUN and his wife Martha Caldwell Calhoun married Nancy Needham de Graffenried, sister of his brother William Calhoun's wife. Their children were: MARTHA CALHOUN (who married Dr. Bon-

ner); CATHERINE CALHOUN (who married Dr. William Tennent); EDWARD CALHOUN; LUDLOW CALHOUN; FRANCIS AUGUSTUS CALHOUN; BENJAMIN ALFRED CALHOUN.

Of the foregoing:

EDWARD CALHOUN, married Frances Middleton and had JOHN FRANCES CALHOUN who married Rebecca Noble and had Frances Calhoun, Susan Calhoun, Caroline Calhoun, Rebecca Calhoun (married Robert Shiver) Rosa Calhoun, Patrick Calhoun, and Andrew Pickens Calhoun); PATRICK EDWARD CALHOUN (who died young); EDWIN CALHOUN (who married Sallie Tillman and had Kate Calhoun (married L. C. Haskell) John Calhoun, Edwin Calhoun, Frances Calhoun, Lalla Calhoun, Arthur Calhoun, Charles Calhoun, Eunice Calhoun); ·IDA CALHOUN (who married Charles Alexander) and ROSA CALHOUN (who married her sister's widower, Charles Alexander.)

LUDLOW CALHOUN married Margaret Teague. Their children were LUDLOW CALHOUN, Second, NANCY NEEDHAM CALHOUN; JOHN CALDWELL CALHOUN (who married a Miss Gilmer); PATRICK CALHOUN; EUGENIA CALHOUN (who married Robert Middleton); THOMAS CALHOUN; FRANCIS A. CALHOUN; EDWARD CALHOUN; ARTHUR CALHOUN; BENJAMIN F. CALHOUN (who married ―――――――― and had a son, Arthur Ludlow Calhoun who lived in Beaumont, Texas) and ELLA CALHOUN (who married S. B. Mays).

FRANCIS AUGUSTUS CALHOUN, married Laura Jones, of Georgia. Their children were CATHERINE JENNA CALHOUN; BENJAMIN A. CALHOUN (who married Josie Tucker of Texas, and had Etta Virginia Calhoun, Francis A. Calhoun, Patrick Calhoun and Carrie Lou Calhoun); CORNELIA CALHOUN (who married Edward Yarborough); Emma Calhoun (who married George C. Graves); PATRICK L. CALHOUN (who married Ida Hankinson); FRANCIS AUGUSTUS CALHOUN, Second; THOMAS JONES CALHOUN; KATE CALHOUN (who married Marshall P. DeBruhl); and LOUISE CALHOUN.

BENJAMIN ALFRED CALHOUN, son of PATRICK CALHOUN, son of PATRICK CALHOUN, married Miss Yarborough.

DEADERICK FAMILY
(DIETRICK)

The Deaderick family of Tennessee traces its ancestry to David Dietrick, a native of Wurtemburg, Germany, who emigrated to America in 1747. He settled first in Philadelphia, but soon moved to Winchester, Frederick County, Virginia, which was settled by Pennsylvania Germans in 1732. David Dietrick married about 1752 or 3 Rosanna Boucher, daughter of Michael Boucher, a descendant of Jacob Boucher, to whom arms were granted in Germany in 1450. From Cartwell's History of Frederick County and Shenandoah Valley Pioneers we find that Michael Boucher, a German, subscribed to Oath of Parliament for naturalization in Frederick County, at the June term of court 1744. Cartwell says on page 492 "The Bucher (Booker) Family found about Newtown as one of the pioneers, and also in the western section of the County, often spell the name Boogher. They furnished soldiers for all the wars during the history of the County.

From an alphabetical list of the Poll of Frederick County July, 24, 1758, Colonel George Washington and Colonel Martin were elected Burgesses. David Deaderick's name appears as having voted for both as did also James Knight, Christopher Wendel, August Wendel, and Val Wendel, Virginia Historical Magazine, Vol. VI., page 163 .

David Deitrick was a German Lutheran. He was one of the founders of the historic old Stone Church of Winchester, and his name appears upon the ancient Latin document bearing date, April 16, 1764, taken from its corner stone. His will made in 1767, was recorded in the Court of Frederick County, May 4, 1768. The body of the will is written in English, but the signature is in German characters.

The name Dietrick signifies Master Key. Dietrick Von Bern, King of the Ostragoths from 454 to 526, was the founder of a powerful and influential house in South Germany and it is from him that the Dietricks of Wurtemburg claim descent. The descendants of David Dietrick have Anglicized the name to Deaderick.

After the death of David Dietrick, his widow Rosanna Boucher Dietrick married Dr. Samuel May, an Englishman, from whom she was later divorced. Their children were Samuel May, Second; Dr. Francis May; and Rosanna May who married ———Perry, of Staunton and had two sons, George and William Perry.

The Virginia Enumeration for 1782 gives Samuel May as a resident of Fredrick County, having in family eight white souls and four slaves. Mrs. Rosanna Boucher Dietrick May was living in Winchester in 1810. In 1806 David Deaderick, of Jonesboro, Washington Co., Tenn. made a trip to Baltimore and Philadelphia to buy goods for his store at Jonesboro. In a letter to his wife dated Baltimore, April........1806 he speaks of having visited his mother in Winchester. This letter with other heirlooms including a minature of David Deaderick, Second, by the famous Peel is the property of Mrs. Adelia Scott, of Knoxville, Tenn.

The children of David Dietrick and Rosanna Boucher Dietrick were:

I David Deaderick, Second.
II George Michael Deaderick.
III Susannah Deaderick.
IV John Deaderick.
V Thomas Deaderick.
VI Elizabeth Deaderick.

DAVID DEADERICK, Second

David Deaderick, Second, oldest son of David Deitrick, was born in Winchester, Virginia, October 10, 1754, and it is from him that the family in East Tennessee is descended. He was fourteen years old when his father died. At the beginning of the Revolution, he enlisted as a private in the Continental Army and served three months under Colonel John Neville. He was in the 8th Virginia Regiment, commanded by General Peter Muhlenburg. The regiment was commonly called the German Regiment. He was promoted, became adjutant of his regiment and, before the close of the war, was made Colonel of a regiment of Virginia militia. How's History of Virginia p. 469 Smith's History of Virginia, 1st Ed. His wife Margaret Anderson Deaderick was granted a pension for his Revolutionary services. In the first census of Virginia, 1782, David Deaderick's name is given as the head of a family consisting of five white people. This is the only Deaderick given in the whole state of Virginia. In 1784, David Deaderick married Nancy Knight of Winchester. She was a daughter of James Knight, a Revolutionary soldier. She died in 1787, leaving one son, William Haney Deaderick.

The next year, David Deaderick, with his little son, left Virginia and removed to Jonesboro, Tennessee, where he established himself as a merchant. When Washington College was established, in 1795, by a bill passed by the Territorial Assembly at Knoxville, David Deaderick was appointed one of the incorporators. He heads the list of eleven commissioners appointed by the legislature to manage the affairs of Jonesboro, April 23, 1796. He represented Washington and Car-

DEADERICK

ter counties in the State Senate in 1799. In 1795 he married as his second wife, Margaretta Anderson of Jonesboro. Six children were born to this marriage.

David Deaderick died in Jonesboro, October 23, 1823, and is buried there. His monument bears this inscription: "An honest man is the noblest work of God."

The children of David Deaderick, Second were:

By his first wife, Nancy Knight Deaderick
William Haney Deaderick.

By his second wife, Margaretta Anderson Deaderick
David Anderson Deaderick
Amanda Frances Deaderick
Eliza Ross Deaderick.
Joseph Deaderick.
John Franklin Deaderick
James W. Deaderick.

WILLIAM HANEY DEADERICK

William Haney Deaderick, son of David Deaderick, Second, and his first wife, Nancy Knight Deaderick, was born in Winchester, Virginia, November 30, 1785.

He received the best education obtainable in those days. He studied medicine and began the practice of his profession in Rogersville and Greenville. For a period he lived in Jefferson County, Tennessee, where he married, March 26, 1807, Penelope Hamilton, daughter of Colonel Joseph Hamilton and granddaughter of Colonel Alexander Outlaw, both pioneers of East Tennessee. She died April 10, 1836, and is probably buried in the Hamilton graveyard, at Rural Mount, Jefferson County, Tennessee, eight miles south of Morristown.

Dr. Deaderick married a second time Mrs. Lois Ashworth. Dr. Deaderick was highly regarded in his profession. In 1810, he performed the notable operation of removing the jawbone. This was before the introduction of Anaesthetics in surgery. His original notes for his operation are now the property of Mrs. Fannie Cleage McCleary.

A document of interest to those whose ancestors lived in Jefferson County, Tennessee is the Parish Register of St. Paul's Presbyterian Church, near the Nollichucky River.

In this register are enrolled the names of Deadericks, Hamiltons, Campbells, Inmans, Blackburns, Bradfords and many others.

The church was organized in April 1818. One of the first members enrolled was William H. Deaderick, June 20, 1818. William

NOTABLE SOUTHERN FAMILIES

Haney Deaderick and Penelope Deaderick were admitted on examination.

Birth Record:
To William H. Deaderick, March 29, 1818, Joseph Hamilton Deaderick, Baptisms August 8, 1819, Penelope H. and Eliza Ann Deaderick.

In 1820 the Register shows William H. Deaderick was attached to the New Salem Church.

Later Dr. William Haney Deaderick moved to Athens, Tennessee, where he bought a farm which he called Prospect Hill. The main portion of this farm he deeded to his daughter, Eliza Van Dyke and it is now known as the VanDyke Place. He erected a brick house on the corner of his farm nearest the town of Athens and continued the practice of medicine until his death, October 29, 1857.

The children of Dr. William H. Deaderick and Penelope Hamilton Deaderick were.

1 Penelope Hamilton Deaderick.
2 David Deaderick, Third.
3 Eliza Ann Deaderick.
4 Thomas Scott Deaderick.
5 William H. Deaderick, Jr., died in infancy.
6 Frances Nelson Deaderick.
7 Robert Hamilton Deaderick
8 William H. Deaderick.
9 Alexander Hamilton Deaderick.

Of the foregoing:

Penelope Hamilton Deaderick born March 20, 1809, married November 6, 1825, Victor Morceau Campbell. Their children were Kate Deaderick Campbell (who married S. B. Temple) Margaret Deaderick Campbell (who married Hamilton Hale); Loretta Deaderick Campbell.

David Deaderick, Third, born December 26, 1811, went to Texas in the 30's and was in the War of Independence of the Republic of Mexico in 1836. He was in the battle of San Jacinto under General Sam Houston. He died in Athens, Tennessee in 1840.

Eliza Ann Deaderick, born May 1, 1814 married May 25, 1833, Thomas Nixon VanDyke, born January 22, 1803, died 1891. They lived at "Prospect Hill" near Athens, McMinn County, Tennessee. Their children were:

(1) Penelope Smith VanDyke, born August 21, .834, died August 11, 1907 (who married in Athens Tennessee February 15, 1856 Thomas Alexander Cleage born August 24, 1835 died December

DEADERICK

12, 1900. After their marriage they removed to Chattanooga. They had William Deaderick Cleague, Thomas A. Cleague, Jr., Richard VanDyke Cleage, Nellie Cleage; Sue Coffin Cleage; Francis Cleage; Hamilton Cleage; Anna Mary Cleage; Letitia Cleage; Jose Cleage. Of these: William Deaderick Cleage married his cousin Josie Sloss, a descendant of Judge David Campbell and had Mary Louise Cleage (who married E. E. Crum, of Mobile, Alabama), and married for his second wife Carrie Clinton, and had five children who reside in Memphis, Tennessee. Thomas A. Cleage, Jr., married his cousin Mamie Deaderick, daughter of Frank Deaderick and grand daughter of Judge James A. Deaderick and had Deaderick Cleage, Van Dyke Cleage, Edith Cleage, Penelope Cleage, all of whom live in St. Louis, Missouri. Richard Van Dyke Cleage married Mrs. Lula Stover. Sue Coffin Cleage married James Whiteside Johnson, of Chattanooga and had Penelope Van Dyke Johnson who married Samuel Boyd Allen, of Knoxville and has one child, Penelope Van Dyke Allen; Thankful Anderson Johnson who married Frank C. Davies, of Chattanooga and has two children John L. Davies Jr. and Sue Davies and now resides in Youngstown, Ohio; Raymond Hamilton Johnson who died unmarried at the age of twenty years; Helen Johnson, who married William Polk Flower, Jr., A. M. Johnson, Second; Thomas Johnson and Foster E. Johnson. Frances Hamilton Cleage married Dr. Wilber W. McCleary of Chicago and has one child, Josephine McCleary. Anna Mary Cleage married Clarence Dumas, of Arlington, Alabama, and they now reside in Mobile, Alabama. Letitia Cleage, Josie Cleage, and Nellie Cleage died young.

(2) William Deaderick Van Dyke born October 20, 1836 married Anna Mary Deaderick third child of Judge James A. Deaderick and Adeline McDowell Deaderick. He was a Major in the Confederate Army. Later he practiced law in Chattanooga where he died August 1, 1883. Their children were Annie Clifton Van Dyke; Thomas Nixon Van Dyke, who married Maud Farquhar and has Louise VanDyke and William Nixon Nixon VanDyke; Frances Lavinia Van Dyke who married Milton B. Ochs and has VanDyke Ochs and Adolph S. Ochs, Second, both officers in the United States Army and Margaret Ochs; and Cary Shelby VanDyke.

(2) Letitia Smith VanDyke, born October 12, 1838, died young.

(4) Richard Smith VanDyke born October 14, 1840 was a Major in the Confederate Army 1st Tennessee Cavalry and was wounded in battle near New Market, Virginia. He died in Lynchburg, Virginia, November 14, 1864, at the residence of his cousin, John William Murrell.

NOTABLE SOUTHERN FAMILIES

(5) John Montgomery VanDyke born October 7 1842 was Captain of 59th Tennessee Mounted Infantry Confederate States Army. He was killed while in command of the Regiment in battle on the September 2, 1864 near Darkville, Va.

(6) Frances Lavinia Van Dyke, born October 8, 18‸‸.

(7) Thomas Nixon VanDyke Jr. born November 11, 1846 died February 3, 1863 at Prospect Hill. He volunteered October 4, 1862 in Captain Blavin's Company 63rd Regiment Tennessee Volunteers Confederate Army and died from illness contracted in camp at Cumberland Gap, February 3, 1863.

(8) Margaret Josephine VanDyke born August 3, 1849 married May 23, 1871, Hugh T. Inman, of Atlanta, and has Annie Inman (who married John Grant, and has Margaret Grant married Richard Wilmer; William Grant; Hugh Grant, Jr., and Ann Grant. Josephine Inman (who married Hugh Richardson and has three children among them Hugh Richardson, Jr.,) Edward Inman, (who married Emily McDougal. Their children are Hugh Inman and Edward Inman Jr. Hugh Inman died young. Louise Inman died young.

(9) Mary Hamilton Van Dyke, born April 4, 1853, married October 4, 1881, George M. Battey, of Rome, Georgia, and had George Battey, Mary Battey (who married George Bonney, of Atlanta); Dr. Hugh Battey, and Adrienne Battey.

Robert Deaderick Van Dyke, born March 7, 1861, married Sue Gwaltney, of Rome, Georgia, and has Marion Van Dyke; Robert Van Dyke, Jr., William Van Dyke and Ann Van Dyke.

William H. Deaderick, Jr., born May 1, 1816, died December 12, 1818.

Thomas Scott Deaderick, born August 28, 1826, was a soldier in the Mexican War.

Robert Hamilton Deaderick, born January 21, 1829, served in the Confederate Army and died unmarried.

Joseph Hamilton Deaderick, born March 29, 1819.

Margaret A. Deaderick, born October 17, 1821, married John L. Bridges and had no children.

By his second marriage to Mrs. Lois Ashworth, December 13, 1836, Dr. William H. Deaderick had one child, Mary McKim Deaderick, who was born January 24, 1838, who married Uriah Lusk York, of Bristol, Tenn. Their children were William Deaderick York, of Bristol, Martha York, Mary Deaderick York, who married Rhea Crawford, and lives in Knoxville, and Lois York.

Dr. William H. Deaderick died October 29, 1857, at his home in Athens, Tennessee.

David Deaderick

DEADERICK

DAVID ANDERSON DEADERICK

David Anderson Deaderick, the first child of David Deaderick, second, and his second wife, Margaretta Anderson Deaderick, was born at Jonesboro, Tennessee, 1799. He married first in 1816, Adelaide Eliza Jackson, a daughter of Samuel Jackson, a Revolutionary soldier and pioneer merchant of Elizabethton, Tennessee. They had one child, Adelaide Deaderick, who married Reverend Dr. Lyon, an eminent Presbyterian minister, and had several children, among whom were: Dr. A. A. Lyon, of Nashville, and Mrs. John Childress, of Nashville. After the death of his wife, Adelaide Eliza Jackson, in 1820, David Deaderick married Sarah A. Helms, who died soon after giving birth to a son, whose name was William Deaderick. (He died in 1835.) David A. Deaderick married July 21, 1831, for his third wife, Elizabeth Crozier. A few years after this marriage David A. Deaderick moved from Jonesboro to Knoxville. In 1839 he was elected Cashier of the Southwestern Railroad Bank, of Charleston, S. C., which established a branch in Knoxville that year. In 1849 David Deaderick, in company with 150 Knoxvillians, departed for the gold fields of California. He remained in the West about two years, and returned to Knoxville. He died August 27, 1873, and is buried in Old Gray Cemetery. The children of David Anderson and Elizabeth Crozier Deaderick were:

John Crozier Deaderick.
Margaret Frances Deaderick.
Robert Von Albade Deaderick.
David Deaderick.
Annie Deaderick.
Alice Deaderick.
Inslee Deaderick.
Oakley Deaderick.
Chalmers Deaderick.

Of the foregoing:

John Crozier Deaderick has never married and lives in North Carolina. Margaretta Frances Deaderick married Frank Alexander Ramsey Scott, of Knoxville. Their children are Elizabeth Crozier Scott, James Alexander Scott, Margaretta Naomi Scott, David Deaderick Scott, Frank Ramsey Scott, Annie Scott, Mary Scott, John B. Scott, Clarence Scott, Frederick Scott, and Edith Scott. David Deaderick Scott married Ada Meek, the only daughter of Judge J. Monroe Meek. They have one child, Elizabeth Meek Scott. They reside in Greeneville, Tennessee. Annie Scott married F. F. Nance. They have one child, Margaretta Nance. They reside in Morristown, Tennessee.

NOTABLE SOUTHERN FAMILIES

Robert Van Albade Deaderick, third child of David Anderson Deaderick and Elizabeth Crozier Deaderick, married Josephine Davis. They are both dead and left no children.

David Deaderick, fourth child of David Anderson Deaderick and Elizabeth Crozier Deaderick, died in 1857 unmarried.

Annie Deaderick, fifth child of David Anderson Deaderick and Elizabeth Crozier Deaderick, married Carrick W. Park. Their children were:

David Deaderick Park, who died young, and Bettie Park who married Dr. Stephen S. Willard. They have two children, Madeline Willard and Stephen H. Willard. They make their home in Calonia, California.

Alice Deaderick, sixth child of David Anderson Deaderick and Elizabeth Crozier Deaderick, married Charles McClung. Their children are Pleasant Miller McClung (who married Margaret Dobbins and lives at Water Valley, Mississippi), Deaderick McClung and Lillie McClung (who married Kenneth R. Scott, of Knoxville), Charles McClung died some years ago. Mrs. Alice Deaderick McClung makes her home in Georgia.

Inslee Deaderick, seventh child of David Anderson Deaderick and Elizabeth Crozier Deaderick, married Martha A. Nichols. Their children are: Alice Deaderick (who married Moses Grainger, a professor in the University of North Carolina, Chapel Hill, and has one child, Fanny Moses Grainger), David Anderson Deaderick, second, and Inslee W. Deaderick, who is a prominent farmer in the southern part of Knox County, near Shooks.

Oakley Deaderick, eighth child of David Anderson Deaderick and Elizabeth Crozier Deaderick, married Margaret E. Dykes. They live in Knox County. Their children are Elizabeth Jane Deaderick, Inslee Chalmers Deaderick, Paul Stuart Deaderick and Oakley Raymond Deaderick.

Chalmers Deaderick, ninth child of David Anderson Deaderick and Elizabeth Crozier Deaderick, is a well known doctor of Knoxville. He married Rebecca Williams, a descendant of Joseph Williams of Revolutionary fame.

Amanda Frances Deaderick, second child of David Deaderick and Margaretta Anderson Deaderick, was born in Jonesboro, about 1800. She married Dr. David Nelson, a physician of Jonesboro, who became a leading minister of the Presbyterian Church. Their children were: Rosa Nelson, who married Dr. Clapp, Emma Nelson, who married ─────── Williams, Laura Nelson and Dr. Eugene Nelson, who lives at Springfield, Illinois.

Eliza Rosa Deaderick, third child of David and Margaretta Anderson, was born at Poplar Hill, Jonesboro, Tennessee, April 30, 1802.

DEADERICK

She died in Knoxville, October 15, 1866. She married June 7, 1825, General Alexander Anderson, a son of Honorable Joseph Anderson (a brother of Margaretta Anderson Deaderick) and Only Patience Outlaw, daughter of Colonel Alexander Outlaw and his wife, Penelope Smith. Colonel Outlaw was one of the pioneers of Tennessee and took an active part in the early history of the State. The children of Eliza Rosa Deaderick Anderson were:

Cornelia Geraldine Anderson who for many years had a private school in Knoxville.

Joseph Anderson died young.

Margaretta Anderson, who married Jacob S. Stuart, a native of Washington County, Tennessee, and a grandson of Captain James Stuart, Speaker of the House of Representatives in the first legislature in the State of Tennessee. Jacob S. Stuart died in Knoxville in 1874 and Margaret A. Stuart died in 1890. Both are buried in Old Gray Cemetery. Seven children were born to them: Annie Elizabeth Stuart (who married Jason B. Kelley and had Addie Kelley, Nora Kelley and Margaret Kelley); Rosa Stuart (who married Charles W. Irby and has six children, Charles W. Irby, Jr., Edna Rembert Irby, Margaret Stuart Irby, Stuart Chalmers Irby, Lois Irby and Philip Erskine Irby. Charles W. Irby, Jr., married Grace Weldon and has two children, Gertrude and Elizabeth); Fannie May Stuart (who lives in Knoxville, Tennessee); Hampden Stuart (who died unmarried); Adelia Stuart (who married, firstly Frederick North, of Asheville, North Carolina, and married secondly ———— Southern, a Baptist minister); Jacob Gerald Stuart (who married Fanny Wray, daughter of Dr. W. A. Wray, and has one child, Frances Stuart); and James D. Stuart (who married Miss D. E. Lanny, of Savannah.

The descendants of Jacob S. Stuart are eligible to the Sons and Daughters of the Revolution through Captain James Stuart, who had charge of a company of home guards in Washington County, Tennessee. His company had charge of the district from Greasy Cove to Duggers Fort, which was located on the St. John property near the village of Watauga, Tennessee. Colonel Hugh Montgomery, of Salisbury District, North Carolina, was the father of Captain James Stuart's wife. Montgomery Stuart married Hester Thompson, of New Jersey, whose ancestors took an important part in the early history of that state.

Rose Anderson, fourth child of Eliza Rosa Anderson and Alexander Anderson, died young.

Fanny Von Albade Anderson, fifth child of Eliza Rosa Anderson and Alexander Anderson married Thomas B. McMillan, of Camden, Alabama. For several years they made their home in Knoxville. Their children were: Von Albade McMillan (who married Virginia Spitza and has Virginia McMillan, Fay McMillan, Thomas B. McMillan, second, Frances Lucile McMillan, Alexander Von Albade McMillan and David Thomas McMillan (who married Ella Jenkins); and Lorene McMillan (who married Major J. S. Robins.)

Alexander Anderson, sixth child of Eliza Rosa and Alexander Anderson, died young.

Joseph Anderson, seventh child of Eliza Rosa and Alexander Anderson, died young.

David Deaderick Anderson, ninth child of Eliza Rosa and Alexander Anderson, married Fanny Deaderick, daughter of John Franklin Deaderick. They had two sons who died in youth. David Deaderick Anderson served as Judge for one of the Knox County Courts for several years.

Adelia Anderson, tenth child of Eliza Rosa and Alexander Anderson, married James Foster Scott. They had six children, namely: Alexander A. Scott, Rosa Naomi Scott, James Foster, Jr., Kenneth W. Scott, Ethel Lee Scott, and Edwin Ramsey Scott. The Scott descendants of David Deaderick are also descendants of Dr. T. A. Ramsay, one of the earliest settlers of Knoxville, and a soldier in the Revolutionary Army. The mother of F. A. R. Scott and J. Foster Scott was a sister of the late Dr. J. G. M. Ramsay, author of the Annals of Tennessee.

Alexander A. Scott married Stella D. French. Their children are: Dorothy Scott and Alexander A. Scott, Jr., James Foster Scott, Jr., married Fanny George, of Texas. Kenneth W. Scott married Lillie McClung, daughter of Charles McClung and Alice Deaderick McClung. Their children are Alice Scott, Margaret Scott, Kenneth W. Scott, Jr., Charles McClung Scott and Benjamin Scott. They live in New Mexico.

Ethel Lee Scott married J. F. Thomas. They make their home in Cauzan City, Colorado. Dr. Thomas is pastor of the First Presbyterian church in that city. Their children are: Theodore Thomas and Scott Thomas.

Edwin Ramsay Scott married Adelia Anderson.

Joseph Deaderick, fourth son of David and Margaretta Anderson Deaderick, was born at Poplar Hill, Jonesboro, Tennessee, May 12, 1804. He died October 18, 1835, and is buried on the Deaderick lot at Jonesboro, near his father. He married Emiline Anderson.

John Franklin Deaderick, fifth child of David and Margaretta Deaderick, was born at Poplar Hill October 21, 1806, and died at Jonesboro, September 12, 1884. He received his early training in his father's store at Jonesboro. In 1840 he was appointed by Judge Thomas L. Williams, (chancellor for East Tennessee), Clerk and Master for Washington County, which position he held twenty-seven

DEADERICK

years. In 1870 he removed from Jonesboro to Knoxville where he lived for several years, but returned to Jonesboro shortly before his death. He married Rebecca Williams, daughter of Judge Joseph Lanier Williams and his wife Susan Taylor Williams, and granddaughter of Colonel Joseph Williams, of Granville County, North Carolina. Rebecca Williams Deaderick died near Jonesboro, in 1857. Thirteen children were born to them, namely: Joseph Deaderick, David Deaderick, William V. Deaderick, Sue L. Deaderick, Mary Frances Deaderick, Eugene Deaderick, Eliza Rosa Deaderick, Isadore A. Deaderick, Katherine Deaderick, Thomas O. Deaderick, and Cornelia Deaderick.

Of the foregoing:

Joseph Deaderick never married. He enlisted in Captain Zed Millet's company in the Confederate Army and died August, 1861.

David Deaderick married Florette Nelson, of Illinois. Their children are Ernest Deaderick, who lives in Missouri, Bertha Deaderick, who lives in California and Nina Deaderick. After the death of his wife David Deaderick married Eva Clarkson, of Rogersville, and had one child, Margaret Deaderick, who lives in Morristown, Tennessee. David Deaderick died January 25, 1906.

William V. Deaderick married Eva Jackson, daughter of General Alfred Jackson, of Jonesboro. William V. Deaderick was a lawyer of note. After the War Between the States he formed a partnership with his uncle, James W. Deaderick and his cousin, James G. Deaderick, which lasted until James W. Deaderick was elected to the Supreme Bench in 1870. William V. Deaderick lived in Blountville, Tennessee. He was a member of the Constitutional Convention of the State of Tennessee, in 1870. He died September 27, 1883.

Sue Deaderick has never married. She makes her home with her brother, Dr. Eugene Deaderick, at Poplar Hill, the Deaderick place at Jonesboro, Tennessee.

Mary Frances Deaderick married Judge David D. Anderson. They had two sons, Roy H. Anderson and Frank Deaderick Anderson, both of whom are dead.

Eugene Deaderick married Rebecca Williams. They had seven children. Dr. Eugene Deaderick practised his profession in Knoxville for many years, but several years ago returned to Jonesboro, where he lives at Poplar Hill.

Eliza Rosa Deaderick married, as his second wife, Edward Rogan. She died October 24, 1899, leaving no children.

Isadore A. Deaderick was the first wife of Edward Rogan. She died November 20, 1893, leaving two children, Carrie Rogan and Sue Rogan, who live at Johnson City.

Thomas O. Deaderick married Josephine Heiskall, daughter of

Colonel William Heiskall, of Knoxville. Their children are: William Heiskall Deaderick, a physician of Mariana, Arkansas, John F. Deaderick, of Lexington, N. C., Louise Deaderick (who married Reverend A. C. Carr, a noted Presbyterian minister), and Edith Deaderick. Thomas O. Deaderick was for several years a professor at the University of Tennessee. Later he was Professor of Latin and French at Southwestern University at Clarksville, Tennessee.

Cornelia G. Deaderick, called Nina, married R. B. Glenn, of North Carolina, who served as Governor in 1904 and 1906. They have two children, Charles C. Glenn and Rebecca Williams Glenn.

James W. Deaderick, seventh child of David Deaderick and Margaretta Anderson Deaderick, was born at Jonesboro, November 25, 1812. He was educated at Jonesboro and at East Tennessee College, afterwards the University of Tennessee. Later he attended Center College at Danville, Kentucky. There he met and married Adeline Shelby McDowell, daughter of Dr. Ephriam McDowell. Sarah Shelby McDowell. (She was a daughter of Governor Isaac Shelby, of Kentucky one of the Heroes of King's Mountain, and a leader of a Kentucky regiment on the Canadian border in the War of 1812). James W. Deaderick began life as a merchant at Cheek's Cross Roads, Jefferson County, Tennessee, in 1833. Later he entered the legal profession and in 1851 was elected on the Whig ticket to represent Carter, Johnson, Sullivan and Washington Counties in the State Senate. In 1866 he moved from Jonesboro to Bristol where he practiced law. In 1870 he was elected to the Supreme Bench. In 1875 he was chosen by the Supreme Judges, Chief Justice of Tennessee. He was re-elected in 1878 and held the position until 1886, when he declined re-election. He retired to his home in Jonesboro, where he died October 7, 1890.

The children of Judge James W. Deaderick and Adeline McDowell Deaderick were: Arthur V. Deaderick, Shelby M. Deaderick, Anna Mary Deaderick, James G. Deaderick, David Franklin Deaderick, William Wallace Deaderick, Alfred Shelby Deaderick, Lewis Deaderick, Charles C. Deaderick and Adeline McDowell Deaderick.

Of the foregoing:

Arthur V. Deaderick married Addie Walker. Their children are James W. Deaderick, second, Hugh McDowell Deaderick, Mary E. Deaderick, Lula C. Deaderick, Charles C. Deaderick and Monroe Deaderick. Captain Arthur V. Deaderick and his family live at Unaka Springs, Unicoi County, Tennessee. James W. Deaderick, second, married Sabra E. Johnson. They live at Scarboro, Tennessee, near Oliver Springs and their children are: Mary E. Deaderick, Anna Deaderick, Louise Deaderick, Ada Deaderick, William Deaderick, Rachel Deaderick, Arthur V. Deaderick, Jr., and Clara Deaderick.

DEADERICK

Hugh McDowell Deaderick married Carrie E. Clarkson. (They have three children: Mary Clarkson Deaderick, William Clarkson Deaderick, and George M. Deaderick); Mary E. Deaderick married James M. Brown. (Their children are: J. Fred Brown, Fanny Brown, and Adeline Brown. They reside in Philadelphia, Pennsylvania); Lula Clifton Deaderick married William M. Martin. Their home is in Bessemer, Alabama. Their children are: Deaderick Martin, Lee Martin, Shelby Martin, Elizabeth Martin, Sabra Martin and Willie Clifton Martin; Charles C. Deaderick married Maud Martin. (They live at Jonesboro, Alabama. Their children are: Thomas Deaderick, Alfred Deaderick and Mary E. Deaderick; Monroe M. Deaderick married Hazel Miller; Shelby Deaderick married August 20, 1861, Louise Brown, of Washington County, Tennessee, who was the daughter of Colonel Bird Brown and Louise Rebecca Sevier, daughter of John Sevier, second, son of Governor John Sevier. See Sevier Family. (They have one son, Wallace Deaderick); Anna Mary Deaderick married her cousin, Major William Deaderick Van Dyke. They made their home in Chattanooga, where Major Van Dyke practiced law. Their descendants have been given; James G. Deaderick married Elizabeth Sears. (They have two children, Ella Deaderick and Horace Deaderick). James G. Deaderick was elected third lieutenant of Company B. 19th Tennessee Infantry, Confederate States Army. He rose to the rank of Lieutenant Colonel of his regiment. At the close of the war he entered into partnership with his father and they practiced law in Bristol. When his father was elected to the Supreme Bench, James G. Deaderick returned to Jonesboro and practiced law there until the death of his father. He has since removed to California; David Franklin Deaderick moved to Quincy Illinois, where he was Mayor at one time. (He married Nannie Haines, daughter of William Haines, of Washington County, Tennessee. Their children were: Mamie Deaderick, who married her cousin, Thomas A. Cleage, Jr., and lives in St. Louis, Missouri, and Fannie Deaderick, who married ——————; Nannie Deaderick who married Frank H. Betts, of Utica, New York; Olive Lavenia Deaderick who married Edward H. Martin, of Utica, New York; Frank Deaderick, Carrie Deaderick who married Dr. Potts, of St. Louis, Missouri, and Fred Deaderick, of St. Louis); William Wallace Deaderick is a lawyer. (He married Sarah Hardin, of Kentucky. Their children are: Sallie Deaderick, Annie Deaderick, Mary Deaderick and Robert Deaderick); Alfred Shelby Deaderick was a prominent lawyer of Jonesboro, Tennessee. (He married Carter Lester, of Virginia. Their children are: Kate Deaderick, Adeline Deaderick, Day Deaderick, James Deaderick, and Felicia Deaderick); Louis Deaderick resides in Washington County, Tennessee. (He married Nannie Bayless. Their children are: Adeline Deaderick, Bird

Deaderick, and Mary Deaderick); Charles Deaderick lives in Hamilton, Missouri. (He married Lou Anderson and has one child, Pauline Deaderick); Adeline McDowell Deaderick married Judge John A. Moon, of Chattanooga, present congressman from the Third District and in Congress continually for twenty years. (They have two children, Anna Mary Moon, who is not married, and Lieutenant Deaderick Moon, of the United States Army, who married Elise Chapin, only daughter of Edward Young Chapin and Elise Hutcheson Chapin, and their child is named Mildred Carrington Moon.)

The Deadericks as a family were Presbyterian. The First Presbyterian Church at Jonesboro has numbered them among its members for more than a hundred years. When the present brick church was built, they were among the most liberal contributors. This church was dedicated Friday, August 16, 1850, by the Reverend Rufus P. Wells. It was long known as the Hebron Church, which was organized in 1790.

The Deaderick homestead at Jonesboro is called "Poplar Hill." It occupies the top of the hill in the center of the town. David Deaderick built his home on the hill top and his office and store were just below it on the main street of the first town in Tennessee.

The charming old brick house, approached by a box wood hedge, a century old, is now the home of Dr. Eugene Deaderick and his sister, Miss Sue Deaderick.

The Deaderick family was Southern in sympathy in the War Between the States and many of its members were in the Confederate Army. David O. Deaderick had three sons with Colonel H. M. Ashby in the Second Tennessee Cavalry, C. S. A., namely, Robert V. Deaderick, Inslee Deaderick and Oakley Deaderick. J. Franklin Deaderick also had three sons in the Confederate Army, namely, William V. Deaderick, Joseph W. Deaderick and J. W. Deaderick. Judge James W. Deaderick had five sons in the Confederate Army, namely, Captain Arthur V. Deaderick, Company I. 19th Tennessee Infantry, Shelby M. Deaderick, Second Lieutenant of Captain Gillespie's Company, 19th Tennessee Infantry, Wallace Deaderick, who was severely wounded in the Battle of Murfreesboro, James G. Deaderick, who was orderly sergeant in Company B., 19th Tennessee Infantry, and Alfred S. Deaderick, who was also in the Confederate Army.

II GEORGE MICHAEL DEADERICK

George Michael Deaderick, second child of David Deaderick, first, and Rosannah Boucher Deaderick, was born in Winchester, Virginia, about 1756. He probably married in Virginia. He emigrated to Tennessee about 1790, and settled in Nashville where he became a very

DEADERICK

prosperous merchant. He was President of the Old Tennessee Bank in 1810. Deaderick Street in Nashville is named for him. He served under General Andrew Jackson in the Battle of the Horseshoe Bend in 1812. He died in 1816, leaving one son, George Michael Deaderick, Jr., and an adopted son, Fielding Deaderick. His will, dated November, 1816, was recorded March, 22, 1817, at Nashville. It was protested at the January term, 1817, by David Dunn, of Grundy County, guardian for George Michael Deaderick, Jr., minor. This very interesting document mentions the following relatives, son, George Michael Deaderick, Jr., adopted son, Fielding Deaderick, Elvira I. Searcy, Susan D. Searcy, Marcia F. McLean, daughter of Bennett Searcy, nephews, George Murrell and George M. Perry, brother David's children, including William, Sister Murrell's children, Sister Perry's children, Samuel M. Perry, George Perry, Nephews William Windle and William P. May and George M. D. Cantrell, David S. Deaderick, son of brother Tom Deaderick, four sons of deceased niece, Elizabeth Searcy. The Executors were Stephen Cantrell, Jr., Jesse Warton and Robert Searcy.

III. SUSANNAH DEADERICK.

Susannah Deaderick, daughter of David Deaderick, first, and his wife, Rosannah Boucher, was born in Winchester, Frederick County, Virginia. She married David Wendell, or Windle. Their children were: David Wendell, second, (who married Sarah Neilson); Rachell Wendell (who married J. P. Wiggins); Rosannah Wendell (who married Judge Howell); Polly Wendell (who married Bennett Searcy) her daughter was Marcia F. McLean; and Juliet Wendell, born April 28, 1787, in Winchester, Virginia; died in Nashville July 3, 1839, married January 2, 1803, Stephen Cantrell, Jr., born March 10, 1783, in Sumner County, Tennessee; died September 25, 1854, near Pine Bluff, Arkansas. (Their children were: George Michael Cantrell, born October 9, 1807; Mary Ann Cantrell, born 1808, married Dr. T. J. Howard, of Franklin, Tennessee. Emmeline Susannah Cantrell, born 1810, married, 1830, Alexander Cassidy, moved to Waco, Texas; Elizabeth Searcy Cantrell, born 1812, married 1830, Abraham VanWyck, of New York); David Wendell; Matilda Carter Wendell (who married William Mason); William Armour Wendell; and Margaret Armstrong Wendell.

IV. JOHN DEADERICK.

John Deaderick, son of David Deaderick, the first, and his wife, Rosannah Booher Deaderick, was born in Winchester, Frederick

County, Virginia. He was associated in business with his brothers in Nashville, but died shortly after his arrival in Tennessee.

V. THOMAS DEADERICK.

Thomas Deaderick, son of David Deaderick and Rosannah Booher Deaderick, was born in Winchester, Frederick County, Virginia, in 1765, and moved with his family to Tennessee. He married about 1790, before coming to Tennessee, Ann Julia Dangerfield, of the distinguished Virginia family of that name.

Their children were:

(1) David Samuel Deaderick, born February 22, 1792; died June 24, 1823.
(2) Mary Caroline Deaderick, born March 8, 1793.
(3) Ann Julia Deaderick, born April 6, 1795.
(4) William Murrel Deaderick, born August 22, 1797; died October, 1798.
(5) Emily Rosannah Deaderick, born July 15, 1799.
(6) Loretta Charlotte Deaderick, born June 29, 1801.
(7) Leroy Dangerfield Deaderick, born November 29, 1803.

Of the foregoing:

Mary Cary Caroline Deaderick, daughter of Thomas and Julia Deaderick, born March 6, 1793, married March 1811, James Clem, born October 19, 1786, died June 15, 1826. Their children were Catherine Julia Ann Clem, born December 6, 1811, (who married September 28, 1828, William M. Brown); William Thomas Clem, born April 11, 1813; John Eason Clem, born September 10, 1817; Eliza Augusta Clem, born March 27, 1821; and Frances Narcissa Clem, born August, 1825; died August 12, 1827.

Julia Deaderick, daughter of Thomas Deaderick and Julia Ann Dangerfield Deaderick, married John Eason. Their daughter, Julia Eason, married William Lowry and had children: John Lowry, who died unmarried; Virginia Lowry married Ruben Arnold, William Lowry, who died unmarried, Robert James Lowry, who married Emma Harkham and is one of the leading citizens of Atlanta, Georgia, and is a banker and a capitalist of that city. Fannie Tolbert Lowry married James Henry Porter, of Atlanta, (her children are William Porter Lowry, who married Annie May Crass, of Chattanooga, and has Margaret Porter; and Julia Lowry Porter, who married Edward Bates Block, of Atlanta). Mary Lowry married Robert Campbell Clark, Alice May Lowry married Walter A. Taylor, of Atlanta, Georgia; Leila Prentice Lowry married James Freeman, Julia Lowry married Thomas Bent Meador, of Atlanta, Georgia.

DEADERICK

Emily Deaderick, daughter of Thomas Deaderick, and Julia Ann Dangerfield Deaderick, married twice; first, Captain James Stewart, U. S. A., and second, John Drennan, who served in the Mexican War.

Loretta Charlotte Deaderick, daughter of Thomas Deaderick and Julia Ann Dangerfield Deaderick, married Captain David Thompson.

David Deaderick, son of Thomas Deaderick and Julia Ann Dangerfield Deaderick, served as a Captain in the Creek War in 1817, under General Jackson and distinguished himself for gallantry and bravery.

Leroy Dangerfield Deaderick, son of Thomas Deaderick and Julia Ann Dangerfield Deaderick, became a physician. He moved to Mississippi where he died unmarried.

Thomas Deaderick married again after the death of Julia Dangerfield Deaderick and had several children. He died October 15, 1831, aged sixty-six.

VI. ELIZABETH DEADERICK.

Elizabeth Deaderick, sixth child of David Deaderick, the first, and Rosannah Boucher Deaderick, was born in Winchester, Frederick County, Virginia, in 1766. She died in Lynchburg, Virginia, March 17, 1841. She married John Murrell, born July 27, 1766. He died May, 1842. They lived in Lynchburg, Virginia. Their children were:

Harding Murrell, who died unmarried.
David Gamble Murrell, who married Alice Tate.
John Dobbins Murrell, who died unmarried.
Rosanna Eliza Murrell, who married Samuel Slayton.
Onslow Glenmon Murrell, who married Elizabeth. (Their children were: John D. Murrell, married Jenny Ross, granddaughter of the famous Cherokee Chief, John Ross. They moved from Lynchburg to Louisiana and settled at Bayou Gould where they owned a large sugar plantation, and Kate Murrell, who married Mr. Ashe, of Lexington, Mississippi).
William Murrell died young.
George Michael Murrell, born April 8, 1808, died March 30, 1894, was the father of George Ross Murrell, of Bayou Gould, Louisiana.

GAINES

For the early history of the Gaines family, as given here, we are indebted chiefly to Major Richard V. Gaines, of Mossingford, Virginia, who devoted many years to the study of this family and traced it through an unbroken line to Brychan, who became King of Wales early in the fifth century and reigned until his death in A. D. 450. His lineage gave to Wales some of the foremost men in her annals and the history of Wales is, in a large measure, the record of the achievements of his descendants, a few of whom were: Beli the Great, Emperor of Great Britain; Cadwalader, great grandson of Beli; St. David, patron saint of Wales; Roderic the Great, from whom descended King George V., of England; Howel the Good, who prepared the first system of civil law which was put into operation in the territory now embraced in the British Realm; Cradoc, of Llancarvon, the historian; Sir Rhysap-Thomas, who commanded the forces under the Earl of Richmond, and by his skill and gallantry at the battle of Bosworth, where Richard III. was slain, placed Richmond (Henry VII.) upon the throne; David-ap-Gwillam, the father of Welsh poetry, and Llewellyn the Great, the last and probably the greatest of Welsh kings, whose reign extended from 1194 to 1240. His administration of affairs caused a great literary and educational revival in Wales, and his achievements in arms were not less signal and masterful. To no one man does Wales owe more for the deep foundation of her indestructible, invincible national spirit than to Lllewellyn the Great.

The Reverend Theophilus Jones in his history gives Brecon City, Wales, as the home of the family at the earliest known period of its history and also gives the genealogy of the family and many valuable facts concerning it. From Howel the Good the line is traced to Einon Sais (who had lived in England and inherited the estate of Castle Einon Sais), his son Howel and his son, Llewellyn-ap-Hoel, the father of Roger, Griffith, Richard, William, Helen and David-ap-Llewellyn, later known as David Gam, a conspicuous and potential personage in Wales in the early part of the fifteenth century, a man of courage and judgment; of dauntless spirit and soldierly tact. By his personal daring on the Field of Agincourt (1415) he saved the life of Henry V., but was himself mortally wounded. He was knighted by his King just before he died. He entered the King's military service as David-ap-Lllewellyn, but having a squint eye, the word signifying

GAINES

it, "Gam," was applied to him and he was knighted Sir David Gam and herein we find the origin of the name Gaines. The name remained Gam through two generations. His great grandson added "es" and thereafter it was Games; which form was adhered to in Wales, but in England it became Ganes, Gaynes and finally Gaines. Thomas Jones, an eminent genealogist, in 1599, makes this important statement: "From this Sir David Gam all ye Games of Brecknogshire, all ye Vaughns, and all ye Herberts of South Wales are descended and ye most part of all the nobility of England."

William Herbert and the Earl of Pembroke were great grandsons of Gladis, daughter of Sir David Gam. They were the friends and patrons of Shakespeare, and it was at Wilton, the home of the Earl of Pembroke, that King James, on December, second, 1603, first witnessed a performance of one of Shakespeare's plays. The Herberts took an active part in the early settlement of America, and were members of the Virginia Company organized by Sir Walter Raleigh. Morgan, the eldest son of Sir David Gaines (Gam) was great-great-grandfather of Sir John Gaines (1559-1606) of Newton, County of Brecon, Wales, from whom the Gaines family of Virginia is believed to descend.

The children of Sir John Gaines were Catherine, Thomas, John, Walter, Richard and Elizabeth Gaines.

From Virginia Land Office and State Library records we find that six members of the Gaines family had located in the colony prior to 1650, one of whom, Thomas Gaines, is believed to have been son of Sir John Gaines and father of Daniel, Robert, Thomas and James (of 1620.)

DANIEL GAINES.

Daniel Gaines married Margaret Bernard and had (1) Elizabeth (2) Bernard, (3) Margaret (who married Ralph Rowzee (4) Mary (who married John Smith.)

Elizabeth, daughter of Daniel Gaines and Margaret Bernard Gaines, married John Catlett, Jr., and had Rebecca Catlett who married Francis Conway and they were parents of Eleanor Rose Conway, who married James Madison and had James Madison, second President of the United States.

Bernard, son of Daniel and Margaret Bernard Gaines married Martha Taylor, daughter of George Taylor. Two of their children were George Gaines and Daniel Gaines, second, who married, firstly, Mrs. Mary Doyle and had Mary Gaines (who married James Jameson and had Mary Jameson).

JAMES GAINES.

James Gaines (1620) said to be son of Thomas and grandson of Sir John Gaines, of Newton, is believed to have been father of Richard Gaines who died in Culpeper County, Virginia, in 1750. The children of this Richard Gaines were Francis Gaines, James Gaines, William Henry Gaines, Thomas Gaines, John Gaines and Mary Gaines, and some genealogists claim that Roger and Richard Gaines were also of this family. Roger married a Miss Rawlings, and Richard also married a Miss Rawlings and had twelve sons, of whom Henry (born about 1733) married Mrs. Stipp (nee Wood.) One of their children, Richard Gaines, (born 1752) married Frances Jolly; their son, James Gaines, married Margaret Close and had a son, Reuben Gaines (who claimed relationship to General Edmund Pendleton Gaines).

Francis Gaines, son of Richard Gaines (of Culpeper) married Dorothy, and had (1) Dorothy, (2) Susannah, who married a Mr. Carter (3) Elizabeth, who married a Mr. Yates and they were grandparents of Mrs. H. L. Kinnison, (4) Anna, who married a Martin; (5) Sallie, who married a Brassfield; (6) William; (7) Lucy, and (8) James Gaines.

James Gaines, son of Richard Gaines, of Culpeper County, Virginia, married about 1730 Mary Pendleton, born 1717, died 1803, younger daughter of Henry Pendleton and Mary Bishop Taylor Pendleton. They had twelve children, namely:

(1) Henry Gaines.
(2) James Gaines, Second.
(3) Richard Edward Gaines, married Elizabeth Broadus.
(4) Edmund Pendleton Gaines, married Mrs. Tabitha Rucker.
(5) Joseph Gaines.
(6) William Gaines.
(7) Francis Gaines.
(8) Thomas Gaines.
(9) Mary Gaines, married a Herndon.
(10) Sarah Gaines married James Broadus.
(11) Catherine Gaines married William Broadus.
(12) Isabella Gaines.

Of the foregoing:
Richard Edmund Gaines, who married Elizabeth Broadus, had a daughter, Elizabeth Broadus Gaines, who married George Clayton.

Francis Gaines, son of James and Mary Pendleton Gaines, married Elizabeth Lewis and their son, Thomas Lewis Gaines married Lucy Patterson Henderson; their son, John Wesley Gaines, married Frances

GAINES

Maria Wair and their son is John Wesley Gaines, second, of Nashville.

James Gaines, Second, son of James and Mary Pendleton Gaines, married Mildred Pollard and had five children: (1) Nancy (who married a Mr. Mathews); (2) Mary (who married a Mr. Daniels); (3) a daughter who married a Mr. Garlick; (4) Benjamin, and (5) Abner Gaines, who married, in 1792, Elizabeth Matthews and had (a) Mildred Pollard Gaines (who married a Mr. Davies and had a son, R. G. Davies, who married as his first wife a Miss Gibbs, and had seven children; James, Charles, Harpin, Fannie, Cornelia, Allen and Fulham Davies.) Another child of Abner and Elizabeth Matthews Gaines was John Pendleton Gaines, Third Territorial Governor of Oregon (who married Elizabeth Kincaid, and had Abner Pendleton Gaines, who married Mary Ellen Looney. Among their children are Chester, Richard L., Wilbur, John Pendleton, Ida (who married a Mr. Wagnon); Hattie (who married ─── Sims) and a daughter (who married ─── Job.)

Henry Gaines (1731-1811) son of James and Mary Pendleton Gaines, married twice; firstly, Martha George and secondly, Sarah Churchill. One son by the first wife was George Gaines (who married Susannah Groves and had a son, William Gaines, who married Janette Watts; their son was Joseph Addison Gaines, who married Martha Lyne and their son was Albert Winston Gaines. Another son of Henry Gaines' first marriage was Richard Gaines (who married Mrs. Rebecca Gatewood Barrett; their daughter, Mary Gaines, married John Neal; their daughter, Catherine Neal, married Mr. Hughes, and they were the parents of Mary Gaines Hughes.) Other children by Henry Gaines' first marriage were: Elizabeth, (who married Mr. George), Nancy, William, Thomas and Augustine Gaines. By the marriage of Henry Gaines to his second wife, Sarah Churchill, he had Gabriel Gaines, Churchill Gaines, Fannie Gaines (who married ─── Bowler) and Mary Gaines (1768-1852) who in 1793 married John Clark (1767-1844), son of James Clark and Mildred Gatewood, and had eight children: (1) Henry James Clark, (see record later); (2) Mildred Clark, (1796-1860) who married James Wilkerson Mansfield (1794-1853) (soldier in War of 1812 and son of Robert Mansfield) and had eleven children. (a) William Wesley (d.y.) (b) Susan Mourning Mansfield (who married firstly: Pressly Allen Reese; and had Pressly Frances Reese (who married Peter Deroy, and had seven children.) Susan Mourning (Mansfield) Reese married secondly, Horatio Ford, and had (1) George Alexander Ford (who married Charity Bemiss); (2) Eliza Ellen Ford (who married Henry C. Thornbro); (3) Edna Amanda Ford (who married Antoine De Larque; (4) John Wilkerson Ford (who married

NOTABLE SOUTHERN FAMILIES

Belle Watkins); (5) Robert Lafayette Ford (who married Cornelia Van Ausdall); (6) Mildred Jane Ford (who married Chauncey Cobb.) (c) Mary Virginia Reese (who married Green Cole Reese and had (1) William Allen Reese (who married Mary Ann Smith and had Bessie and Grover C. Reese); (2) Susannah Jane Reese (who married Isaiah J. Kimberlin and had Minora Reese Kimberlin (who married Bal. Fielder, and has Byrd Joe Fielder, who married Frank White Livingood), and Mary R. Kimberlin (who married W. A. Harvey and has Helen who married Clyde McGee.) (3) Cornelia Ellen Reese (who married Armistead A. Neal and had Virgil, Ardell L., and May Pearl Neal) (4) Henry Clark Reese (who married Catherine Gregg); (5) Robert Joel Reese (who married Catherine Morgan); (6) Narcisso Belle Reese (who married Sherwood and had Lulu, Newell, Ralph, Lee and Catherine Reese; (7) Charles Melvin Reese (who married Julia McNay and had Roy Cole Reese); (8) Albert Smith Reese)who married Addie West and had West Reese and Ella Reese.) (d) Nancy Elizabeth Mansfield (who married Peter Baker, and had James, Ross and Robert Baker, who married Nannie Wilson and had Mabel, Ray, and Eunice Baker.) (e) Martha Jane Mansfield (who married Mortimer Jackson, one child was J. R. Jackson.) (f) Sarah Ann Mansfield (who married Benjamin B. Wyatt and had (1) Louise Mildred Wyatt (who married Dr. J C. Cassidy); (2) James Henry Wyatt; (3) .Margaret Ellen Wyatt who married Jasper W. Wyatt and had Margaret Wyatt); (4) Brunetta Eugenia Wyatt (who married David T. Byrd; (5) Emma Wilkerson Wyatt who married Henry Machen and had Harry, Marguerite and Florence Machen); (6) Fannie Belle Wyatt (who married Walter Byrd); (7) Sallie P. Wyatt (who married Needham Sykes); (8) Edward Sterling Wyatt (who married ———— and has a son, Hugh Wyatt. (g) Louisa Anne Mansfield (1832-1906) (who married Dr. Henry Owsley (1816-1901) and had: (1) Lee (who married and had twelve children); (2) Luella (who married A. R. McGintie and had two sons); (3) Alvin Clark Owsley (who married Sarah Blount and had eight children: (1) Eunice Owsley (who married J. C. Wright and has one son); (2) Louisa Sophia; (3) Jessie Owsley (who married Mr. Boney and has one son); (4) Alvin Mansfield Owsley, of Denton, Texas; (5) Stella Lee Owsley; (6) Clark Owsley; (7) Charlotte Warmouth Owsley, and (8) Henry Owsley.) (h) Ellen Z. Mansfield (who married Lyman C. Littlefield and had (1) Charles Benjamin Littlefield (who married Theodosia C. Webb and had (1) Maud Ellen (who married Sterling Price Agee); (2) Charles Webb and (3) Rose Arnott Littlefield; (2) William Wallace Littlefield (who married Rebecca Simpson and had Edith and Norah Ellen Littlefield); (i) Robert A. Mansfield (who married Aurelia J. Halleck and had Elnora (who married Mr. Bogan and had two sons): William, Sidney, A. W., Carrie, Jennie, Walter and Minnie Mansfield); (j) John Clark Mansfield (who married Margaret Maxwell and had Robert John and James Wilkerson Mansfield (who married Bridget Welch and their daughter, Etta Mansfield married, firstly William Francis Miller and had Edward Roland Miller, who married Edna Hassinger; married secondly Paul Hodge DeMange (First Lieutenant A. T. 87 Division.) (3) Thomas Pendleton Clark, (4) William Fountain Clark, (5) Mary Jane Clark (who married Zachariah Glass, of Kentucky, and had (a) John Pendleton Glass (who married Emma Conrow Ayres), (b) Susan Jamison Glass (who married Jack West and had Alice West (who married Benjamin Moore and had Lizzie Moore (who married Fleming Clardy and has two children), (c) James C. (called "Posey") Glass (who married Margaret Gant and had (1) James C., Jr., (2) William A., (who married Rose Dade), (3) Sallie (who married Edgar McPherson) and (4) Annie Glass; (d) Mary Jane Glass (who married James S. Phelps), (e) Elizabeth Glass (who married Bathurst E. Randolph), (f) Virginia Glass (who married Samuel C. Mercer), (g) Julia Glass (who married John Jefferies McComb.) (6) Joseph Clark (who married Frances Downer, one child was Mary Clark, who married Robert C. Slaughter, and had (1) Coleman Clark Slaughter, of Nashville, and (2) Francis Downer Slaughter (who married William Rhode Hurt and had two children (a) Helen Hurt (who married Stuart Brezee and has Berry Hurt and Harrison Pendleton Brezee); (b) Harry Garner Hurt (who married John Carter Walker and has Coleman Carter Walker and Helen Walker), (7) Eliza Francis Clark (who married firstly; Mr. Brown; secondly, Dr. Frank Bell. (8) Sarah Ann Clark (who married Henry Durett and had Mary Elizabeth, John Clark and Henry Durett, Jr.)

Henry James Clark (1794-1874), (in War of 1812), oldest child of John and Mary Gaines Clark married firstly, (in 1815) Mary Lewis Mansfield; secondly, Mrs. Mary Brown Bell.

Mary Lewis Mansfield (1795-1857) was daughter of Robert Mansfield (1762-1833), Revolutionary War Soldier) and wife, Mourning (Clark) Mansfield (1763-1831) (daughter of Micajah Clark, Jr, and wife Mildred (Martin) Clark.) The children of Henry James and Mary Lewis (Mansfield) Clark were:

(1) Elizabeth Jane Clark (who married John Price Beatty and had (a) Lycurgus Beatty (who married Mona Branch and had Nina and Guy Beatty), (b) Mary Eliza Beatty (who married Lomas Gant and had (1) Lizzie Ellen Gant (who married William Shirley), (2) Laura Etta Gant (who married Homer J. Clark), (3) Ruth Moore

Gant (who married Charles C. Craig), (c) Helen Louise Beatty (who married Ira Hall), (d) Laura Melinda Beatty (who married Joseph B. Ramp and has Oliver Ramp.) (e) James Robert Beatty (who married Emma Moorhouse and had Ray, Minnie, Mary, Clara, Louise, Dee, Price and Amy Beatty), (f) Oliver Pleasant Beatty (who married Zona McKinney and had Fred, Oliver and Elizabeth Beatty.)

(2) John Pleasant Clark (1817-1898) (who married Mary L. Muldrow and had (a) George Henry Clark (who married Marietta M. Lackland and had (1) John Pleasant, Jr., (2) Ida Longuey; (3) Marguerite Lackland and (4) Henry Grant Clark), (b) Mary Belle Clark (widow of Samuel Sterling Craig and has Charles Carroll Craig), (c) John Muldrow Clark (1855-1893) who married Hattie Flye and had (1) Harry Brown Clark (who married Emma Belle Faxon), (2) Mary Emma Clark (who married Fred M. Gifford), (3) Jennie Flye Clark (who married Bert Wright), (c) Edward William Clark (who married Josie C. Cudworth and had Louis John, Walter Price and Jennie Crystal Clark.)

(3) Robert Mansfield Clark (1819-1865) (who married Cynthia Mills Dickinson (1821-1891) and had twelve children: (a) Henry Dickinson Clark (1839-1913) (a soldier in Civil War, and for many years beloved pastor of Christian Church in Mt. Sterling, Kentucky, married Melissa McElhinney and had (1) Maude Mansfield Clark, wife of Prof. William M. Forrest (U. of V.) and has a son, Clark Forrest.) (2) Claude McElhinney Clark, (3) Lawrence Clark, (4) Ruby (an adopted daughter married Walter Mackie); (b) Mary Gertrnde Clark (1844-1917) (who married Robert Moffet Allison Hawk and had (1) Henry Clark Hawk (who married Ida Whitmer. Their children are Lucy and Clark Hawk), (2) Hannah Gertrude Hawk, (3) Egbert Burgess Hawk (who married Osyth Lamoreaux); (c) Cynthia Elizabeth Clark (1843-1884) (who married Lafayette Tweed Blair and had (1) Mary Idella Blair who married John F. Sherman and had: Harold, Roger, Walter, Mary Olive and Elizabeth Sherman); (2) Robert Ashton Blair and (3) Harvey Blair); (d) Susan Jane Clark (who married Oliver Perry Darst and had, (1) William J. Darst (who married Hattie Gilbert), (2) Walter Darst (who married Lou Gilbert), (3) Bert Darst (who married Mary Shaw), (4) Bertha Darst (who married F. G. Switzer), (5) Arthur Darst (who married Clara Day); (e) Emily Augusta Clark (who married William Henry Crow); (f) Mildred Ann Clark (1851-1912) (who married John Taylor Smith and had (1) Austin Smith, (2) Mary Blanche Smith (who married Dr. Latta), (3) Hal Clark Smith, (4) Bert Smith); (g) Robert Mansfield Clark (who married Emma Louise Russell); (h) Amelia Virginia Clark (who married John Asbury Coleson and had (1) Esther Mills Coleson, (2) Charles

GAINES

Thomas Coleson, (3) Margaret Elmira Coleson), (4) Robert Clark Coleson, (5) Marian Olive Coleson.)
(4) William Wallace Clark, (1821-1851) (died unmarried.)
(5) Virginia Ann Clark (1823-1900) married Charles Towar Boggs (1812-1902) and had eight children; one of whom (a) Amelia (widow of Norman T. Gassette) lives in Paris, and with her daughter, Grace G. Gassette, was closely identified with the work in American Ambulance Hospital at Neuilly-Paris, from the beginning of the World War until November, 1916, when Miss Gassette became Directrice-Technique in the Franco-American Corrective Surgical Appliance Committee; a position for which her wide experience during the war eminently fits her. In June, 1917, the highest honor France bestows for military or civic service, the Cross of the Legion of Honor, was given to Miss Gassette in recognition of her heroic original work in aid of the wounded soldiers of France. In November, 1917, Miss Gassette was made Honorary Member of the 109th Infantry Regiment, with title of Corporal Brancardiere and decorated with the fourragers of the Croiz de Guerre which the 109th had received for bravery in the Battle of the Aisne. In November, 1917, Mrs. Gassette received the Medaille d'Honneur from France for two years continuous service in the American Ambulance Hospital), (b) Mary Elizabeth Boggs (1842-1874) (who married Edward Mendsen and had Charles Frederic Mendsen (who married Calista Louise Bryant and had Jessie (who married Edwin Childs Conover and had John Charles Conover), (2) Nellie Mendsen (who married Frederick A. Leland and has Henry Sherman, Dorthea, Marion, Charlotte and Mary Leland); (3) Edward Boone Mendsen (who married Cornelia ─────────, and has John Mendsen), (c) William Mansfield Boggs, (1846-1914) (who married Lillian Newman and had (1) Georgia Virginia (who married Lewis James Morganstern, and has Lewis James Morganstern, Jr.) and (2) Lillian Mansfield Boggs); (d) Emma Virginia Boggs (widow of Melville R. Doty) has children, (1) Lois Cornelia Doty (who married James Wetherell); (2) Bessie Virginia Doty (who married Walter Deitz Connor and has Melville Doty Connor), (3) Harold Darius Doty (who married Kathleen Herely and has Mary Jane Doty); (e) Helen Moore Boggs, widow of Charles Robert Stouffer, has daughters; Edith Aiken Stouffer (who married Jackson Kemper Dering and has Jackson Kemper Dering, Jr.) and Leita Dorothy Stouffer (who married firstly: Clayton Sedgwick Cooper and had Dorothy, Virginia and Gwendolyn Price Cooper and married secondly John Dean Purdy, Second, and has John Dean Purdy, Third); (g) George Towar Boggs (who married Grace Legrow Tobin and they have (I) Norman Towar (who married Ethel Fitzhugh and has three children), (II) Allen Dearborn (who married Muriel Abbott

NOTABLE SOUTHERN FAMILIES

Closson) (III) Mildred (doing war work in France) and (IV) George Arthur Boggs (with Motor Truck Division in France); (f) Fanny Iglehart Boggs (married Albert Greene Lester and their children are: Helen (who married Emory S. Rockwell and have an adopted son, Lester Rockwell) and Ruth Lester (with Hospital Unit 13 in France).

(6) James Thomas Clark (1825-1850) married Louisa Stephenson, cousin of Adlai Stephenson and had (a) Edgar Poe Clark (who married Margaret Wineteer and had (1) Myra Clark, (2) Vernon Mansfield Clark (who married Vivi Lewis and has four children, (3) Cora Clark, (who married Charles J. Weld): (b) Flora Clark (who married John H. Brubaker and had Flora Belle Brubaker (who married Frank Mohr and has children: Adele, Ethel, Marjorie, Louise, and John Alden Mohr).

(7) Louise Mildred Clark (1826-1878) married her cousin John David Clark; children are: (a) Joseph Henry Clark (Civil War Veteran) who married Jennie Elizabeth Mallett and had Fannie, Joseph, Horace, Ella, Frank, George, Cora and Robert; (b) Ella Clark (who married James Stewart and has (I) William Clark (served in Cuban War), (II) Lottie Bell, (III) Charles Oliver, (IV) Harry C., (V) George Albert, (VI) Fannie Louise and (VII) Ella Manita Stewart); (c) Frank (who married Mary E. Dormer); (d) Lee (who married Olive Gambell and has son Nelson Clark); (e) Albert Garth (who married Carrie Rindlaub and has Eva and Albert Clark); (f) Clara Clark (who married Wilbur Mosena and has children: Wilbur, Roscoe, Elizabeth, Albert, Ralph, Beulah and Eva Mosena).

(8) Martha Augusta Clark (1828-1903) who married William Dupre' Waynick (1823-1880). Their children were (a) Mary Susan Waynick, (1850-1918) (who married Moses Folsom and had Robert Gilman Folsom); (b) Albert Gallatin Waynick (who married Florence Myrtle Watkins and had Elizabeth Avery Waynick (who married Frederick Burton Ruble and had Frederick Warren and Herbert Waynick Ruble); (c) Gertrude Waynick (who married Abner W. Johnstone; children: Dwight and Howard Johnstone); (d) Emma Isadora Waynick (who married John Skinner; children: Ralph, Jessie and Martha Skinner); (e) Clara Mabel Waynick (married Abner Goodhue and has Hugh, Paul and Burt Goodhue); (f) Harlan Dupont Waynick, (who married Chassie——————————— and has Mark Anthony Waynick and Ella Waynick); (g) Robert Mansfield Waynick (who married Emilie ——————— and had Robert Waynick); (h) Laura Jay Waynick (who married Will Livingston Ag-

GAINES

new; their children are Dupre Livingston Agnew (in Aviation Corps) and Clark Mansfield Agnew); (i) Martha May Waynick (who married Edward J. Watson).

(9) Emma Houston Clark (1830-1906) (who married Thomas Bazil McLure (1828-1897) and had five children; (a) Helen Isora (d. 1916) who married John William Vance; no children); (b) Elizabeth Jane McLure (who married John Irvin Armour and has (I) Frank Clark Armour (who married Delora Minor); (II) Nellie Armour and (III) Margaret Genevieve Armour); (c) William Frank McLure (d. unm.); (d) Joseph Eugene McLure (d. unm.); (e) Emma Permelia McLure (who married Charles Edward Vance (cousin of her sister's husband) and has Myra Louisa Vance and Charles Clark Vance (who married Anna Christina Block and has Charles Clark Vance, Second, and Frederick Lawrence Vance).

(10) Henry Samuel Clark (1831-1898) (who married Frances E. Cassidy and had three children: one of whom George Alfred Clark married Manita O Bacon, and has Mary Elizabeth and Antoinette Cassidy Clark).

(11) Charles Anderson Clark (1833-1902) who married Sabrina Smith (1834-1889). Their children were (a) Harry Lee Clark (1857-1917) (who married Etta V. Harsh and had Veda Almira Clark (who married Jacob Petsch, August 2, 1911); (b) Frank Wendell Clark (who married Katie A. Tuttle. Their children are (I) Amy Grace Clark, (who married Frederick A. Rice); (II) Mary Josephine Clark (who married Carl Sutorius and has Clark and Helen Sutorius); (III) Jennie Gertrude Clark (who married Joe Wesley Fitts, and has Joe Wesley Fitts, Jr.); (IV) Frank Wendell Clark, Jr. (Battalion F. 63rd Artillery.)

(12) Mary Catherine Clark (1835-1914) who married Uriah Shelby Hodge (1816-1881) and had, (a) Mary Louise Hodge (1853-1909) (who married Edgar Antoine DeMange and had (I) Ralph Charles DeMange (who married Emma Bradley Ewing) and (II) Paul Hodge DeMange (1st Lieutenant 312th Ammunition train, 87th Division, who married Mrs. Etta Mansfield Miller). (b) Virginia Eliza Hodge (who married Joseph Fletcher McNaught and has (I) Helen Fairfax McNaught (who married Edward Hamilton Geary, son of the late Major William Geary) and (II) Carl Shelby McNaught (who married Ruth Taylor and their children are Nancy and Joseph Taylor McNaught); (c) Alice L. Hodge (who married William E. Rossney); (d) Amelia Gertrude Hodge (died young); (e) Minnie Mansfield Hodge (who married Robert William Loudon. Their son William Hodge Loudon married George Jenckes Wilson); (f) Lillian Hodge (who married Francis Allen Bell. Their daughter is Mary Catherine Bell); (g) Emma Hodge (1870-1901) (married

NOTABLE SOUTHERN FAMILIES

Owen T. Reeves. Their child Marian Reeves died young); (h) William Clark Hodge (1874-1882); (i) Julia Fairfax Hodge.

(13) (Died young).

(14) Susan Maria Clark (1840-1893) married Park Worden (no children).

Henry James Clark (son of John and Mary (Gaines) Clark married (in 1860) as second wife, Mrs. Mary Jane (Brown) Bell (1829-1914). Their children are (1) Alonzo Bell Clark (who married Nettie Seibert; one child Bonnalyn B. Clark); (2) Amelia Julia Clark (who married Frank Ewins. Their children are: John A. Ewins (who married Irene Comfort Werner) and Mary Louise Ewins); (3) Albertine Francis Clark (who married Charles E. Blankinship. Their children are (a) Leta C. Blankenship (who married Robert Austin Ward and they have (I) Wallace Howard, (II) Alice Esther, (III) Martha and (IV) Robert Elnore Ward); (b) Dean Francis Blankinship (who married Grace Coriell and their children are (I) Francis Aurelia, (II) Charles and (III) Don Robert Blankenship); (c) Nellie Blankenship (who married Albert James Earl and have Charles Edward, and Nellie Albertine Earl), (d) Clark Blankenship); (IV) Nellie Mansfield Clark (who married S. E Altom and their son is Lawrence Dale Altom (who married Eunice Marfin).

WILLIAM HENRY GAINES

William Henry Gaines, son of Richard Gaines of Culpepper County, Virginia, and brother of James Gaines the First, was a member of the House of Burgesses of Virginia. He married Isabella Pendleton, a sister to his brother's wife Mary Pendleton and a daughter of Henry Pendleton and Mary Bishop Taylor Pendleton. They had ten children namely:

I Benjamin Gaines
II William Henry Gaines
III Richard Gaines, married Jemima Pendleton.
IV Thomas Gaines, married Susannah Strother.
V Robert Gaines, married Elizabeth Long.
VI James Gaines, married Elizabeth Strother.
VII Anne Gaines, married Lieutenant Peter Steinberger.
VIII Isabella Gaines, married a Brown.
IX Philip Gaines.
X Frances Gaines, married Thomas Botts.

William Henry Gaines, Second, son of William Henry First and Isabella Pendleton Gaines was a soldier of the Revolution.

GAINES

Frances Gaines who married Thomas Botts had a son Benjamin Botts, who married Jane Tyler and their son was the Honorable John Minor Botts of Virginia, Member of Congress.

Thomas Gaines, fourth son of William Henry and Isabella (Pendleton) Gaines, married Susannah Strother, daughter of Francis and Susannah (Dabney) Strother and grand, daughter of William and Margaret (Thornton) Strother); they had at least nine children: James Strother, who married Judith Easley and among their children were: John Strother Gaines, who married Letitia Dalton Moore, his cousin, and they had twelve children, of whom Amanda Melvina Fitz-Alan Gaines, married Charles A. Rice and had several children: Hugh Brown Rice, Susan Letitia Rice (who married John Baird Clotworthy, late of Hillman, Georgia. They had three sons: Charles W. Clotworthy (who married Mabelle Affleck), Hugh Alexander Clotworthy (who married Salome Geiger Bell), and John Baird Clotworthy, Jr.) and the Rev. Dr. William A. Rice, of New York, Susan Letitia Gaines (who married Wylie Neal and their daughter, was Parmelia Gaines Neal, (Mrs. John Abernathy); William Dabney, who married Helen Toulmain and had a son Dr. Edmund Pendleton Gaines, who married his cousin, Mary Toulmain; Francis Henry Gaines, who married May Henry and had an only child, Ellen Gaines, who married Thomas St. John; and George Woodson Gaines, Richard Thomas, Elizabeth Strother, Susannah Dabney, Henry Pendleton, Francis Henry and Francis Thornton Gaines. George Woodson Gaines, son of James Strother and Judith (Easley) Gaines, married Sarah Rhea and had (a) William Strother, (b) Robert James, (c) Augustus Pendleton, (d) Elizabeth McCuin and (e) John Rhea Gaines who married three times: firstly, Sarah Rice (a sister of Charles Rice, q.v.), secondly Elizabeth M. Blair and thirdly, Harriet Craig. By the first wife he had (1) Dr. Francis Henry Gaines (Founder and President of Agnes Scott College), who married Mary Lou Lewis and has a son Dr. Lewis Gaines of Atlanta); (2) Dr. William Strother Gaines of Spokane, Washington (who married Laura Brown and has (I) Sue Brown Gaines (who married Edward Franklin Betz and has William Edward Betz), (II) Sarah Rice Gaines (who married Reese B. Brown (III) Harriet Pendleton Gaines (who married Thomas W. Secrest, and has William Gaines Secrest), (IV) Mable J. Gaines, (V) Minnie L. Gaines (who married J. Howard Shubert). By his second marriage John Rhea Gaines had a daughter, Mary Gaines, who married William Magill, of Chattanooga and had children: Elizabeth, Sadie, William and Ensign Alexander Magill. John Rhea Gaines by his third marriage had three daughters: Anne Rhea, who married Charles Clark; Susan Rice, who married Francis Knox Hutcheson; and Louise Gaines, who married John Gates.

NOTABLE SOUTHERN FAMILIES

Elizabeth McCuin Gaines, daughter of George Woodson and Sarah (Rhea) Gaines, married Dr. Franklin Bogart and their sons are Dr. Walter Gaines Bogart and Dr. William M. Bogart of Chattanooga. Dr. Walter Gaines Bogart married Lurella Magill and has two children, Elizabeth Bogart who married T. C. Olney and Frank Bogart who married Roberta Stauffer, Dr. William M. Bogart married Miss Thompson and has Josephine, Eleanor and Franklin Bogart; Elizabeth Strother Gaines, daughter of Thomas and Susannah (Strother) Gaines, married the Rev. Munford Smith; their daughter, Adaline Smith, married, in 1838, David Warren Smyth and they had a daughter, Susan Victoria Gaines Smyth, who married, in 1855, William A. Payne; their son is William Jefferson Payne of Richmond, Virginia.

James Gaines, sixth son of William Henry and Isabella Pendleton Gaines was born in 1742 and died in 1830; he was a Captain of the Culpepper County, Virginia, Minute Men (in which also served his cousins, Henry and Nathaniel Pendleton, Jr.) He was also a Member of the Convention of North Carolina for the Ratification of the Constitution of the United States and of the North Carolina Legislature. Captain James Gaines was one of the two favorite nephews of Judge Edmund Pendleton, to whom the latter left most of his property, consisting of an estate of six thousand acres of land, most of which is now in Sullivan County, Tennessee, and thirty slaves. Captain James Gaines moved in 1788 and settled upon this estate; he was twice married; firstly, in 1762, to a Miss White; and, secondly, in 1776, to Elizabeth Strother, daughter of Francis and Susannah Dabney Strother and sister to his brother's wife, Susannah Strother. By the first marriage he had one daughter, Margaret Gaines who married Samuel Edgeman.

Child of Captain James Gaines by his first wife, Miss White:
I Margaret Gaines, married Samuel Edgeman.

Children of Captain James Gaines by his second wife Elizabeth Strother:
I Susannah Gaines, died unmarried.
II Elizabeth Gaines, married Samuel Moore.
III Lucy Gaines, married David Childress.
IV Francis Henry Gaines, died unmarried.
V James Taylor Gaines, married Anne McMinn and Frances Rogers.
VI Frances Gaines, married Charles Lynn.
VII Edmund Pendleton Gaines.
VIII Behethland Gaines, married James Lyon.
IX Agnes Gaines, married Joseph Everett.
X Nancy Anne Gaines, married Nathan Ashworth.

GAINES

XI George Strother Gaines, married Anne Gaines.
XII Patsey Gaines, married Benjamin Everett.
XIII Sarah Gaines, died unmarried.

Of the foregoing:
I Susannah Gaines died unmarried.
II Elizabeth Gaines married Samuel Moore; their daughter Letitia Dalton Moore, married her cousin, John Strother Gaines, son of James Strother Gaines and his wife, Judith Easley.
III Lucy Gaines married David Childress, an uncle of Mrs. James Knox Polk.
IV Francis Henry Gaines died unmarried.
V James Taylor Gaines (1793-1883) married firstly Anne McMinn, only daughter of Governor McMinn, of Tennessee, by whom he had no children and married secondly Frances G. Rogers, daughter of Joseph and Mary (Ames) Rogers, of Rogersville, Tennessee. Their children were (1) Mary Elizabeth (who married James McKinney, son of John A. McKinney, (born in Coloraine, Ireland and wife Elizabeth (Ayer) McKinney born in Alva, Maine), and (2) Frances. Children of Charles James and Mary E. (Gaines) McKinney were (1) Frances, (who married Joseph M. Logan (no issue), (2) Elizabeth (who married Robert Spurrier Howard-Smith of Germantown, Pennsylvania. Their children were (a) Logan Howard-Smith, (b) Robert Spurrier Howard-Smith (died young), (c) Elise Howard-Smith). (3) Mary Gaines McKinney (who married James McKinney Phipps and had (a) Ann Phipps (who married Colonel Samuel Lee King and had (I) Samuel Lee King, Jr., (II) J. McKinney Phipps King (d.y.), (III) John G. King and (IV) Charles Logan King), (b) Charles McKinney Phipps (who married Anne Sevier Morrison and had Mary McKinney and Margaret Sevier Phipps), (c) Kenneth Logan Phipps (died aged 22), (d) James Gaines Phipps (married Mabel Sevier Morrison (sister of his brother's wife), their children were Kenneth Logan Phipps and James Gaines Phipps, Jr.) (e) Mary McKinney Phipps (d.y.), (f) James McKinney Phipps, Jr. (g) Frances Logan Phipps (who married Arthur S. Cosler and had Arthur S. Cosler, Jr.), (h) Elise Phipps (who married George Felix Phillips.) (4) Susan McKinney (who married William George Nice of Rogersville. Their children (a) Charles McKinney Nice (who married Helen Gilberta Adams of Philadelphia and had Mary Willis Nice and Helen Adams Nice), (b) William George Nice, Jr. (d. y.), (c) Frances Logan Nice (who married Robert Emmet Howe of Shamrock, Kentucky, and had William George Howe), (d) Susan McKinney Nice (who married Dr. Jacob Schultz, of Middleboro, Kentucky), (e) Mary Elizabeth Nice (who married Kenneth Kenner and had Susan Nice

NOTABLE SOUTHERN FAMILIES

Kenner). (5) Charles James McKinney, Jr. (who married Lady Percy and had (a) William Percy McKinney, (b) Mary McKinney, and (c) Charles James McKinney, Third.

VI Frances Gaines married in 1837, Charles Lynn, of Kingsport, Tennessee; six of their children were: John Bell Lynn, who died in 1914; Martin Fleming Lynn, who married Samuel Cloud; Frances Rogers Lynn, who married Thomas Graham Houston; Catherine Jane Lynn, who married Frederick Cushman; Mary Elvira Lynn, who married George Logan; and Eliza Allen Lynn, who married Willis McLaughlin.

VII Edmund Pendleton Gaines was born March 20, 1777, and died June 6, 1849; he was a distinguished General in the War of 1812 and was voted a sword by the Legislature of Tennessee for his victory over the British at Fort Erie, Canada, August 15, 1814; he was also voted swords by the Legislatures of New York and Virginia and a Medal by the United States Congress. General Gaines married three times: firstly, Frances Toulmain, a daughter of Henry Toulmain, first Territorial Judge of the Alabama portion of the Mississippi Territory: secondly, Barbara Blount, a daughter of William Blount, Governor of Tennessee (see Blount family), and, thirdly, Mrs. Myra Clark Whitney, the daughter of Daniel Clark (a native of Ireland who came to New Orleans in 1776 as Consul) and his wife, Zulime Carrier des Granges, a Creole. Mrs. Myra Clark Gaines became celebrated for her litigation with the city of New Orleans in order to inherit the property of her father, worth millions of dollars, much of which she recovered. By his marriage to Barbara Blount General Gaines had a son, Edmund Pendleton Gaines, Jr., late of Washington, D. C.

BEHETHLAND GAINES

Behethland Gaines married James Lyon and had one son, the Honorable Francis Strother Lyon, was a member of the United States Congress and later a member of the Confederate States Congress and President of the Convention of Alabama which in 1861, adopted the Ordinance of Secession; he married Serena Glover, and had: (a) Ida A. Lyon, who married Dr. William Mecklenburg Polk, (a son of Leonidas Polk, the "Fighting Bishop"); their son Francis Polk Lyon (Counsellor of the Department of State) married Elizabeth Sturgis Potter; Helen Gaines Lyon (daughter of Francis Strother Lyon), married Zachery Canty Deas. Another son of James and Betheland (Gaines) Lyon was James Gaines Lyon, (who married Rosina Fisher and moved to Alabama; their daughter, Sarah Behethland Lyon, married the Honorable Charles King Foote, and their daughter, Helen Gaines Foote, married the Honorable Richard Henry Clarke, of Mobile, Alabama, member of Congress, etc. Their daughter, Helen Gaines Clarke married Henry George Smith. William Henry Lyon, another son of James and Behethland (Gaines) Lyon married Elizabeth Armstrong. Their son, Thomas Armstrong Lyon, married Mary Coffee Hearst and their daughter, Mary Lyon, married George Warren Quarles. A daughter of Behethland Gaines Lyon and James Lyon, was Christina Harmon Lyon, who married Joseph Martin and had John Lyon, Elizabeth, Edmund Pendleton, James Gaines, Augustine, Sarah Ann, Mary Frances, William Francis, Martha Josephine, Margaret Isabella, Amanda G. Misa, and Joseph Martin, most of whom married and had children.

(9) Agnes Gaines, daughter of Captain James Gaines and Elizabeth Strother Gaines was born in 1780 and died in 1816. She married in 1797, Joseph Everett, a son of Benjamin and Ann Dennis Everett, of Delaware, and a brother of her sister's husband, Benjamin Everett. After her death he married her cousin Phoebe Childress, a daughter of David and Lucy Gaines Childress. By his marriage to Phoebe Childress, Joseph Everett had five children; (see record of Phoebe, third child of David and Lucy (Gaines) Childress.) By his first marriage he had nine children:

(1) Nancy Laton Everett, who died young.

(2) Elizabeth Strother Everett, (married Samuel Patton, (had nine children: Agnes Patton, died unmarried; George Patton died unmarried; Samuel Patton married Margaret McDonald; Joseph Patton; Susan Patton, married Hugh B. Campbell and had two children, George Campbell married Elizabeth Rogers and Mary Campbell married Ira Dillman, and has one child, Louise Dillman; Mary Patton married Bryan Nesbit; Benjamin Patton died unmarried; Alfred Everett Patton died unmarried; James Gaines Patton married firstly Mary Foster, secondly Katherine Gray and thirdly Martha Thompson.

(3) Susan Dabney Everett married in 1816 James O'Brien whose father was a Revolutionary soldier. Three of the sons of James and Susan Dabney (Everett) O'Brien died unmarried prior to the War Between the States. The youngest son, Alfred Gaines O'Brien, enlisted as a private soldier in the 13th Mississippi Regiment, Confederate States Army, and after being wounded several times was Colonel of the Regiment when the war ended. Years ago the widow and children of Colonel Alfred Gaines O'Brien resided at Kosciuska, Mississippi. The daughters of James and Susan Dabney (Everett) O'Brien were Eliza O'Brien, Sarah O'Brien and Mary O'Brien. Eliza O'Brien married Governor William Gannaway Brownlow, of Tennessee. They had seven children, namely: Susan Brownlow, John Bell

NOTABLE SOUTHERN FAMILIES

Brownlow, James Brownlow, Mary Brownlow, Fannie Brownlow, and twin daughters, Annie Brownlow and Caledonia Temple Brownlow.

Susan Brownlow married Daniel T. Boynton and had four children: Lucile Boynton (who married Clarence A. Benscoter and has Daniel Boynton Benscoter); Edmee Boynton (who married Louis D. Huntoon); Ilia Boynton (who married Franklin Pierce Swindler and has Franklin Pierce Swindler, Jr., and Jean Swindler); Dr. Emerson Boynton (who married ———— ———— and has Daniel E. Boynton, Lewis D. Boynton and Charles G. Boynton);

Colonel John Bell Brownlow married Fanny Fouche and had three children: William Gannway Brownlow, second (who married for his first wife ———— Park and has Fanny Park, married Len G. Broughton, Jr., and married for his second wife, Isabelle Williams); John F. Brownlow (who married ———— and has John F. Brownlow, Jr., and Mary Brownlow); and Jennie Brownlow (who married Edward Ashe and has Jane Brownlow Ashe.)

Colonel James P. Brownlow married ————.

Mary Brownlow married Henry M. Aiken and had Fannie B. Aiken (who married Frank Carrahan and has Elizabeth Carrahan); William B. Brownlow Aiken, Horace Aiken, Halmer Aiken, Frank Aiken, Eliza Brownlow Aiken and Henry M. Aiken, Jr.

Fannie Brownlow married George G. Latta and had Georgia Latta; William Brownlow Latta, Ernest Latta and Vivian Latta.

Annie Brownlow married William F. Patrick and had William F. Brownlow Patrick.

Calendonia Temple Brownlow married John C. Hale and had John Boynton Hale.)

(4) Alfred W. Everett, born November 4, 1804, died July 12, 1859, (married Sarah Comer Griggs Mann, of Alabama, and had Joseph Leonard Everett, died young; John Griggs Everett, died in War Between the States, Sarah Eugenia Everett married Dr. Robert F. Dominick; and had Mattie Comer Dominick, (who died young). Annie Robinette Dominick, who married Francis Marion Lavendar, of Greensboro, Alabama, and had Margaret Everett Lavender, John Robert Lavender and Francis Marion Lavender, Junior. At the age of fifteen Alfred W. Everett went to General Edmund Pendleton Gaines to make his home. He was familiar with several Indian dialects and was connected with the transportation of the Indians from Mississippi to their reservation.

(5) Sarah Ann Everett (daughter of Joseph and Agnes (Gaines) Everett, married Dr. Robert Patton, son of John Adams and Mary (Kelso) Patton, of Rockbridge County, Virginia. Their thirteen children were: (1) Susan Gaines Patton (who married Littleton

GAINES

Henderson Rogan and had six children: Robert Patton Rogan, Sarah A. Rogan, who married Robert Ambrose Wood, son of Reverend John and Eliza Lynn Wood and had seven children: (1) Effie Davis Wood, (2) Eliza Lynn Wood, (3) Leonard Whitney Wood (who married firstly, Louise Pendleton); secondly, Mrs. Emily (Taylor) Canfield), (4) Susan Rogan Wood (who married the Reverend Dr. John Rankin Herndon and had two children: Sarah Eliza Herndon and Margaret Rogan Herndon); (5) Littleton Henderson Wood, who married Stella Luikart, (6) Ada Lee Wood (who married William Franklin Taylor and had three children: Mary Lee Taylor, Lillie Taylor and William Franklin Taylor, II. (7) Reverend John Ambrose Wood (who married Leonora Whitaker and had a daughter Sarah Katherine Wood, (c) Katherine Rogan died young, (d) James Whitney Rogan, D. D. (1854-1916) (who married Lillie Jackson, daughter of General Alfred and Katherine Taylor Jackson, no children), (e) John Patton Rogan (who married Frances Young and had a daughter, Sarah Rogan, (f) Alice Lee Rogan died unmarried; (2) James Strother Patton, an officer in Mexican War, who married Susan Vance. Their children were William Kirkpatrick Patton and Florence Patton (who married her cousin, William Jordan (q. v.) son of Reverend Thomas and Helen Everett Jordan.) (3) John Adams Patton (who married Denise Patton, daughter of Dr. Samuel Patton, of Kingsport, Tennessee.) Their children were (a) Samuel Patton, (b) Robert Patton, (c) Joseph Everett Patton; (4) Ann Adelaide Patton (d. unm.) (5) Agnes Everett Patton (who married Nelson P. Jordan, of Iowa), (6) Mary Kelso Patten (d.y.) (7) Myra Clark Gaines Patton died young; (8) Rebecca Patton (d.y.); (9) William Kelso Patton (who married Cornelia E. Powell and had (a) Robert Lee Patton (who married Adelaide Broyles and had (1) Catalina, (2) Maude and (3) Robert Patton, died young; (b) William Lamont Patton (1867-1908) (who married Ida Phipps and had (1) Pauline; (2) Hugh, died young; (3) Clyde; (4) Minnie, (5) Carl, (6) Reed, and (7) Cornelia Patton); (c) Charles Sloane Patton (who married Ida Woodring and had (1) Helen. (2) Pansy; (3) Rachel, and (4) Charles Sloan Patton, Jr. (d) Anne Elizabeth Patton, (e) Claude Patton, (d.y.), (f) Wade Hampton Patton (who married Agnes Self and had: (1) Cornelia Patton, (2) James Duncan Patton, (3) Wade Hampton Patton, Jr., (4) Mary Ruth Patton, and (5) Marjorie Lee Patton), (g) Minnie McFarland Patton (who married Vincent Morgan Thomas and had: (1) Cornelia Shelby Thomas, (2) Hazen House Thomas, died young; (3) Vincent Morgan Thomas, Jr.) (10) Joseph Perry Patton, who died young); (11) George Patton (who married Mary Vance, a niece of his brother's wife, Susan Vance), (12) David Nelson Patton died

NOTABLE SOUTHERN FAMILIES

young; (13) Eliza Strother Patton(daughter of Robert and Sarah Anne Everett Patton married Francis Alexander Kelly. (a son of Judge John Alexander and Martha Peck Kelly, of Marion, Virginia.) Their children were (a) Martha Kelly (who died young; (b) Robert Patton Kelly (who married Langborne Nowlin Cosby (daughter of William Woodson and Mary Langborne Nowlin Cosby), and had a son, Robert Patton Kelly, Jr.), (c) Francis Marion Kelly (who married Dorothy Elizabeth Mitchell (daughter of Daniel McRae and Martha (Wooton) Mitchell, and had one child Dorothy Mitchell Kelly), (d) Frederick Strother Kelly (who married Rebecca Chisholm Ammons(daughter of James D. and Rebecca Chisholm Ammons), (e) Josephine Hull Kelly, (f) Ann Kelly, died young (g) Professor John Alexander Kelly of the University of Virginia, (h) Ruby Kelly, who,died young.)

Letitia Moore Everett(daughter of Joseph and Agnes (Gaines) Everett) married John Adams Patton, a brother of her sister's husband, Robert Patton. They had three children: (1) Sarah Everett Patton (Mrs. Hunt), (2) Susan Gaines Patton (Mrs. Evans) and (3) Robert Patton.

Lucy Gaines, daughter of Captain James and Elizabeth Strother Gaines, married David Childress. Their children were (a) James Childress; (b) Elizabeth Childress, and (c) Phoebe Childress. James Childress married Letitia Gaines and had (1) Elizabeth Childress (who married Duke Gibson and had (1) Olivia Gibson, who married David Kinkaid, (2) Josephine Gibson, who married Charles Clark, a Canadian, (3) Jerry. Gibson (married ———), (2) Louise Childress married Jesse Childress, (3) Lucy Childress married Colonel John Talbert Keyes and had: (1) Mary Virginia Keyes (b. 1844); (2) Theona B. Keyes (b. 1845) (3) Letitia C. Keyes (d. inf.) (4) Martha E. Keyes, (5) George A. Keyes, (6) John M. Keyes, (7) Letitia Gaines Keyes), (4) Behethland Childress (who died unmarried) (5) Matthew Moore Childress (married ——— and had Letitia Gaines, Tabitha, and Matthew Moore Childress, II.) (6) George Childress(married Sarah Norton; no issue), (7) Letitia Dalton Childress (married David Waterman and had (1) Olivia Waterman; (2) William Waterman; (3) Ann Waterman; (4) Letitia Waterman and (5) Samuel Gaines Waterman, (b) Elizabeth Childress married William Nelms. Their children were (1) David Wallace Nelms (who married Lavinia Clyce (no living issue); (2) John Henry Nelms (who married Letitia V. Pendleton, children were: (I.) Myrtle Nelms (who married Dr. Joseph Campbell and had (A) Joseph Campbell, Jr., (B) James Preston Campbell and (C) Allen B. Campbell); (II.) Kathleen Nelms married Dr. Z. E. Dee; (III.) Virginia Nelms; (IV.) Helen Nelms (married Edward

GAINES

E. Tarr and had Virginia F. Tarr): (3) Joseph Monroe Nelms (who married Helen Hoffman and had Bruce Nelms and a daughter), (c) Phoebe Childress (married Joseph Everett (whose first wife was her Aunt Agnes Gaines.) Their children by this marriage were: (1) Adeline Everett (who married Andrew Gibson and had Elizabeth Gibson (who married John Richardson), and Joseph Perry Gibson (who married Susan Emmert), (2) Lucy Helen Everett (who married Reverend J. Thomas Jordan and had: (I.) Alice Virginia Jordan (d.y.), (II.) Gordon William Jordan (who married firstly, his cousin, Florence Patton (daughter of James Strother Patton) and had Hugh K. Jordan, Hattie Jordan and Perry Everett Jordan.) Gordon William Jordan married secondly: Lelia Patton and had Elizabeth Jordan (who married ——— Jewell); married thirdly: Virginia French.) (III.) Phoebe Jordan (d.y.). (IV.) Everett Jordan (d.y.) (V.) Hugh Chapman Jordan married Agnes Hatcher and had Meta Jordan and Helen Everett Jordan); (VI.) Oscar Perry Jordan married Nannie Wysor Morehead and had Oscar Perry Jordan, Jr. (U. S. N.) (VII.) Andrew Henry Jordan married firstly Ella Darst and had Harry Darst Jordan, married secondly Virginia Whitman and their children were Virginia Elizabeth Jordan and Margaret Jordan. (VIII.) David Childress Jordan married Mamie Edmondson. Their daughter, Helen Jordan, married George Brandon. (IX.) Thomas Lee Jordan (unm.), (X.) Barbara Helen Jordan married Dr. R. H. Wooling, (3) Joseph Perry Everett (b. June 7, 1820) married Jane Ayer Smith, niece of Elizabeth (Ayer) McKinney, whose son, Charles James McKinney, married Mary Elizabeth Taylor (daughter of Francis Taylor and Frances (Rogers) Gaines.) Their children were: (I) Charles Smith Everett (who married Julia King and had Lillian C. Everett); (II.) Joseph Dennis Everett (b. Jan. 5, 1840) who married Caroline E. Southworth and had Alice Couch Everett(died aged 14); (III.) John McKinney Everett (who married Carrie Van Wagner and had (A) William van Wagner Everett (who married Mary Brown and had a daughter), (B) Eula Everett (who married Clarence Wimpenny and had William Baker Wimpenny), (IV) Henry Childress Everett (d. inf.), (V.) Sarah Ann Everett (who married Dr. J. D. Bryan and their children were Perry Everett, Arthur and Esther Bryan), (VI.) Thomas Andrew Everett (who married Harriet Wait and had George Wait Everett); (4) Virginia Everett who married Thomas Perry (no issue), (5) Barbara Everett (who married Rev. Henry Procter Waugh and had I. R. Virginia Everett Waugh (who married (in 1879) John M. Boyd and had (A) Henry Everett Boyd (d. 1899) (B) Eula Lee Boyd (who married Frank P. Cogdal and has Ruth Elizabeth Cogdal); (C) Elizabeth Boyd (who married Ralph C. Chestnutt); (c) Behethland Childress (who married Joseph Powell), (d) Reverend Edward Childress, (e) Henry Childress.

(6) Isabella Pendleton Everett (married John Graham, son of James and Margaret Rodgers Graham. They had nine children, namely: Mary ,Frances Graham; James Gaines Graham; Margaret Rodgers Graham; Isabella Graham; Myra Clark Graham; Alfred Everett Graham; John Graham, Junior; Edmund Pendleton Graham; Emma Graham, who is the only surviving member of the family. She resides in Bloomington, Illinois. Only the eldest child, Mary Frances Graham, married. She married James Montgomery Allison Higgins Howe, son of Joshua Owen Howe and Lucinda Allison Howe. Their children were

(a) Walter Howe, (1846-1915) Brigadier General, U. S. A., who married Elizabeth Dunn, daughter of Samuel and Margaret Batterton Dunn, and had Judge Walter Dunn Howe, of El Paso, Texas, (who married Marie Hobson Shelton and has Harriet Elizabeth Howe, Marion Shelton Howe, Walter Shelton Howe, Ethel Irene Howe).; Professor George Maxwell Howe, of Colorado College (who married Frances Chamberlain, and has Frances Elizabeth Howe) ; and Alfred Graham Howe, Commander U. S. N., who married Hilda Gregory and has Hilda Haywood Howe.

(b) Alice Howe married W. L. Polk, of Vicksburg, Mississippi, and has Walter Howe Polk; married Lillian Montgomery; Susan Polk; Mary Polk; Lancaster Polk; Paul M. Polk married Alice Dunning; and Clara G. Polk married George W. Roberts.

(c) Joshua Owen Howe married Ella Wetherby and had Ross Maxwell Howe, died young; Owen Chalmers Howe, of Boston, married Charlotte Kendall and has three children; Louis P. Howe, of Rockford, Illinois.

(d) Alfred Graham Howe married Mary Belle Jennings and had Alice Howe; married Dr. Charles Eller, of Albuquerue, New Mexico: Hazel Howe married Dr. Homer Curry, of Bloomington, Indiana; Irene Howe married Professor Karl Fischer, of the University of Pennsylvania; Lucille Howe; and Willafred Howe married Ralph Wellons. They are missionaries at Lucknow, India.

(e) James Howe.

(f) Lucy Isabella Howe.

(g) Minnie Howe married Judge Frank E. Hunter, of El Paso, Texas, and has Herbert Howe Hunter, who married Pearl Ellis and has one child.

(h) Lillian G. Howe married James B. Troutman, of Chicago.

(i) John Montgomery Howe married Lula Sears and has Cecile Howe; married Harry Benner, of Chicago, and James Howe.

GAINES

(7) Martha Gaines Everett died young.
(8) Letitia Moore Everett married John Adams Patton.
(9) Mary Frances Everett married William Lynn.

(X.) Nancy Anne Gaines married, in 1809, Nathan Ashworth and settled in Louisiana.

(XI.) George Strother Gaines married Anne Gaines.

XII. Patsey Gaines married Benjamin Everett. Of their children four left descendants; (1) James Taylor Gaines, (2) John Ray, (3) Elizabeth Strother, who married David Hite, and (4) George Gaines.

James Taylor Gaines Everett m. Elizabeth Hite. They had five children, as follows: (1) David B. Everett (m.) (I.) Caroline Dugy; (II.) Ann Gutherie), (2) Gaines Meek Everett m. Ada Dent) (3) James C. Everett (m. Frances Vincent) (4) Francis Strother Everett (m. Alice Russell), (5) Eleanor E. Everett (m. Dr. Virgil Russell.

XIII. Sarah Gaines, born 1789, died, unmarried, 1870; she was named for her mother's grandmother, Sarah Jennings, said to have been a sister of William Jennings, the intestate English millionaire, whose estate was settled after a century in the courts, in favor of Earl Howe.

Richard Gaines, son of William Henry and Isabella Pendleton Gaines, married his cousin, Jemima Pendleton, daughter of Philip and Martha Pendleton, and granddaughter of Henry and Mary Bishop (Taylor) Pendleton. They had eleven children: Lucy (Mrs. Botts) Rowland, Jemima (Mrs. Speak), Benjamin, Nathaniel, James, Judith (Mrs. Chancellor), Anne (Mrs. Crigler), John Cooke, Elizabeth (Mrs. Benjamin Thomas), and William Henry Gaines, III. (who married Jane Botts and had at least four sons: Richard, Nathaniel, Cornelius, who married Susan Foster; and Augustine Gaines, who was a soldier in the War of 1812 and married a daughter of Captain Brawner, of Maryland.)

The King and Queen County Virginia, records mention under date of 1776, Harry Gaines, who was a brother of Lieutenant Gaines, of "Green Way," King William County, and of Robert Gaines, of the "White House," King and Queen County; he, Harry Gaines, lived at Providence and died in 1789. He married Elizabeth Herndon and had seven children: (a) Benjamin, who lived at "Plain Dealing," and married Sarah Garlick; they had four children (1) Mary Anne, (who married her cousin, Richard Gaines, and inherited "Plain Dealing"), (2) Myra, (who married George Carlton, of "Carlton's Store"), (3) William Fleming Gaines, III., and (4) Sarah Jane (who married Major John Henry Steger), (b) Henry (Harry) Gaines, Jr., (of whom later), (c) Robert Beverly, (who married Lucy Gaines, his cousin, a daughter of William Fleming Gaines of Greenway; and they had three children, Sarah, Herndon and Lucy Gaines, all of whom died unmarried), (d) William Fleming Gaines, Jr. (who died young) (e) Martha Fleming Gaines (who married Robert Baylor Hill and they had a daughter, Catherine Gaines Hill who married Samuel Peachy Ryland), (f) *Elizabeth Herndon (who married Captain Thomas Miller, of Powhatan County, Virginia, and died without issue), (g) John Gaines (who lived at Providence. He was Commonwealth Attorney for Virginia, never married). Henry Gaines, Jr., who was called "Harry" married Myra Muse and lived at "Woodlawn." They had five children: Juliet (who married Thomas Nelson Carter; Cornelia, (who married Dr. Meade), Henry Mortimer (who died unmarried), Martha Elizabeth Gaines (who died unmarried) and Sarah Anne Gaines (who died unmarried.) Ambrose Gaines, of Culpeper County, Virginia, had a son, Matthew Ambrose Gaines, who moved to Tennessee and married Margaret Luttrell, daughter of James Churchwell Luttrell, First, and Margaret Armstrong Luttrell. (See Luttrell and Armstrong Families). They had five children, namely: James Luttrell Gaines, M. M. Gaines, Martha Gaines, Mary Gaines, and Ambrose Gaines, Third.

Of the foregoing:
M. M. Gaines I have no record of him.
Mary Gaines married ――― Bearden.
Martha Gaines married Richard Bearden.

Ambrose Gaines, Third, married Mary Towns and had six children, namely: George Towns Gaines (who married ――― and had Ethel Smith Gaines and Katherine Woodville Gaines); Margaret Gaines (who married Garland Buffington); Etta Gaines (who married H. B. Hogan); Blanche Gaines (who married F. J. Hoyle); Mary Towns Gaines (who married Reuben S. Payne); and Ambrose Gaines, Fourth (who married Edith Lucie Jenks and has Margaret Gaines, Ambrose Gaines, Fifth, Edith Jenks Gaines, and Mary Towns Gaines.)

James Luttrell Gaines was a gallant officer of the Confederate Army and lost his arm in the service. He married Belle Porter, daughter of Erasmus Porter and had five children: Ambrose Porter Gaines, Matthew Gaines, Lillian Gaines, (who died young); and James Luttrell Gaines, Second.

It should be mentioned here that various members of the Gaines family in England and in Wales were knighted by different sovereigns and as a rule each one adopted his own coat of arms and crest; consequently there is some confusion on this subject in Works of Heraldry. In Dunn's "Heraldic Visitation of Wales," which was prepared by order of the King, are given the Coat of Arms and the genealogy of the family in Wales. We therefore give the one described by Dunn

GAINES

as that of 'the Gaines family; "A field of silver a black lion with a crown on its head." This was the COAT OF ARMS of Sir John Gaines, but many of the descendants of Sir David Gaines bore his arms: Sable, three spear heads argent, gonttes de sang a chevron argent. Another Gaines COAT OF ARMS is described as follows: "Argent, two chevrons gules. CREST: Out of a ducal coronet or, a lion rampant sable."

HOWARD FAMILY

The Howard family is given by Burke and other authorities as the oldest and most illustrious in the world. The Head of the House of Howard is the Duke of Norfolk, Premier Duke of England, with precedence of all save the Princes of the blood, and with hereditary honors and titles that would fill a page. The present Head of the House, the little Duke, is only ten years old. The late Duke was married twice, and this child is the son of his second wife. By an odd chance the little boy, heir of the House of Howard and Premier Duke of Great Britain is also a descendant of a Colonial Governor in America, John Winthrop. Through his mother, the Dowager Duchess of Norfolk, he is in the tenth generation from Governor John Winthrop.

The history of the Howards goes directly through English history for a thousand years, and through other lines of the family centuries further still, to the time indeed when history begins to be chronicled.

Hereward was of a Saxon Family living in the Reign of King Edgar, 957 to 973. They were Lords and Earls. Duke Oslac was their close kinsman and their daughters were married to reigning families. Hereward's son was the great Lord Leofric and Leofric's wife the famed Lady Godiva of Coventry. They had a son, Hereward the Banished, one of the famous characters in early history. Charles Kingsley's "Hereward the Last of the English" is the story of young Hereward. A daughter of Leofric and Godiva was married to a son of Siward the Strong Arm. The Armstrong Family is from Siward.

Hereward the Banished was permitted to return. He had a son, Hereward, and a grandson, Hereward, who married Wilburga. Hereward and Wilburga named their son Robert. Robert's son was John, who married Lucy Germond. They had a son, William de Hayward or Hereward, who was Chief Justice. It will be seen that the name Hereward had become Normanized to de Hayward, and from that it became in time Howard.

William de Hayward, the Justice, married twice, firstly, Alice Ufford who died without children, and second, Alice Fitten, who was mother to John Howard who married Joan de Cornwall, sister to Sir Richard de Cornwall. Their son was another Sir John Howard.

The foregoing pedigree is from Burke. Some students of the family history, however, begin the line with Robert and his son, John, who married Lucy Germund, and was father to William de Hayward, the Justice. Still others give William himself credit for being head of the family line. From his name, however, all authorities agree.

HOWARD

Burke, however, is authority and his record, page 1128, of the Peerage, reads:

"Ingulf and Mathew Paris concur in stating that Howard, or Hereward, was living in the reign of King Edward, 957 to 973, and that he was a kinsman of Duke Oslac, and that his son, Leofric, was the father of Hereward, who was banished by the Conquerer. The very ancient book of the Church of Ely, 'Historia Ecclesia Eliensis,' entirely confirms this statement. It appears that Hereward was subsequently allowed to return and it is certain that his family returned to Wigenhall and other portions of their inheritance in Norfolk. Hereward's grandson, Hereward or Howard and his wife Wilburga, in the reign of Henry II., granted a carucate of land in Torrington, in Norfolk, to the Church of Len (Lynn) and directed that prayers should be said for the souls of Hereward, his father, and of Hereward, the Banished, or the Exile, his grandfather. Robert Hereward, the son of Hereward, was seized of Wigenhall, Torrington and other estates in Norfolk and was the father of John Hereward or Howard, of Wigenhall, who by Lucy Germund, his wife, was the father of Sir William Howard, Chief Justice of the Common Pleas, from 1297 to 1308.

Sir John married Alice de Boys, daughter of Sir Robert de Boys, and their son was Sir Robert who married Margery Scales, daughter of Robert, Lord Scales. They had a son, Sir John, who married Margaret, daughter of Sir John Plaiz, and no sons surviving, married for his second wife, Alice, daughter of Sir William Tendring. They had a son, Sir Robert, who married Lady Margaret Mowbray, daughter of Lord Mowbray and heiress of the Mowbrays.

With this marriage to Lady Margaret Mowbray, begins the great record of the Howards, for through her they heired titles and estates innumerable.

Lady Margaret Mowbray was the elder daughter of Thomas de Mowbray by his wife, Elizabeth, daughter and co-heir of Richard FitzAllen, Earl of Arundel and cousin and co-heir of John Mowbray, Duke of Norfolk. Thomas de Mowbray was a son and heir of Lord John Mowbray by Elizabeth Segrave (a direct descendant of Robert de Vere, who signed Magna Carta as surety for King John.) John de Mowbray was directly descended from Henry de Bohun, Roger Bigod, Hugh Bigod, William de Mowbray, Gibbert de Clare, Richard de Clare, John de Lacies, Saber de Quincey and William de Albina each of whom signed Magna Carta as surety for King John. Lord de Mowbray, was a Crusader and fell in Battle in 1368.

Elizabeth Segrave's father, John Lord Segrave married Margaret of Brotherton, daughter and heir of Thomas Plantagenet, called Thomas of Brotherton, son of King Edward I., and his second wife, Margaret of France, daughter of Phillip II., called Phillip Le Hardi, King of France.

Margaret of Brotherton (Plantagenet) was created Duchess of Norfolk, and she claimed through her father the office of Earl Marshall of England and was called the Marechale. She was the daughter of Thomas of Brotherton and his wife Alice, daughter of Sir Roger Halys.

Thomas of Brotherton (Plantagenet) was the son of Edward of England and his second wife Margaret of France, daughter of King Phillip II, of France, called Le Hardi. Thomas was born in Brotherton Castle, and was called of Brotherton. He was the son of Edward I, who was the son of Henry III, who was the son of King John, who was the son of Henry IV (and Eleanor of Aquitaine) who was the son of Empress Matilda, who married for her second husband, Geoffry Plantagenet, Count of Anjou and first of the name Plantagenet because of a sprig of the broom plant which he wore in his cap. Geoffry was the son of Fulk, Count of Anjou and King of Jerusalem.

Matilda was the daughter of Henry I, and he the son of William the Conquerer, whose queen was a descendant of King Alfred. From Edward I the genealogical lines are so many and so accurate that they are bewildering. Suffice it to say that the family is descended from Charlemange, King Alfred, William the Conqueror, Rollo, all the early French Kings and heroes, and countless English and Saxon heroes.

Thomas of Brotherton, son of Edward I, was Earl Marshall of England and his daughter and heir was Margaret of Brotherton who claimed the office and was called the Marechale. She was created Duchess of Norfolk. She married John Mowbray and her son Thomas Mowbray became the first Duke of Norfolk of the Mowbray line. There were four Mowbray Dukes of Norfolk, when the male line failing, the title reverted to the first Duke's daughter, Margaret Mowbray's descendants.

Margaret Mowbray had married Sir Thomas Howard, as stated before, and their son, Sir John Howard, became by right of his mother the Duke of Norfolk. He is the first Duke of Norfolk in the Howard line and in history is always called the First Duke of Norfolk (though four Mobray Dukes and the Duchess Margaret of Brotherton had preceded him).

Sir John Howard, the First Duke of Norfolk, son of Sir Robert Howard and the Lady Margaret Mowbray married Katherine Moleyns, daughter of William Lord of Moleyns.

Their son, Thomas Howard, was first Earl of Surrey by which title he acquired fame and after his father's death became the Second Duke of Norfolk. He is often called also the Victor of Flodden and

HOWARD

is famous in history for that battle. He married firstly Elizabeth Tilney, daughter and heiress of Sir Frederick Tilney, and widow of Sir Humphrey Bouchier, and married secondly Agnes Tilney a cousin of his first wife. A number of children by both wives left descendants though the Ducal line comes through the first wife, Elizabeth, as does also the Southern family in America.

Thomas Howard, the Third Duke was the eldest son. The American family traces through the third son, Lord Edmund Howard. He married Joyce Culpepper, daughter and heir of Sir Richard Culpepper, A daughter of the couple was Katherine Howard, one of the ill fated Queens of Henry VIII, (another was her first cousin Ann Bolyn, daughter of Lady Elizabeth Howard and Sir Thomas Bolyn. Queen Elizabeth was the daughter of Ann Bolyn).

Margaret Howard, daughter of Lord Edmund Howard and Joyce Culpepper, married Sir Thomas Arundel, and they became protestants in the reign of Henry VIII. In the next reign, that of Edward VI, Arundel was accused of conspiracy and was beheaded and his property sequestered. They had one son, Matthew, and this Matthew assumed his mother's name of Howard as his own was temporarily under a cloud and with Mary's accession to the Throne and Crown, the Howard prestige was greater than ever. His great uncle, Thomas Howard, was Duke of Norfolk and Counsellor of State to Queen Mary. The use of surnames was not yet so fixed a habit but that a man might take one at his convenience, and the assumption of the mother's name was a frequent occurrence.

Matthew, son of Margaret Howard and Sir Thomas Arundel married Margaret Wiloughby, and had a son, Thomas, who was a soldier of fortune in Europe. He married twice, firstly, Lady Marcia Wriothesley, by whom he had Thomas, William and Elizabeth Howard, and secondly, Ann Thoroughgood. By his second marriage he had three sons, Matthew, Thomas and Frederick, who being younger portionless off-spring had to seek fortunes for themselves. Emigration to America, the Land of Promise, was the spirit of the day and in company with the family of their mother, who had been Ann Thoroughgood they all came to America and to Virginia. The only daughter, Ann Howard, married Cecil Calvert, Lord Baltimore.

MATTHEW HOWARD

Matthew Howard eldest son of Thomas Arundel or Thomas Howard, was settled in Virginia before 1623, on the East bank of the Elizabeth River near the present Parish of Norfolk. He had a large tract of land and several white servants. He received a grant of land in 1638. He was a close friend, neighbor and evidently kinsman of Edward and Cornelius Lloyd. His first wife by whom he seems to have had no children was named Elizabeth. His second wife, the mother of several children was named Ann and she was possibly Ann Hall, as Richard Hall seems to have been an inmate of Matthew Howard's household and bequeathed his estate to Matthew and his children. Matthew Howard's sister, Ann Howard, daughter of Thomas Arundel Howard and Ann Thoroughgood was married to Cecil Calvert Lord Baltimore, and the intimacy between the two families probably prompted the removal of the entire Howard connection from Virginia to Maryland in 1649. Matthew Howard's name is not mentioned after that date in the Maryland records but it is believed that he emigrated there and it is a certain fact that all his children did. They all settled around Annapolis, and each appears frequently in the Maryland records.

The children of Matthew Howard and his wife Ann Howard were Henry Howard, Philip Howard, Samuel Howard, John Howard, Cornelius Howard, Matthew Howard, Second, Ann Howard, who married a Phillips, and Elizabeth Howard, who married a Ridgeley.

Cornelius Howard, the fifth son of Matthew and Ann Howard became the most prominent member of the family in early Maryland affairs. He was born about 1630, in Virginia and he died in Maryland in 1680. He married Elizabeth, a daughter or granddaughter of Lawrence Todd. In his will, made in 1680, he mentions his children, Joseph Howard, Cornelius Howard, Second, Sarah Howard, Elizabeth Howard and Mary Howard. In his will he lists his estate as including: Howard's Hope, South side of Severn, Howard's Hardship, Howard's Hill, Hockley Branch, Tuckahoe on Clapstack River, Howard and Porter's Range.

His will is witnessed by Phillip Calvert and John Howard. He was perhaps married to a daughter of Joshua Owen before he married the granddaughter of Lawrence Todd.

He was an ensign in the Maryland Militia in 1661, (Maryland Archives) and was a member of the House of Burgesses 1671 to 1675, (Maryland Archives.) All his descendants are eligible to the Colonial Societies. When he made his will in 1630, his eldest son was not yet eighteen years of age and his second son was also a minor. This establishes the approximate date of the birth of Joseph Howard, the eldest son, as about 1663, and the second son, Cornelius Howard, Second, as about 1665.

Cornelius Howard, Second, son of Cornelius Howard, First, and Elizabeth (Todd) Howard was born about 1665 in Maryland. He married Mary Hammond. His children were, Charles Howard, Cornelius Howard, Third, James Howard and John Howard.

Charles Howard, son of Cornelius Howard, Second, and Mary

Thomas Howard
Second Duke of Norfolk
Probably on the morning of the Battle of Flodden

The Southern family is descended from the Second Duke through his third son, Lord Edmund Howard

After the Painting by C. Hallmandel

HOWARD

Hammond Howard, married Mary ———. His son was Benjamin Howard.

Proofs of the line of descent in the Howard family may be found in J. D. Warfield's "Founders of Anne Arundel County." See the following pages: Matthew Howard page 7-11-29-30. Cornelius Howard (First) 71. Cornelius Howard (Second) 76. Charles Howard 76. Benjamin Howard 76.

After Benjamin Howard, who married Prudence Sater, the descent as given is in the family Bibles and private papers now in possession of his descendants.

Benjamin Howard served in the War of the Revolution. The records in Washington show that Benjamin Howard served as a private in Captain Henry Gaither's Company First Maryland Regiment, commanded by Colonel John H. Stone, Revolutionary War. He enlisted March 3rd, 1777, and his name is borne on the Company rolls for February, 1799, dated Middlebrook, March 3rd, 1779, with remarks showing him in command.

Benjamin Howard married Prudence Sater and with her name another long and interesting family connection must be traced. She was born November 25, 1743 and died September 22, 1822. She was the second child and eldest daughter of Henry Sater and his wife Dorcas Towson.

HENRY SATER

Henry Sater was born in England in one of the Western Shires in 1690 and was of Danish extraction. He came to America in 1709, and first settled in Virginia. He subsequently removed to Maryland and became a well known colonist in that Province. He established an estate ten miles north of Baltimore from grants of land received from Lord Baltimore. He was probably of family and position before he emigrated to America, as he possessed large means and lived in an almost princely style upon his large plantation. There is no record of his having performed military service, though it is believed that he did serve his country and that his grants of land were in recognition of military service.

He married twice, first, Miss Stephenson, by whom he had no children and secondly, Dorcas Towson, by whom he had a large family. Dorcas Towson was a daughter of William Towson. Henry Sater died May 1754, in the forty-sixth year of his age. He was a distinguished colonist and his gift of the the first Baptist Church in Maryland and one of the first in America is most interesting. He made a deed of the land to the Baptist denomination "to the end of the world." That shows his generous public spirit as well as his devotion to religion.

His six children were, George Sater, Prudence Sater, Henry Sater, Discretion Sater, John Sater and Joseph Sater.

William Towson, father of Dorcas Towson, who married Henry Sater was born in Germany (in Munich it is believed about 1695. He emigrated to London and there married Catherine Allen, a descendant of Oliver Cromwell. With his wife he came to America and established a place now known as Towsontown. After the death of Catherine Allen Towson he married for his second wife Dinah Wilmot, He died June 1772. His children were: Ezekial Towson, Rachel Towson, Dorcas Towson, John Towson, Thomas Towson, Ruth Towson, Catherine Towson and Charles Towson. The child of William Towson and his second wife Dinah Wilmot Towson was Abraham Towson. Towsontown is near Baltimore.

Numbers of the Towson connection married Cromwells, all kinspeople, and all probably as a result of the first marriage of William Towson to Catherine Allen, a descendant of Cromwell. Ezekial Towson (son of William and Catherine Allen Towson) married, firstly, Sarah Cromwell and secondly, Ruth Cromwell, his mother's kinswomen. Sarah was a daughter of Joseph and Comfort Cromwell and Ruth was probably her sister.

Joseph Cromwell had a brother, William Cromwell and they are said to be direct descendants of Sir Oliver Cromwell of Hinchenbrook, great uncle to the Protector. William Cromwell's will is dated May 9, 1753, Anne Arundel County Province of Maryland. William Cromwell's wife was a Wilmot, a sister to Dinah Wilmot, who was William Towson's second wife.

General Nathan Towson, Paymaster General U. S. A. grandson of William Towson and Catherine Allen Towson was also a descendant of the Cromwell families through his mother who was a Cromwell, daughter of a Richard Cromwell. Some authorities give her as a granddaughter of Henry Cromwell, son of the Protector, but Henry's son, Richard, died unmarried according to genealogists. The same English genealogists, Waylen and others, state that the Cromwell family of America is not directly descended from Oliver Cromwell the Protector, but from an older branch, though doubtless the same family. This refers to those by the name Cromwell, as male heirs of the famous Protector could not have been in America. Catherine Allen, however, does not come under this general statement, as she was living in London when she married William Towson, and she does not come in the male line which is thoroughly known to genealogists.

Our records say positively that William Towson married Catherine Allen in London, and that she was a descendant of Oliver Cromwell, the Protector. Though it is not so stated I have always believed that Catherine was a granddaughter of Oliver's son, Henry Cromwell, Lord

Lieutenant of Ireland, and a man of distinguished ability. Henry's daughter, Elizabeth, married her mother's first cousin, William Russell, and had born to her fourteen children. The Russells fell upon evil times financially, and William escaped his numerous creditors by dying, leaving Elizabeth with many surviving children, though several of her sons died early. Of the fourteen only ten names are known. "The widow with her children fled to London." The Restoration had thrown all the Cromwells into disfavor, and as Elizabeth and her children were in very straightened circumstances, their consequent obscurity has prevented genealogists from picking up all their name and histories. I believe that one of the daughters of this Elizabeth Cromwell (or possibly a granddaughter) married William Towson. Catherine Allen may have been a middle name, the use of middle names was beginning them to be a custom, or she may have been a young widow by the name of Allen when she married William Towson.

Her daughter, Dorcas Towson was born about 1720, showing that she must have been married about 1715 or 1718, and a search of the marriage records in London about that date might show more data concerning her.

The family of Elizabeth Cromwell Russell is the only one of the Protector's descendants which is identified with London. Also many, if not all the others are pretty well accounted for.

Despite their poverty the kinship was doubtless fully recognized, and when Catherine Allen Towson and her prosperous young husband, William Towson established in America, near Baltimore, a plantation home, it became a journey's end for emigrating Cromwells and a meeting place for other Cromwells of the older branch already established in Maryland. The result was a series of marriages, as chronicled above, Ezekial Towson's marriage, to two Cromwells, Ruth and Sarah, and many other alliances.

Henry Cromwell, fourth son of the Protector, (born 1623, died 1674) developed faculties which proved him a worthy son of such a sire. Rapin's observation that had he succeeded to the Protectorate instead of his elder brother, Richard Cromwell, history would have worn a different tinge has been accepted by all historians. Henry Cromwell married Elizabeth, daughter of Sir Francis Russell, Baronet. Henry died in 1674. His widow styled the "good Lady Cromwell" survived him thirteen years. Their daughter, Elizabeth married her mother's first cousin, William Russell (grandson of Sir William Russell) August 30, 1681.

By the way, it is because of a Cromwell, Thomas Cromwell, next to Oliver most noted of the name, that we are able to give dates of births, marriages and deaths in early English history. It was he who ordered that all parish churches should keep such records and it is entirely due to him therefore that after 1588 authentic dates may be obtained. This Thomas Cromwell and his sister, Catherine, were children of Walter Cromwell. Catherine married Morgan Williams, and her descendants took the name Cromwell as Thomas had already given it fame. Henry VIII knighted her son, Richard Williams as Richard Cromwell. The Protector is from this family.

BENJAMIN HOWARD

Benjamin Howard was born February 17, 1742. His tombstone relates that he was born on Long Island, but this probably means an Island in Maryland.

He married Prudence Sater September 21, 1762, in Baltimore County, Maryland, and it is believed by his descendants that this was a run away marriage, for Miriam Isbell Turnley was told by her mother that it was an elopement. To lighten the gravity of this genealogical statement be it observed just here that Prudence having run away with Benjamin Howard named her daughter Discretion! and further that Discretion ran away as you will see if you read more of this family story.

Prudence and Benjamin Howard went to Wilkes County, North Carolina to reside. When the Wilkes was divided into two counties, their homestead was thrown into Caldwell County and there it is standing now in a very good condition.

Benjamin Howard died June 4, 1828, and is buried on his home place.

Prudence Sater Howard died September 22, 1822, and is buried beside her husband on the home place.

Benjamin Howard and his wife, Prudence Sater Howard had twelve children, namely:

(1) Discretion Howard, born July 29, 1764, (who married Thomas Isbell).

(2) Phillip Howard, born January 6, 1766.

(3) Mary Howard, born 1768.

(4) George Howard, born February 4, 1770.

(5) Sarah Howard, born October 21, 1771.

(6) Elizabeth Howard, born February 1, 1774.

(7) Rachel Howard, born December 27, 1776.

(8) Rebecca Howard, born February 10, 1778.

(9) Benjamin Howard, Second, born March 11, 1780, married Betsey Walker, lived and died July 21, 1825, in Wilkes County, North Carolina, and had a son, George R. Howard.

HOWARD

(10) Cornelius Howard, born April 7, 1782, married Delhia Hagler.

(11) Nancy Howard, born February 20, 1784, married Joseph Callaway. They had a son Thomas H. Callaway.

(12) Prudence Howard, died in infancy.

From these come literally hundreds, aye, thousands of descendants. The line best known to the writer is that of Discretion Howard, afore mentioned, who ran away when she became of marriageable age, despite her name "Discretion" following her mother's example.

Discretion Howard is said to have been beautiful with magnificent red hair and a character that matched the vividness of her hair, for on several occasions she displayed remarkable courage and quickness of judgment.

Once when the Tories sought her husband, who had escaped from them and had arrived breathless at his home just ahead of them, she pushed him into place and went on calmly milking a white cow, as though her heart was not beating its life out in anxiety.

They asked if she had seen a rebel go by and she truthfully replied that she had not, and continued to milk the cow.

So they passed by and Thomas Isbell was saved.

Thomas Isbell was known as "Captain of the Lighthorse," but no proof to that effect has been found. However, his sword which he carried throughout the Revolution, and described as a very sharp, three sided spear which fitted into a cane with buck horn handle was burned when the home of his granddaughter, Mrs. Caroline Tucker Johnston was destroyed in 1895.

The marriage of Discretion Howard to Thomas Isbell brings into the family another interesting line. James Isbell, first of the Isbells in America emigrated from England. His wife was Frances Tompkins Livingston. Their eldest child was born September 27, 1748. Presumably they were married in 1747. It is possible that they were married in Virginia. They lived for many years in Albemarle County, Virginia, where their children were all born. About 1778 they moved to Wilkes County, North Carolina.

James Isbell died November 2, 1780, in Wilkes County, North Carolina. His wife, Frances Tompkins Livingston Isbell died January 2, 1784, in Wilkes County, North Carolina. They had ten children, six sons and four daughters and had the honor of having six sons in the Battle of King's Mountain, namely, John Isbell, Livingston Isbell, Thomas Isbell, Francis Isbell, James Isbell, Second, and William Tompkins Isbell, who was only fifteen years old. Only two other families can boast such a record, the Seviers with seven members of the family and the Shelbys with four. Note: As Martha Parkes, a granddaughter of Livingston Isbell, married her cousin, Benjamin Isbell, a son of Thomas Isbell, several of the Isbell lines are descended from two of the foregoing heroes of Kings Mountain.

FRANCES TOMPKINS LIVINGSTON ISBELL

Frances Tompkins Livingston, was born probably about the year 1727. She was the daughter of ———— Livingston and ————. In Virginia say 1747 she married James Isbell. Her eldest son, John Isbell, was born September 27, 1848. Another son, Thomas Isbell, was born in Albemarle County, Virginia, June 27, 1753. The family continued residing in that county until about the year 1778, when they removed to Wilkes County, North Carolina. She died there January 2, 1784. The Livingston family probably lived in Virginia, prior to the marriage of Frances. She had six sons and four daughters.

The children of James and Frances Tompkins Livingston were:

(1) John Isbell, born September 27, 1748.
(2) Milly Isbell, born April 2, 1750.
(3) Livingston Isbell, born November 17, 1751.
(4) Francis Isbell, born February 12, 1755.
(5) Thomas Isbell.
(6) Edith Isbell, born November 17, 1756.
(7) Mary Isbell, born August 21, 1758.
(8) James Isbell, Second, zorn April 3, 1760.
(9) Elizabeth Isbell, born October 19, 1762.
(10) William Tompkins Isbell, born September 19, 1765.

Of the foregoing I have only the full record of Thomas Isbell and a partial record of Livingston Isbell.

(3) Livingston Isbell, the third child of James and Frances Tompkins Livingston Isbell was born November 17, 1751, in Albemarle County, Virginia. As his brother Thomas Isbell made his first enlistment in the war from Albemarle County, Virginia, it is possible that Livingston Isbell also first went into the Army in Albemarle County. Later, October 7, 1780, he was in the Battle of King's Mountain, from Wilkes County, North Carolina, where the whole family of Isbells had by that time emigrated. He married, about the year 1774, ———— Martin and had at least one daughter, Frances Isbell, whom he evidently named for his mother, who married Ambrose Parkes. Their daughter, Martha Parkes married Benjamin Isbell as will be seen.

HOWARD

THOMAS ISBELL.

(5) Thomas Isbell, fifth child of James and Frances Tompkins Livingston Isbell was born in Albemarle County, Virginia, in 1753, June 27th.

At the time of his enlistment in the Army of the Revolution, 1776, he still resided in that county.

Thomas Isbell with his five brothers fought under Colonel Cleveland in the battle of King's Mountain, October 7, 1780.

At that date the youngest brother was fifteen, the oldest thirty-two, and the family resided in North Carolina, where Cleveland's troops were mustered.

Of Thomas Isbell's service we have this information.

The Pension Records show that Thomas Isbell was a private in Captain Thomas Walker's (afterwards Captain William Henderson's) Company, Ninth Virginia Regiment, Colonel George Mathews commanding, Revolutionary Army.

He enlisted, date not stated, to serve two years from April 10, 1776, and his name is borne on the rolls to and including January 1778, when he is reported honorably discharged, date not shown.

The widow's pension was allowed for his services as a private in the Virginia troops for the period of two years.

Residence of soldier at enlistment, Albemarle County, Virginia. Date of application for pension by widow January 26, 1843.

Benjamin Isbell writes that his father, Thomas Isbell, served five years in the War of the Revolution. It is probable that after the demoval of his father's family to North Carolina, (between the years 1776 and 1780) he entered some command in that state. He was in the Battle of King's Mountain.

February 21, 1782, Thomas Isbell married Discretion Howard, who lived in Wilkes County, North Carolina.

His homestead, built of solid walnut logs, where he died October 27, 1819, was torn down in 1897.

Thomas Isbell and his wife, Discretion, were members of the King's Creek Baptist Church, Wilkes County. It was burned only a few years since.

In Thomas Isbell's will he makes repeated mention of his "beloved wife Discretion."

Thomas Isbell and Discretion Howard Isbell had nine children, namely:

(1) Prudence Isbell.
(2) Benjamin Isbell.
(3) John Isbell.

NOTABLE SOUTHERN FAMILIES

(4) Frances Isbell.
(5) Livingston Isbell.
(6) Elizabeth Isbell.
(7) Thomas Isbell, Second.
(8) Mary Isbell.
(9) James Isbell.

Of the foregoing:

(1) Prudence Isbell, born 1783, married Ambrose Carelton.

(2) Benjamin Isbell. His record follows:

(3) John Isbell, born February 11, 1788.

John Isbell (son of Thomas) who died unmarried about 1824 had been given that tract of land around Ducktown but the burning of the courthouse with all records at Madisonville soon afterwards destroyed all proofs and left the family nothing on which to base claims for his estate.

(4) Frances Isbell, born July 2, 1791, died October 23, 1871, married September 25, 1808, Micajah Ferguson. They had several children: Matilda Ferguson, Horton Ferguson, Linville Ferguson, Salena Ferguson, Savannah Ferguson, Livingston Ferguson, Finley Ferguson, Stanford Ferguson, Kilby Ferguson, Jane Ferguson and Olive Ferguson, all of whom married and left children.

(5) Livingston Isbell, born April 15, 1749, died ————; married Mary Edwards and had three sons, namely: Thomas Isbell (who died unmarried); Bolling Isbell, who died unmarried) and Louis Isbell, (who married and left one son).

(6) Elizabeth Isbell, born November 1796, died July 19, 1884, married October 11, 1818, Nimrod Ferguson and had eleven children, namely: Thomas Leeland Ferguson, Milton Ferguson, Polly Elmira Ferguson, Vina Ferguson, John Wycliff Ferguson, Pinckney M. Ferguson, Casburn Ferguson, Caroline Ferguson, James N. Ferguson, Sarah Catherine Ferguson and Discretion Rebecca Ferguson, almost all of whom married and left children.

(7) Thomas Isbell, born January 29, 1800, married Lucinda Petty and had two children, James M. Isbell and a daughter.

(8) Mary Isbell, born December 21, 1803, died January 6, 1891, married August 16, 1829, Joseph Tucker, ninth child of William and Nancy Grider Tucker, and had six children, namely:

George Livingston Tucker.
Jane Elizabeth Tucker.
Isabelle Minerva Tucker
Martha Caroline Tucker.

HOWARD

Julia Discretion Tucker.
Frances Rutelia Tucker.

Of the foregoing:

George Livingston Tucker, married Minerva McKamy Frazier and had: Mary Emily Tucker, died young; Hannah Minerva Tucker, (married Dr. W. W. Cunningham and had George T. Cunningham and Ethel Cunningham); and Julia Frazier Tucker, died young;

Jane Elizabeth Tucker, (who married John Hall and had ten children: (1) George Tucker Hall, married Abigall Grant and had an infant, died young, Anna Lou Hall married William Rodgers and has William Rodgers, Second, and Virginia Rodgers; and John Grant Hall; (2) Delano Tucker Hall, who married Cynthia Taylor and had Velma Hall, and Clapman Hall; (3) Joseph Tucker Hall married Leonie Barnett; (4) Emmett Tucker Hall married Annie Brown and had Annie B. Hall, married Coleman Rodgers, and Jane Hall; (5) Ney Tucker Hall, who married Tulie McKamy and had Ruth Hall, married Oscar Reynolds and John McKamy Hall, married Isabelle Williams; (6) Lea Tucker Hall, married Lizzie Stewart and had John Stewart Hall; (7) John Tucker Hall, died young; (8) Fate Tucker Hall, married Emma Acobert for his first wife and married for his second wife Icie Bryant Hall, the widow of his brother Isbell Tucker Hall and had by her Isbell Hall; (9) Isbell Tucker Hall married Icie Bryant as her first husband and had Icie Belle Hall; (10)

Isabelle M. Tucker married Christopher Lafayette Hardwick April 3, 1851, and had twelve children: (1) Frank Tucker Hardwick married Caroline McCutcheon and had Wallace McCutcheon Hardwick, married Lucy Maddox and has Frank Tucker Hardwick Second; Johnnie Millard Hardwick, married John McChesney Hogshead and has Frances Caroline Hogshead; Frances Tucker Hardwick married Emmett S. Newton and has Martha Caroline Newton; (2) Joseph Henry Hardwick married Cooksey A. Harris and had Harrie B. Hardwick, married Oscar A. Knox and has Adela Knox, married Joseph Jarnagin, and Irene Knox; and Christopher Lafayette Hardwick, Second, married Clyde Johnston; (3) John Millard Hardwick, (who died unmarried); (4) James Oscar Hardwick, married Ida Ruff and had C. Lafayette Hardwick, married Ruby ———, Irene Hardwick married Fred Beekham and had Ida Beekham; Laura Belle Hardwick; Julia Hardwick, John Houston Hardwick, died young, and Garland Reeves Hardwick; (5) George Lee Hardwick, married Fannie McCutcheon, a sister to his brother Frank's wife, and had Lollie Belle Hardwick, married David Sullins Stuart and has Mary Frances Stuart and Hardwick Stuart; Margaret Hardwick, married Hal B. Moore and has Martha Frances Moore, George Lee Hardwick

NOTABLE SOUTHERN FAMILIES

Second married Elizabeth Pyott and has George Lee Hardwick, Third, and James Hardy Hardwick; Cicero McCutcheon Hardwick, who is not married; Jennie May Hardwick, who is not married, Frank Tucker Hardwick and Frances Hardwick; (6) Nora Isbell Hardwick, married John C. Ramsey and had Maynard Ramsey, married Edith Robinson and has Maynard Ramsey, Second; (7) Margaret Julia Hardwick, married James Leonidas Caldwell as his first wife and had four children: James Lafayette Caldwell, died young; Joseph Hardwick Caldwell married Kathleen Pound and has two children: Joseph Hardwick Caldwell, Second, and James Leonidas Caldwell, Second; Margaret Caldwell married Mark Charles Morrison; and Lafayette Hardwick Caldwell, who is not married; (8) French Montgomery Hardwick died young; (9) Houston Lafayette Hardwick died unmarried; (10) Julius Holmes Hardwick married Estelle Jones and had two children, Florine Hardwick, married Robert L. Smith and Richard Holmes Hardwick, (11) Fannie Lucretia Hardwick, died young; and (12) Anna Belle Hardwick, married Reeves Brown and has Reeves Brown, Second.

Martha Caroline Tucker, married Emmett R. Johnston and had Eugene Johnston, Mary Alice Johnston, (who married M. L. Beard and had Frankie Beard, Carrie May Beard and Frank Beard); Esther Johnston; Joseph Tucker Johnston, (married Ella Wehunt and had Caroline Johnston); Carrie Belle Johnston; and French Johnston.

Julia Discretion Tucker married James McGhee and had Benjamin McCarthy McGhee; Horace G. McGhee, (married Hattie Huntington and had Mildred McGhee, Edwin McGhee H. C. McGhee, Second).

Frances Rutelia Tucker married Columbus A. Mee.

(9) James Isbell, born September 12, 1806, married March 19, 1833, Rutelia Houston, a descendant of the Armstrong and Calhoun Families, and had five children, namely: Houston Isbell, (who died unmarried); Thomas Livingston Isbell, (who married Mattie Norris and had three children: Rutelia Houston Isbell, married W. H. Lane and has one child Rutelia Lane, William Isbell who died and Moss Isbell who died unmarried; Margaret Isbell, (who married Major Joseph Hardie and left no children); and Alice Isbell (who married her cousin, William Park Armstrong; and had four children: William Park Armstronk, Second, who married Rebekah Sellars Purvis and has five children: Rebekah Purvis Armstrong, William Park Armstrong, George Purvis Armstrong, Ann Elizabeth Armstrong and Jane Crozier Armstrong; Houston Churchwell Armstrong married Mina Lamar and has three children, Houston Churchwell Armstrong, Second, Alice Isbell Armstrong, and Mina Cary Armstrong; Margaret Armstrong, married Ainslee Power Ardagh and has five children, Margaret Ardagh, Ains-

lee Power Ardagh, Second; Anne E. Armstrong, who married Thomas Stoo Johnston and lives in New Orelans) ; and Fannie Isbell, who married William Boynton and had William Boynton, Second, and Dwight Boynton.

(2) Benjamin Isbell, the second child of Thomas and Discretion Howard Isbell, married Martha Parkes, who was his first cousin once removed, as she was the granddaughter of Livingston Isbell, brother of Thomas Isbell. A brief record of her families is therefore inserted here.

About 1670 there was living in Virginia Thomas Parkes. He had two sons.

(1) John Parkes who had seventeen children of whom ten were sons, George, (grandfather of E. M. Parkes, of Memphis) and others most of whom settled in North Carolina, and one went to Georgia. George was the youngest child of the seventeen.

(2) Thomas Parkes, who lived in Wilkes County, North Carolina, and had six children all of whom were sons.

(1) John Parkes, the eldest son moved to and died in Tennessee.
(2) Thomas Parkes the second son remained in Wilkes County.
(3) Reuben Parkes, the third son, died in Tennessee.
(4) Aaron Parkes the fourth son died in Tennessee near Fayette (Fayetteville?)
(5) Ambrose Parkes the fifth son went to Missouri.
(6) William Parkes the sixth son also went west.

The above information was furnished by E. M. Parkes, of Memphis, who says he spent some time with members of the family in Wilkes County, in 1840 en route to school to study medicine in Philadelphio.

It is certain that Ambrose Parkes went to Missouri and there died. Mrs. Missouri Isbell McMillan received her name Missouri from this fact. She was born and named in 1837.

AMBROSE PARKES

Ambrose Parkes, fifth son of Thomas Parkes and has wife ———, married about the year 1790, Frances Isbell, daughter of Livingston Isbell. This marriage took place in Wilkes County, North Carolina. He lived during the Revolution and possibly served in the War.

Ambrose Parkes and his wife Frances Isbell Parkes went to Missouri late in life and probably died there.

Ambrose Parkes gave to each of his daughters a slave. To his daughter Martha he gave "Milly." She survived her mistress many years and was a faithful servant to her children.

NOTABLE SOUTHERN FAMILIES

Children of Ambrose Parkes and his wife Frances Isbell Parkes:

(1) Martin Parkes.
(2) Allen Parkes.
(3) Thomas Parkes.
(4) Martha Parkes, who married Benjamin Isbell.
(5) Susan Parkes, who married Lee Hubbard.
(6) Polly Parkes, who married George Barnes, of Kentucky.
(7) Ambrose Parkes.
(8) Lee Parkes
(9) Cynthia Parkes, who married ———— Barnes.

MARTHA PARKES

Martha Parkes, daughter of Ambrose Parkes and his wife Frances Isbell Parkes, was born April 6, 1799. She married in Wilkes County, North Carolina, February 17, 1918, Benjamin Isbell. It is believed that both the Parkes and Isbell families were members of the Kings Creek Baptist Church of that county. This church was recently burned and its records destroyed. She removed with her husband three years after her marriage, (1821) to McMinn county, Tennessee, where they established a handsome homestead. She had five sons and six daughters. She died July 15, 1840, when only forty-one years old, and is buried on the Isbell place in McMinn county.

FRANCES ISBELL PARKES

Frances Isbell Parkes, daughter of Livingston Isbell and his wife ———— Martin Isbell, was born say about 1770. She married Ambrose Parkes about 1790. Her daughter, who was presumably her fourth child was born April 10, 1779. This information is received from Missouri Isbell McMillan who received it from Prudence Isbell Carleton in February, 1861. Missouri Isbell McMillan also says: "Some of my mother's (Martha Parkes Isbell) brothers settled at or near Lewisburg, Tennessee. Some of the family moved to the State of Missouri, and that is how I came to be named Missouri. When I was the youngest child (1837) mother received a letter from grandmother telling her that she was coming to Middle Tennessee on a visit and for her to meet her there. For some reason it seemed mother felt she could not leave home, and she wrote she could not go. But after the letter was written she grieved so about it that my father had her get ready, and she with babe (Missouri), nurse, Frances and Martin, took the carriage and made the trip, but on getting there, late one evening, found her mother gone. She had left that morning. She

HOWARD

never saw her mother again. Sister Frances told me of this trip shortly before her death."

Thus it will be seen that in 1837, the year of Missouri Isbell's birth, Frances Isbell Parkes was still living and made the trip from Missouri to Tennessee. It is believed that she died in Missouri shortly after this date.

Benjamin Isbell, son of Thomas Isbell and Discretion Howard Isbell, married Martha Parkes, his first cousin, once removed. She was the granddaughter of Livingston Parkes Isbell. They had eleven children, namely:

(1) Miriam Isbell, born February 25, 1819
(2) Thomas Martin Isbell, born March 3, 1821.
(3) Frances Discretion Isbell, born March 11, 1823.
(4) Martha Ann Isbell, born November 9, 1825.
(5) Mary Louise Isbell, born November, 1827.
(6) Sarah Elizabeth Isbell, born September 29, 1829.
(7) James Parkes Isbell, born July 20, 1831; died unmarried April 19, 1850.
(8) Benjamin Howard Isbell, born July 1, 1833; died unmarried September 8, 1864.
(9) John Williams Isbell, born August 7, 1835, died unmarried July 7, 1864.
(10) Lucinda Missouri Isbell, born July 4, 1837.
(11) Dennis Rowan Isbell, born September 1, 1839.

Of the foregoing:

(1) Miriam Isbell, born February 25, 1819, died January 9, 1898, married May 28, 1839, Matthew Jacob Turnley (see Turnley Family) and had eight children: Martha Julia Turnley, (who married December 19, 1867, John McMillan Armstrong (see Armstrong and McMillan Families. Their children were Turnley Armstrong who died unmarried and Zella Armstrong); George Isbell Turnley (who married twice, first Willie Woodward and secondly, Emma Ross and has no children); Mary Turnley (who married John Hughes Reynolds and had six children: Hughes Turnley Reynolds, married Mary Taylor and has two children: John Hughes Reynolds, Second, and Margarhetta Reynolds; William Barton Reynolds died young; Miram Reynolds; May Reynolds, married Raymond Scott and had two children, Reynolds Scott and May Scott; Ruby Reynolds, married William Ogburn and has Reynolds Ogburn; and John Hughes Reynolds, Jr., died young). James Benjamin Turnley (who married Lula Phinizy (see Phinizy Family) and had five children: Louisa Turnley; John Phinizy Turnley, Jane Turnley, married Charles E. Sedberry and left an infant child who died. James Marco Turnley, married Nettie

Brooks and has two daughters, Mary Florence Turnley and Lula Turnley; and William Micou Turnley, married Lillian Crow and has one child Lulu Elizabeth Turnley); William Franklin Pierce Turnley (who married and left one son, Thomas Turnley); Thomas Howard Turnley (who died unmarried); Frances Amelia Turnley (who died in infancy); and Eppie Reynolds Turnley (who married Nathan Calhoun Sayre and has no children).

(2) Thomas Martin Isbell, born March 3, 1821, died June 19, 1859 He married December 21, 1843, Sarah Ann Terry. They had children, among them, Mattie Isbell, who married "Tip" Forrest.

(3) Frances Discretion Isbell, born March 11, 1828, died January 29, 1886, married March 30, 1852, for her first husband John Hughes, who died March 7, 1855, and married for her second husband, 1867, William L. Rice, by whom she had no children. Her two children by her first husband were: Benjamin Isbell Hughes, (who married Sarah Park and had Phebe Hughes, married Capers Simmons; Benjamin Isbell Hughes, Jr., married Frank Hawltiwanger, has two children, Sallie Bonham and Julia Carouthers Hughes; Sophy Hughes, who is umarried, John Hughes, United States Army; Park Hughes, United States Army; Lucian Hughes, United States Army; and Sarah Hughes); and Elizabeth Hughes, (who married Wallace K. Shedden and left Elizabeth Shedden and Mary Shedden).

Martha Ann Isbell, born November 9, 1825, died April 27, 1844, married Robert Houston McMillan (see McMillan family) as his first wife and had two children: James Benjamin McMillan, (who married Cynthia Cunningham and had William Cunningham McMillan; Alice McMillan, Rutelia Isbell McMillan, Mary B. McMillan; and Kitty McMillan); and Alice McMillan, (who is not married).

(5) Mary Louisa Isbell, born November 5, 1827, died ——— married November 5, 1844, Richard Franklin Malone Hampton and had five children: Robert Isbell Hampton, (who married Effie Elizabeth Clabaugh and had Robert Richard Hampton and Elizabeth Clabaugh Hampton, married Charles Alden Rowland and has Charles Hampton Rowland. Robert Isbell Hampton married for his second wife Miss Comer, by whom he had no children); James Hampton, (who died without issue); Frances Hampton (who married Rankin Magill); Emma Hampton (who is unmarried); and Richard Hampton.

(6) Sarah Elizabeth Isbell, born September 29, 1829, died May 28, 1864, married December 26, 1849, Judge Jesse Gaut as his first wife had three sons: Thomas Isbell Gaut, Oscar Gaut and Orlando Gaut. Of these Thomas Isbell Gaut married Mary Lee and had two children: James Gaut who died unmarried and Ione Gaut who married James Mooney of Washington and has six children: Oscar Gaut

married Annie Mills and left three children, Lieutenant Oscar Gaut, Junior, now in France, Orlando Gaut, junor, also a soldier in the United States Army and a daughter Elizabeth Gaut who is married and lives in Texas. Orlando Gaut, son of Judge Jesse Gaut and Sarah Elizabeth Isbell Gaut, died unmarried.

(7) James Parkes Isbell, born July 20, 1831, died unmarried April 19, 1850.

(8) Benjmain Howard Isbell, born July 1, 1833, died unmarried September, 1864.

(9) John Williams Isbell, born August 7, 1835, died unmarried July 7, 1864.

(10) Lucinda Missouri Isbell, born July 4, 1837, died April 25, 1918, at her home in Talledega, Alabama. She married July 9, 1855, Robert Houston McMillan (her sister Martha's widower) as his second wife and had two children, both deceased: Robert Houston McMillan, Second, (who married Sarah Gray and had Robert Houston McMillan, Third, died young, Allen Gray McMillan and Catherine McMillan) and Fannie McMillan, (who married Jesse F Wikle and had Robert McMillan Wikle and Jesse F. Wikle, Second).

(1) Dennis Rowan Isbell, born September 1, 1829, died ———; married December 28, 1871, Emma Callaway. They had two children, John Callaway Isbell and Ernest Isbell.

Other descendants of the Howard family through one of his daughters who married a Callaway, are Mrs. Susan Latimore Kline, of Chattanooga, and her children, Mrs. Isaac Phillips and Captain Franklin Kline, of the United States Army.

KEY FAMILY

The Tennessee family of Key is of Scotch origin, migrating first from Scotland to Pennsylvania and later like so many of the Scotch Irish people to Tennessee. The name of the emigrant was John Key, a name borne by his descendants to this day. He came to America prior to the Revolution, served in that War and was one of the early settlers in what is now Greene County, Tennessee, but was then a part of North Carolina. He married either before or directly after his coming to Tennesse and had two sons, Peter Key and David Key.

David Key married and had a son, John Key, born about 1810, who was a Methodist preacher of renown throughout East Tennessee. John Key married Margaret Armitage, daughter of Isaac Armitage. Margaret Armitage was born in Greene County February 18th, 1814. Her father Isaac Armitage was of an English family that had come from England first to Pennsylvania and later to Tennessee, and he had married Elizabeth Weston, daughter of ——— Weston, a Tennessee pioneer. Margaret Armitage Key died April 12th, 1882.

John and Margaret Armitage Key had four children, three sons and one daughter, namely: David McKendree Key, Summerfield Armitage Key, John Fletcher Key and Elizabeth Key.

Summerfield Armitage Key was born October 14, 1834. He died June 14, 1890. He married in 1871 Mary Divine, daughter of John L. Divine, and his first wife who was Elizabeth Williams, daughter of Colonel Samuel Williams, a Tennessee pioneer whose wife was Rebecca Davis, of Trenton, Georgia. Samuel Williams' father was George Williams, and his father was Samuel Williams, who was a Revolutionary soldier; served at King's Mountain and is frequently mentioned in Ramsey's Annals and other Tennessee histories.

Mrs. Summerfield Armitage Key survives her husband. The three children of Summerfield Armitage Key and Mary Divine Key are John Divine Key, a prominent Chattanooga business man, Elizabeth Key, who married James Francis Johnston of an old and Tennessee family; (they have one son, Summerfield Key Johnston) and Mary Key, who married Pearson B. Mayfield, of Cleveland, and has one son, Pearson B. Mayfield, junior.

Summerfield Armitage Key entered the Confederate Service immediately upon the breaking out of the War Between the States and achieved rapid promotion, rising from a private in the ranks of the Nineteenth Tennessee Regiment. He had the great distinction of being a member of the faithful personal escort of the lamented President

Judge David M. Key

KEY

Jefferson Davis with whom he remained until the capture of the President. Judge Key after the War took up his residence in Chattanooga where he was married to Miss Divine. He became a prominent lawyer, was elected to the General Assembly of Tennessee and was later elected Chancellor. He occupied this office until his death June 14, 1890. He was greatly respected in the community in which he lived so many years and his memory is treated with great honor. The Chancery Court recently hung his portrait in the Court with other distinguished jurists who have occupied the position of Chancellor of the District.

John Fletcher Key, son of John Key and Margaret Armitage Key, made his home in Philadelphia where he was well known. His only surviving child, Miss Nannie Key, resides in Philadelphia.

Elizabeth Key, daughter of John Key and Margaret Armitage Key, married Reverend John Breunner, President of Hiwassee College in Monroe County, Tennessee. Her only surviving child is Arthur Breunner, who resides at Hiawassee.

David McKendree Key, son of John Key and Margaret Armitage Key, was born January 27th, 1824, in Green County, Tennessee. At the breaking out of the War Between the States he immediately offered his services to the Confederacy and was Lieutenant Colonel of the 43rd Tennessee attaining distinction as a gallant and able officer. After the close of the War Between the States President Rutherford B. Hayes appointed him Postmaster General—a position which he also filled with credit, and later he was appointed by President Hayes, United States District Judge. He had the remarkable distinction of being Lieutenant Colonel in the Confederate Army, Chancellor, United States Senator, Postmaster General of the United States and United States District Judge, a position which he held at the time of his death, February 3, 1900.

He married Elizabeth Lenoir (born January 28th, 1838 at Lenoir in Loudon County, Tennessee). She was the daughter of General Albert S. Lenoir, of an ancient Huguenot family, who came from North Carolina to Tennessee. He was a descendant of Waightstill Avery, who was a member of the Mecklenburg Convention that made the Declaration of Independence and was the first attorney-general of North Carolina. The Averys were early settlers in America, Christopher Avery having been born in Salisbury, England, about 1600 having arrived in Massachusetts Bay in 1631, accompanied by his young son, James Avery, born in Salisbury in 1620. Christopher Avery left his wife in England and she never came to America.

James Avery went to Boston in 1643, and there married Joanna Greenslade. They had ten children, one of whom, Samuel Avery (born August 14, 1644) married (in 1886) Susan Palmer, daughter of Major Edward Palmer, and granddaughter of Governor John Winthrop. They had ten children, one of whom was Humphrey Avery (born July, 1699) who married in 1724 his cousin Jerusha Morgan, daughter of William and Margaret Avery Morgan. They had twelve children, one of whom was Waightstill Avery (born May 10, 1741), in Groton, Connecticutt, who is famous in North Carolina annals. He moved from Connecticutt to North Carolina in 1769. He changed the spelling of his name by inserting gh. The name was formerly Wait Still and he was named for Colonel Wait Still Winthrop.

Waightstill Avery married a widow, Mrs. Leah Frank. Waightstill Avery died in 1821.

Mrs. David McKendree Key is also of Revolutionary and Colonial stock through the Lenoirs, as her grandfather, General Lenoir was President of the North Carolina Senate and a Captain of a Company at King's Mountain. Mrs. Key's mother, Catherine Fruling Welcker, was a descendant of German family which came from Germany many years ago and settled in Roane County, Tennessee.

Judge David McKendree Key and Elizabeth Lenoir Key had children, namely, Albert Lenoir Key, John Fletcher Key, David McKendree Key, Junior. (who died young); Lenoir Key, Emma Key, Sarah Key, Katherine Key, Margaret Key and Elizabeth Key.

Albert Lenoir Key is a Commodore in the United States Navy, having graduated at Annapolis. He married Grace Condit-Smith, of Washington, and their two handsome sons bear the family names of David McKendree Key and Albert Lenoir Key, Junior. Lenoir Key married Julia Adams. Emma Key married Colonel William B. Thompson and died without children. Sarah Key married, Zeboim Cartter Patten and has one son, Zeboim Cartter Patten. Katherine Key married Samuel Robertson Read. Elizabeth Key married Garnett Andrews and has four children, Garnett Andrews, the Fourth of his name in a direct line, David Key Andrews, Elizabeth Andrews, and Katherine Andrews. Margaret Key is not married.

The Tennessee Family of Key is probably connected with the Maryland Family which produced the author of the Star Spangled Banner, Francis Scott Key. The emigrant in this Key Family was Phillip, son of Richard and Mary Key of Convent Garden, St. Paul's Parish, London. Phillip Key was born in 1764. When he was between thirty and perhaps forty years of age he emigrated to America, settling in St. Mary's County, Maryland. He was a member of the Provincial Council and his descendants are eligible to the Societies of the Colonies. Phillip Key married twice, first Susannah Gardiner and secondly Thedosia Lawrence Humphries, a widow, though by his second wife he had no children.

He had by his first wife seven children: Phillip Barton Key,

KEY

Richard Ward Key, John Key, Francis Key, Edmund Key, Thomas Key, and Susannah Gardiner Key.

Francis Key, the fourth of the foregoing seven children, married Anne Arnold Ross and they had among other children John Ross Key, who married Anne Charlton. They had among other children Francis Scott Key, the famous author of our National Hymn. He was born August 1, 1779. He volunteered during the War of 1812. During the Bombardment of Fort McHenry, which is near Baltimore, he was on a British ship, having boarded her under a flag of truce, hoping to obtain the release of a friend who had been made prisoner. It was then that he composed the lines which are now famous the world over.

Francis Scott Key married Mary Taloe Loyd and had eleven children. He has many descendants.

LUTTRELL

The Luttrell Family is of ancient origin and in history many distinguished persons bear the name. John Luttrell was Chancellor of the University of Oxford in 1317 and occupied other high offices. Edward Luttrell was an artist of note in the latter half of the seventeenth century and the first years of the eighteenth. He is said to have invented the art of copper engraving.

Thomas Luttrell was head of a long and illustrious line of Luttrells. He was succeeded by his son, Simon Luttrell, who was a gallant offices under King James II. and was a member of the Irish Parliament of 1698 from County Dublin and was appointed Military Governor of the City of Dublin. He was succeeded by his brother, Henry Luttrell, who was also a gallant soldier and became a Major General. He married Elizabeth, daughter of Charles Halkin, of Flintshire. His son, Simon Lutrell, Second, married Maria, daughter of Sir Nicholas Lawes, and was raised to the Irish Peerage first as Baron Irnham, later as Viscount Carhamon, later still as Earl of Carhamon or Carhampton. He named his son, Henry Lawes Luttrell, who is accepted as the greatest Luttrell in Brittain's history. He left no children, however, to succeed to the title which went therefore to his broher, John Luttrell. A sister of these two Luttrells was Anne Luttrell, who married the Duke of Cumberland, brother to King George III. John Luttrell, third Earl of Carhampton, died in 1829, without children, and the title became extinct.

There was, however, another brother of Henry Lawes Luttrell, Temple Luttrell, who attained distinction in public affairs, first going into the Naval service. He died in France in 1803 without children.

Another brother of Henry Lawes Luttrell, first Earl of Carhampton, was James, and, like Temple Luttrell, he adopted the Navy early in life as his particular profession. He commanded the Portland and the Mediator, and in an engagement in December, 1782, with an American squadron, he displayed great courage and resource and is said to have taken his own ship and his prizes safely into an English port.

Henry Luttrell was another scion of the family who achieved fame and he took literature for his forte. He was the friend and contemporary of Thomas Moore and wrote a great deal, though not all he wrote has been published. He lived to a great age, was described as a great wit, an ideal conversationalist and the greatest epigram maker of his day.

LUTTRELL.

During the political upheavals in England, members of collateral branches of the Luttrell family migrated to America. They were younger sons, doubtless, of the family and possibly without fortune other than name and courage. But the first Luttrell mentioned in Tennessee history must have been closely connected with the rich and powerful family of which Henry Lawes Luttrell was the first Earl, and Anne Luttrell, Duchess of Cumberland, for he was evidently a man of wealth and position.

This John Luttrell was associated with Colonel Richard Henderson and "other men of capital," namely Thomas Hart, John Williams, James Hogg, Nathanial Hart, David Hart, Leonard H. Bulloch, and William Johnston. They paid, it is said, ten thousand pounds sterling in merchandise to the Indians for certain lands and at that time 1775, such a sum was an enormous fortune. The purchase was called Transylvania and the nine proprietors at first contemplated a separate and independent Government, but in a memorial addressed to the Continental Congress of 1775, they asked that Transylvania be added to the number of the United Colonies. "Having their hearts warmed with the same noble spirit that animates the colonies and moved with indignation at the late ministerial and parliamentary usurpations, it is the earnest wish of the proprietors of Transylvania to be considered by the colonies as brethren engaged in the same great cause of liberty and mankind."

From the brother of this John Luttrell of the Transylvania purchase the Tennessee family may have sprung.

The land purchased was "all south of the Kentucky River, beginning at the mouth or junction of said river with the Ohio to its source, thence south into Tennessee, until a westwardly line should cross the Cumberland Mountain so as to strike the Ridge which divides the waters of the Tennessee River from those of the Cumberland, and with that ridge to the Ohio River, and with that river to the mouth of the Kentucky River aforesaid."

This interesting estate purshased from the Cherokees included most of the land, or at least a very large portion of the land now known as Kentucky and Tennessee.

The Company took possession on April 20, 1775, but the Governor of North Carolina issued a proclamation declaring the purchase illegal and Virginia did the same. Later the State of North Carolina allowed the proprietors two hundred thousand acres in lieu of their purchase and the State of Virginia declared a similar grant, and the State of Tennessee gave them a similar grant. So, though the proprietors did not own the whole of Tennessee and Kentucky they had a large slice.

NOTABLE SOUTHERN FAMILIES

Judge Henderson opened a land office in Nashville, then the French Lick for the sale of these lands.

John Luttrell who was of Cheatham County, North Carolina, was Clerk of the Crown at Hillsboro, 1770, before the Revolution, a Colonel in the American Army, during the Revolution and he evidently had no children. He willed his land to his widow and to his three brothers, William, Hugh and Thomas of Westmorland County, Virginia. His widow paid William and Hugh cash for their share of the land located in Tennessee. He had married ———— Hart, a daughter of John Hart, of North Carolina.

Begining with the Revolution we have in Virginia four Luttrells, Rodham Luttrell, John Luttrell, Richard Luttrell and Michael Luttrell, all soldiers in that war.

Michael Luttrell moved from Virginia to Illinois after the Revolution and lived there at least until 1855, so that he must have been quite a young man when he served in the Revolution in Virginia.

William and Elizabeth Luttrell were living in Virginia, probably in Amherst County, from about 1788 to 1796. Elizabeth Witt was the daughter of Jesse Witt, a soldier of the Revolution. William Luttrell was born about 1770. He was possibly of the same family as was Richard Luttrell, a soldier of the Revolution in Virginia, as he named his second son Richard Luttrell.

William and Elizabeth moved to Tennessee in 1796 and settled in the "Fork" of the French Broad. Their eldest son was John Luttrell, which again shows the family name.

Their second son and third child was Richard Luttrell, who was born in Virginia, probably in Amherst County, January 6, 1792. He was four years old when the family migrated to Tennessee. When he was just twenty-one his father, William Luttrell, and the oldest brother, John Luttrell died, leaving Richard with the care of his widowed mother and a large family. Despite this he enlisted in Sharp's Company in the Campaign against the Creek Indian and served honorably. His descendants are eligible to the Society of 1812 through his service.

He married November 17, 1817, Mary or Polly Turnley, daughter of George and Charlotte Cunningham Turnley (born December 19, 1797, died July 18, 1831). Richard Luttrell and Mary Turnley Luttrell had seven childen:

(1) William Cunningham Luttrell (born October 2, 1918).
(2) Louisa Jane Luttrell (born December 10, 1819).
(3) John Haynie Luttrell (born May 2, 1821).
(4) Harvey Wilkerson Luttrell (born November 19, 1822).
(5) Charlotte Elizabeth Luttrell (born January 25, 1825).

LUTTRELL

(6) Albert Axley Luttrell (born December, 1826).
(7) Cordelia Matilda Luttrell (born September 1, 1828).

Of the foregoing:

William Cunningham Luttrell, son of Richard Luttrell and Polly Turnley Luttrell, born 1818, married Mary Snow, daughter of Dudley and Priscilla Snow, and their children were: Dudley Richard Luttrell (who married Ella Hicks); Bessie Luttrell (who died unmarried); Annie Priscilla Luttrell (who married Edward S. Farmer and had five children); Lucinda Snow Luttrell; George William Luttrell (who married ——————— Anderson); Cordelia Caroline Luttrell (who married George Washington Brock); Robert McMillan Luttrell (who married Dolly Dodd and had one daughter); Kate Garland Luttrell (who married Prof. Cawthorn and had one or two children).

Louisa Jane Luttrell daughter of Richard Luttrell and Polly Turnley Luttrell, married William Wilson Blaine. They had eleven children, namely: James Wilson Blaine; John Howard Blaine; Robert Alexander Blaine; Richard Blaine; William Henry Clay Blaine; Russell Franklin Blaine; Mary Elizabeth Blaine; Martha Parlee Blaine; Frances Cordelia Blaine; Florence May Blaine; and Vivian Sallie Blaine.

John Haynie Luttrell, son of Richard Luttrell and Polly Turnley Luttrell, married Susan Brock and had twelve children, namely: William Haynie Luttrell; Martha Jane Luttrell; Sarah Cordelia Luttrell; Margaret Joanna Luttrell; Lilbourne Patty Luttrell; Polly Ann Luttrell; Frances Elizabeth Luttrell; John Wilkerson Luttrell; Harvey Elmore Luttrell; George Washington Luttrell; Louisa Matilda Luttrell; Susan Elnora Luttrell.

Harvey Wilkerson Luttrell, son of Richard Luttrell and Polly Turnley Luttrell, married Susan Frances Ellston, and had chidren, namely: Corrie Luttrell (who married Charles L. Sowell and had no children); Oscar Fowler Luttrell (who married Mollie Magill Oden and has three children, Oden Luttrell in the United States Navy, Oscar Forney Luttrell and Frank Alexander Luttrell); Ellston Luttrell (who marriel Lucy Barbour and had five children: Randolph Luttrell, Corrie Luttrell, Annie Laurie Luttrell, Harvey Luttrell and Alton Luttrell); Chester McCallie Luttrell (who married Gussie Harwell and had Juliet Luttrell, Katie May Luttrell, Elizabeth Lynn Lutrell, and Ethel Lucile Luttrell); Bruce Luttrell (who married Lena Crumpton and had Sue Ellston Luttrell, Ralphine Luttrell, Rush Luttrell, Lucy Grace Luttrell and Marcie Luttrell); Rush, Katie, Marcie, Fred, and Frank Luttrell all died unmarried.

NOTABLE SOUTHERN FAMILIES

Charlotte Elizabeth Luttrell, daughter of Richard Luttrell and Polly Turnley Luttrell, died unmarried.

Elbert Axley Luttrell, son of Richard Luttrell and Polly Turnley Luttrell, married Mrs. Nancy Saylor and had no children.

Cordelia Matilda Luttrell, daughter of Richard Luttrell and Polly Turnley Luttrell, was born in Knox County, 1828. She married George Washington Crumbliss, October 30, 1856, at Locustdale. They had nine children, namely: Vivian Walter Dewitt Crumbliss (who married Rosannah Weatherford and had eight sons); James Richard Crumbliss (who died young); Louisa Magnolia Crumbliss (who married Charles L. Leader and had two children); Hugh Marcus Crumbliss; Oscar Leonidas Crumbliss (who married Alice Mary VanDoren and had eight children); Eliphalet Fortunatus Crumbliss (who married and had children); Ida Lavade Crumbliss (who married George Wunderlick); Ola Eugenia Crumbliss (who died young); and Oliver Morteaugh Crumbliss.

JAMES CHURCHWELL LUTTRELL.

James Churchwell Luttrell was a resident of Tennessee early in eighteen hundred. He married, about the year 1803, Martha Armstrong, the Second, daughter of Robert Armstrong, and his wife Margaret Cunningham Armstrong. See Armstrong Family. They had six children.

(1) James Churchwell Luttrell, Second.
(2) Margaret Luttrell.
(3) Martha Luttrell.
(4) Amanda Luttrell.
(5) Robert Armstrong Luttrell, who died young.
(6) Fannie Luttrell who died young.

James Churchwell Luttrell, Second, son of James Churchwell Luttrell and Martha Armstrong Luttrell, married Eliza Carr Bell, daughter of Samuel Bell and his wife, Eliza Carr Bell. They had seven children, namely: James Churchwell Luttrell, Third; Samuel Bell Luttrell; Elizabeth Saunders Luttrell; Martha Armstrong Luttrell; Eliza Bell Luttrell. Mary M. Luttrell and a child that died young.

James Churchwell Luttrell, Third, married Josephine E. Brooks, daughter of General Joseph Brooks and Margaret Almeda McMillan Brooks; (see McMillan Family); and had: Annie Luttrell (who married Joseph Shields and has one daughter, Josephine Luttrell Shields married Leonard Murphy); Libbie Luttrell (who married Benjamin

LUTTRELL

Moore and has Benjamin Moore, Jr., and Margaret Moore); Sophy Luttrell (who married Harry Harmon, Jr., and had Harry Harmon, Third); Fannie Luttrell (who married ——————— Powers and has no children); James Churchwell Luttrell, Fourth; Ernest Luttrell; and Samuel Bell Luttrell, Junior, (who died unmarried).

Samuel Bell Luttrell married Margaret McClung Swan, a descendant of the distinguished McClung family and had Samuel Bell Luttrell (who died young); Margaret Luttrell (who married William B. Sullins and has Samuel Sullins and David Sullins); Jennie Luttrell (who married Charles M. Mitchell and has Margaret Luttrell Mitchell and Mary Mitchell); Mary Luttrell (who married Dr. Thomas A. R. Jones); and Charles Luttrell (who died unmarried).

Elizabeth Saunders Luttrell married Dr. William Morrow, of Nashville, and had nine children, namely: James L. Morrow; Frank Murfree Morrow; Lillie Morrow; Emma Morrow; Sallie Hooper Morrow; Libbie Luttrell Morrow; Ada Murfree Morrow; Walter S. Morrow and Margaret Bell Morrow. James Luttrell Morrow married Jane Ewing and their children are Irene Ewing who married Dr. Essler Hoss, Elizabeth Morrow, who married Arthur Timmons, William Morrow, Jane Morrow, and Orville Morrow. Frank Murphee Morrow married Celeste Baylord and left one son, William Leigh Morrow, who married Dolly Post. Lillie Morrow married Judge J. M. Anderson and has one daughter, Emma Morrow Anderson, who married Harold B. Whiteman. Emma Morrow married John B. Atchison and has Thomas Ayres Atchison, Lillie Morrow Atchison and Emma Morrow Atchison. Sallie Hooper Morrow married T. Ludlow Chrystie and has Elizabeth Ludlow Chrystie, Thomas Witter Chrystie and Frances Nicholson Chrystie. Libbie Luttrell Morrow is not married. Ada Murfree Morrow married D. F. C. Reeves and has Joseph S. Reeves, and Daniel F. Carter Reeves, Junior. Walter S. Morrow is not married. Margaret Bell Morrow married Clarence B. Simpson and has Isabel Simpson and John Morrow Simpson.

Martha Armstrong Luttrell married Stokeley Donelson Mitchell and had three children: Mabel W. Mitchell; William M. Mitchell; and Libbie Luttrell Mitchell (who married John McMillan Moulden and has John McMillan Moulden, Junior, and Margaret Luttrell Moulden).

Eliza Bell Luttrell married Jesse H. Thomas and had Jesse H. Thomas, Junior, and James Luttrell Thomas.

Mary M. Luttrell married Charles E. Griffith and had four children: Charles E. Griffith, Junior; Sallie M. Griffith, Lillian Bell Griffith, and a child that died young.

Margaret Luttrell, daughter of James Churchwell Luttrell and Martha Armstrong Luttrell, married Matthew Ambrose Gaines, son of Ambrose Gaines, of Culpepper County, Virginia. (See Gaines and

Armstrong Families). They had five children, namely: James Luttrell Gaines, M. M. Gaines, Martha Gaines, Mary Gaines and Ambrose Gaines, Third.

Of the foregoing:

M. M. Gaines, I have no record.

Martha Gaines, married Richard Bearden.

Mary Gaines, married ———————Bearden.

Ambrose Gaines, Third, married Mary Winston Towns and had six children, namely: George Towns Gaines (who married ——————— and has Ethel Smith Gaines and Katherine Woodville Gaines); Margaret Gaines (who married Garland Buffington); Etta Gaines (who married H. B. Hogan); Blanche Gaines (who married F. J. Hoyle); Mary Towns Gaines (who married Reuben S. Payne): and Ambrose Gaines, Fourth (who married Edith Lucie Jenks and has Margaret Gaines, Ambrose Gaines, Fifth, Edith Jenks Gaines, and Mary Towns Gaines).

James Luttrell Gaines, was an excellant officer of the Confederate Army and lost his arm in the service. He married Belle Porter, daughter of Erasmus Porter and had five children: Ambrose Porter Gaines, Matthew Gaines, Lillian Gaines, (who died young); and James Luttrell Gaines, Second.

Martha Luttrell, daughter of James Churchwell Luttrell, and his wife, Martha Armstrong Luttrell, married Richard Bearden.

Amanda Luttrell, daughter of James Churchwell Luttrell and his wife, Martha Armstrong Luttrell, married Reverend George Horn and had three children: Sarah Horn (who married James Newman); James Horn (who never married); and William Horn (who married Kate Kelso).

DESCENDANTS OF WILLIAM AND ELIZABETH LUTTRELL.

Just about the time that James Churchwell Luttrell, the First, married Martha Armstrong, a son was born (1803) to William and Elizabeth Witt Luttrell, on the "Forks" of the Holston. They christened the boy James Churchwell Luttrell. The name proves that there was a close connection between the two families, though it has not been determined what that connection was. Possibly William Luttrell was a brother to James Churchwell Luttrell, the First, and the little newcomer was a namesake-nephew. As stated earlier in the Luttrell article the name Churchwell came into the family because of a marriage earlier in its history and the father of William and James Churchwell Luttrell may have had that name or their mother may have been a Churchwell.

LUTTRELL

The family of Richard Luttrell, who married Polly Turnley, is also closely allied with both the families of William and James Churchwell Luttrell.

Richard was not, however, a brother to James Churchwell and William, as he was the eldest brother in his own family and they were both of age and married before he came of age. He was very likely their first cousin. His father and mother are given as William and Elizabeth and like the other William and Elizabeth Luttrell they also emigrated from Virginia.

William and Elizabeth Witt Luttrell emigrated from Virginia to Tennessee about the year ———. They were accompanied by Elizabeth's father, Jesse Witt, who had been a soldier of the Revolution. Jesse Witt and his wife had a number of children of whom we know Elizabeth who married William Luttrell and Abner Witt.

William and Elizabeth Luttrell lived on the "Forks" of the Holston and raised a large family. William Luttrell died about 1814. Some of their children were: Hugh Luttrell, Eliza Luttrell, James Churchwell Luttrell, Matthew Luttrell, and John Luttrell.

James Churchwell Luttrell, born 1803, died 1866, married Eliza Bounds as his first wife and had twin children, Frank and Eliza Luttrell. He married for his second wife, Dicey Ann Murphey and their children were John Luttrell, Lawson Luttrell, Creed Luttrell, James Madison Luttrell, Louisa Luttrell, Brownlow Luttrell and Gideon Luttrell.

James Madison Luttrell married Mary Jane Lockhart McMillan. Their children were Walter Madison Luttrell (who married for his first wife Jennie May Anderson and had Louisa Luttrell and Elnora Luttrell, married Herbert Graf, and married for his second wife A. Mariah Crawford). James B. Luttrell, (who married Rena Good); Laura Elizabeth Luttrell, (who is unmarried); Lucy A. Luttrell (who is unmarried); C. Albertine Luttrell (who married Hugh Lyle Vance); Mary Iva Luttrell (who married Otho Atkin and died in 1901); Anne E. Luttrell (who married Edward Silver Maclin); William Eugene Luttrell (who married Mattie Lee Walling); Ella Luttrell (who is unmarried); Beulah Luttrell (who is unmarried); and Kate Luttrell (who married Harvey A. McBath).

LYLE

The name Lyle is an ancient one. In the Eleventh Century the people of the Isles of Wight and Ely in England and the Isle of Butte in Scotland were called "de Insula." With the Norman conquest the name became "d'l'Isle," and with passing of Norman rule the d was lost and we have "l'Isle and later still the form in common use, Lyle.

It has been claimed that the derivation comes from nobles in the train of William, and this may also be true.

The earliest direct ancestor of the name Lyle whom we know is Samuel Lyle who was living in Ireland where he married Janet Knox in 1680. Of the family of Janet Knox, however, we have earlier record. She was the daughter of John Knox, whose wife was Sally Locke Knox (childless widow of Ephriam Knox), Sally Locke was the daughter of David Locke, whose wife was Mary Wylie, granddaughter of William Wylie, and his wife, Janet Black.

The "earliest Lyle," Samuel and his wife Janet Knox Lyle, occupied a stone house, which is still standing and is occupied by his descendants. It is near Larne, on the west coast of Ireland.

Samuel and Janet Knox Lyle had six children. One of them, James, married Margaret Snoddy (daughter of William Snoddy, and his wife, Jane Adams). James and Margaret Snoddy Lyle had eight children: Elizabeth, Jenny, Matthew, John, James, Robert, Daniel, William. The Southern family, now scattered throughout this country, is descended from four of these seven children, four sons. Three of them, Matthew, John and Daniel, emigrated to America and Robert's son, Samuel, emigrated probably with one of his uncles, or at least as a result of their emigration.

Though living in Ireland in County Antrim, near Larne, on the Irish coast, the family was of Scottish origin, and it is supposed that the emigration from Scotland took place about 1616.

In 1700 there was a general movement in Ireland for emigration to America.

MATHEW LYLE.

Mathew Lyle, first of the emigrant Lyles, son of James Lyle and Margaret Snoddy Lyle, was born in Ireland, about 1711, in the family residence at Browndood, near Larne, in County Antrim. He married, it is said, before he was of age, in 1731, (it is from this tradition that we learn the probable date of his birth) Esther Blair. (Esther Blair was born about 1713, in Ballyvallah, County Antrim, Ireland. She was the daughter of Samuel Blair, and his wife, they were married in 1690, Martha Campbell Lyle, a daughter of a James Lyle, of Toreagh, and his wife, Martha Campbell. James Lyle's father was John Lyle, and his wife was Florence Montgomery. Esther Blair was a descendant on her father's side of Brice Blair of very high lineage. Brice Blair married in Ayrshire, Scotland, Esther Peden, in 1625, and went to Ireland).

About ten years after Mathew Lyle's marriage to Esther Blair they emigrated to Virginia. The exact date is not known, but one of their children, Robert, who died young, was baptized in Larne, in 1740, and on July 30, 1742, Mathew Lyle's name is signed to a petition to Colonial Governor Gooch in Virginia, and he was evidently a resident of some standing in the colony at that time.

He settled on Timber Ridge, in what is now Rockbridge County, Virginia. From Mathew Lyle's marriage to Esther Blair there were born six children, four of whom grew to maturity. (William and Robert died young).

(1) James Lyle.
(2) Elizabeth Lyle.
(3) John Lyle.
(4) Martha Lyle.

Of the foregoing:

James Lyle, first child of Matthew and Esther Blair Lyle, was born in Ireland in 1732, and died in Virginia. He accompanied his parents to Virginia about 1741. He married in Virginia about 1764, Hannah Alexander. Their children were: Joseph, Matthew, Elizabeth, Esther, Margaret, John and Archibald. Of these: Joseph Lyle married Sarah Butt, in 1791, and had children; Mathew Lyle became a Presbyterian minister, married his cousin, Sarah Lyle, and had children; Elizabeth Lyle married her cousin, William Lyle as his second wife and had children; Esther Lyle never married; Margaret Lyle married James Alexander and had children; John Lyle, a physician, went from Virginia to Texas and nothing definite is known of him; Archibald Lyle never married. He commanded a company of cavalry in the war of 1812.

John Lyle second son of Matthew Lyle and Esther Blair, was born in Ireland about 1736; he died in Virginia in 1793, was captain of a militia company in 1778, accompanied his parents to America and married twice in Virginia; first Isabella Paxton, and, second, Frances Stuart. He had three children by Isabella Paxton; John, Esther and Mary Paxton Lyle, and by his second wife, Frances Stuart, he had two children, Alexander Stuart Lyle and Isabella Lyle. (Of these: John Lyle married Nancy Thompkins and had fourteen children, only three of whom, however, married; Esther Lyle married Joseph Paxton and had children; Mary Paxton Lyle married James MacDowell, (son of Judge Samuel MacDowell, and Mary McClung, and grandson of Captain John McDowell, who first settled on Borden's Grant in Virginia, in 1737), and had children; Alexander Stuart Lyle probably did not marry; Isabella Lyle married John McDowell and had a son, William McDowell, who married but had no children.

Elizabeth Lyle, eldest daughter of Matthew Lyle and Esther Blair Lyle, was born in Ireland about 1734, and died in Virginia. She married twice and is ancestress of a large and influential posterity. Numbers of Tennesseans and Georgians claim descent from Elizabeth Lyle. She remained in Ireland, when her parents emigrated to America, with her grandparents and her maternal uncle, Daniel Blair. She married in Ireland, about the year 1750, William Thompson, (died 1759), son of Thomas Thompson (b. 1697, d. 1779), and his wife, Mary Black, (b. 1714, d. 1778), who was the daughter of Samuel Black, (b. 1656, d. 1740), and his wife, Alice Murdock, (b. 1675, d. 1743). Elizabeth Lyle Thompson and her husband, William Thompson, had three daughters, Esther, Jane and Mary. Six years after the death of William Thompson (in 1759), the young widow married (1765) for her second husband, William Thompson's first cousin, Mathew Donald, (son of John Donald, and Margaret Black, Mary Black having been William Thompson's mother). Eliabeth Lyle Thompson Donald and her husband, Mathew Donald, emigrated to America in 1775, bringing with them her three Thompson daughters, Esther, Jane and Mary, and her children by Mathew Donald. Another child, Margaret, was born at sea in 1775 and this establishes the date of their crossing. The children of Elizabeth and Mathew Donald were Mathew Lyle, John, Samuel, Margaret, William Blair, James and Mark. Margaret was born at sea in 1775.

LYLE

Of Elizabeth Lyle's daughters by William Thompson: Esther Thompson (born about 1752) married about 1778, John McShadden; they went from Virginia to Tennessee and settled near Dandridge, and had a large family, namely, James, Thomas, Elizabeth, Jane, John, Mary, Samuel, Esther, Mathew, Archibald Thompson. A large connection of East Tennessee people comes from this family.

Jane Thompson, second daughter of Elizabeth Lyle Thompson, (b. about 1755, d. near Dandridge, Tennessee), married James Walker, and had children: Jane and Elizabeth, (both of whom married and had children), and married a second time Andrew Cowan (who had, by a previous marriage, six children). She had three Cowan children, Joel W., Thompson and Matthew, all of whom married and had children. She married a third husband, Joel Ellis, but had by him no children. Jane Walker, (eldest child of Jane Thompson, by her first husband, James Walker), is the ancestress of the Inman family, through her marriage to John Ritchie Inman, son of Abednego Inman; their children were James Abednego, Mary A. Shadrack Walker, James M., John W., William M., Joel C., Walker P., Elizabeth, Jane, Susan, Hannah, Matilda, Sallie and Mary, which was rather a nursery full, even for those prolific times.

Mary Thompson, daughter of Elizabeth Lyle and William Thompson, was born in Ireland about 1757; she died in 1797. She is frequently called Polly Thompson in the family record. She came with her mother and stepfather to America in 1775. She married Samuel Wear, in Augusta County, Virginia, in 1778. Samuel Wear was a son of Robert Wear. Mary and Samuel Wear moved to what is now Tennessee and settled on Little Pigeon River, Sevier County, Tennessee, which was then a part of North Carolina. For history of Colonel Samuel Wear see Armstrong Family).

Samuel Wear married twice. After the death of Mary Thompson Wear he married Mary "Gilhan," or Gilliland, and had by her several children, though this record deals with the children by his first wife only, namely, Elizabeth, Robert, Rebecca, Samuel, Junior, John and Mary.

Elizabeth Wear, daughter of Samuel Wear, and his first wife, Polly Thompson, was born in Augusta County, Virginia, 1780, and died in Tennessee, 1820. She married Robert Armstrong, the third, son of Robert Armstrong, second, and his wife, Margaret Cunningham. They built a home, which is standing, on the Tennessee River above Knoxville. Their children were Drury Paine Armstrong, who married Amelia Houston); Addison Wear Armstrong, who married Nancy MacMillan); Maria Armstrong, (who married John Brooks); Rutelia Armstrong, (who married Thomas G. Craighead); Charlotte Armstrong, (who married first Samuel Armstrong, and had no children; married second Henry C. Baldwin); Robert Houston Armstrong (who died young); Margaret Cunningham Armstrong (who married Samuel Hannibal Love); Dialthea Perry Armstrong, (who married Pleasant M. Love); James H. Armstrong, (who married Ann Eliza Park); Malinda Armstrong, (who married Samuel Morrow); Samuel T. Armstrong, (who died young), and Elizabeth Armstrong, (who died young). From these sons and daughters comes a large connection.

Robert Wear married Lucretia Thomas and had children. Rebecca Wear married John Witt and had children. Samuel Wear, Junior, married and had children. John Wear, who was also an officer in the War of 1812, married Sussannah Mullendore and had children. He married for his second wife Sarah M. Patty and had children.

Mary Wear, last child of Samuel Wear by his first wife, Polly or Mary Thompson, married Colonel Simeon Perry and had children. Simeon Perry married a second wife.

A very large connection of Tennessee people comes through Samuel Wear's children.

Going back to Elizabeth Lyle, who married first William Thompson, and second Matthew Donald: By her marriage to Donald she had seven children: Mathew Lyle Donald, (who married Mrs. Nancy Walker, nee Caughron or Cawhorn, and had children); John Donald (who married Nancy Paxton); Samuel Donald (who died unmarried); Margaret Donald, who married William Keys, who was a Colonel of an Ohio Regiment in the War of 1812; William Blair Donald, who married Mary Campbell, and was a Captain in the War of 1812; James Donald, who married Jennie McCorckle, and Mary Donald, who married his cousin, Hannah Lyle).

Martha Lyle, fourth child of Matthew Lyle and his wife, Esther Blair, was born about 1740. She accompanied her parents from Ireland to Virginia and married there about 1758, Matthew Houston, son of John Houston and an uncle to General Samuel Houston. Their children

LYLE

were John (who married Rachel Balch); Samuel (who married Nancy Gillespie, married second Mary Mitchell, by whom he had no children, and married third Annie Hutchison, by whom he had no children); Matthew (who married Margaret Cloyd); Robert D., (who died unmarried); Esther (who married her cousin, Major James Houston); and Margaret (who married Captain James Gillespie).

JOHN LYLE.

John Lyle, second of the emigrant brothers and second son of. James Lyle and Margaret Snoddy, of County Antrim, Ireland, was born about 1720, in Ireland. He married in Ireland, Jean Owens, a daughter of William Owens, and his wife, Matilda Knox, (of the same family of Janet Knox, who was John Lyle's grandmother by her marriage to Samuel Lyle in 1680, or about that date). John Lyle and his wife emigrated to Virginia about 1745. They settled on Timber Ridge, now Rockbridge County, Virginia, adjoining the property of his brother, Matthew Lyle. Like all the Lyles, John was a Presbyterian and helped to establish the faith in Virginia. He worked on the Presbyterian Church of Timber Ridge, which was built on lands given by his brother, Mathew. He died in 1758 and was survived for forty years by his widow. Their children were:

(1) John Lyle.
(2) David Lyle.
(3) Martha Lyle.
(4) Elizabeth Lyle.
(5) Sarah Lyle.
(6) Esther Lyle.

Of the foregoing:

John Lyle married Flora Reid, and had children; William Lyle married Nancy Agnes Gilmore and had children; Martha Lyle was left in Ireland with her maternal grandparents, Owens, when John Lyle and his wife emigrated to Virginia, she married in Ireland, Robert Russell and emigrated with him to Virginia. She returned to Ireland, however, and died there; she had children; Elizabeth Lyle married Samuel Ramsey and had children; Sarah Lyle married her cousin, James Lyle, son of Daniel Lyle, the emigrant, and had children; Esther Lyle married Samuel Keys and had children.

DANIEL LYLE.

Daniel Lyle, third brother and emigrant, was born in Ireland about 1715. He was the son of James Lyle and Margaret Snoddy. Daniel Lyle emigrated to Virginia about 1745, when his brothers, Matthew and John, were already settled there. He had a home on Timber Ridge in what is now Rockbridge County, and helped to build the Timber Ridge Presbyterian Church, land for which was given by his brother, Matthew. He married in Virginia, ———— Paxton, and his children were:

(1) James Lyle.
(2) David Lyle.
(3) Robert Lyle.
(4) Samuel Lyle.
(5) John Lyle.
(6) Esther Lyle.

Of the foregoing:
James Lyle married his cousin Sarah Lyle and had children.
David Lyle never married.
Robert Lyle (married Jane Ramsey and had children)
Samuel Lyle married Elizabeth White, a cousin of Hugh Lawson White, and had children, married second Margery Hadley and had children. He was in the Revolution.
John Lyle was a Presbyterian minister and a soldier of the Revolution; he married Sarah Glass and had children.

SAMUEL LYLE.

Samuel Lyle, the fourth emigrant, was a son of Robert Lyle, a brother of the three emigrants, Matthew, Daniel and John and a grandson, therefore, of James Lyle and Margaret Snoddy. Samuel Lyle was born about 1725, near Larne, County Antrim, Ireland. He emigrated to Virginia about 1750, when his paternal uncles had been settled there for some years. For a time he made his home with his uncle, Daniel Lyle, but afterward settled land for himself on Tim-

LYLE

ber Ridge, in what is now Rockbridge County. His first home stood a mile from Fairfield, Virginia. Later he moved northeast of Lexington. He was an important member of the community, Justice of the Peace, Vestryman, etc.; he married Sarah McClung, a daughter of William McClung, and his six children were:

(1) William Lyle.
(2) James Lyle.
(3) Mary Lyle.
(4) Jean Lyle.
(5) Elizabeth Lyle.
(6) Sarah Lyle.

Of the foregoing:

William Lyle married Julia Ann Stuart, and had children. After her death William Lyle married for his second wife, Elizabeth Lyle (his second cousin, daughter of James Lyle and Hannah Alexander). They also had children. William Lyle was a soldier of the Revolution.

James Lyle married Margaret Baker and had one daughter who married Abram Smith, and had children.

Mary Lyle married John Dalhouse, and had children.

Jane Lyle married James Ramsey and had children.

Elizabeth Lyle married Michael Graham, a Revolutionary soldier, and had children.

Sarah Lyle married her cousin, Matthew Lyle, and had children.

This completes a brief account of the Lyles. Each of the lines mentioned can be carried out to the present date.

McADOO

John McAdoo, first of the name in America, was of the stock known as Scotch Irish. He came from Ulster to Virginia in the early part of the eighteenth century. He married perhaps in 1756, at a point where later the Norfolk and Virginia Railway crossed New River, a bride who also was an emigrant from Ulster, whose name seems not to have been preserved.

Their son, John McAdoo the second, was born at that point in Virginia, February 6, 1757, and on September 4th, 1787, he married Martha Grills also a native of Virginia. They removed from Virginia to what is now East Tennessee in the early settlement of the colony. He served in the Revolution and was with John Sevier in the Battle of King's Mountain. John McAdoo, the second, died in his seventy-fourth year, December 26th, 1830, at his home, three and one half miles from Clinton, Tennessee, from an injury he received by falling from his horse. His wife Martha Grills McAdoo died January 8, 1838.

John McAdoo, the second, and his wife Martha Grills McAdoo had five children, one of whom was given the family name of John. He was John McAdoo, the third. Another was William McAdoo. He was born May 28, 1788. John McAdoo the third, was born in Jefferson County, Tennessee, June 21, 1790. He was a soldier under General Andrew Jackson in the Creek War. He married about 1825, Mary Ann Gibbs, daughter of John Gibbs and his wife who was Mary Ann Howard before her marriage.

The Gibbs family came from Scotland to England with the Stuarts, and in Cromwell's time were strong adherents of the royal cause. They left England therefore for the continent, spending some years in Holland and Germany. Nicholas Gibbs, the direct ancestor, was born in Germany in 1735, but was not of German blood. He left Germany for America in the early part of the eighteenth century and stayed for a time in Maryland or Pennsylvania. He then went to North Carolina and there married a Miss England, of Elfland. In 1782 or close to that date he moved again, settling this time in Tennessee. He became prominent in the early history of Knox County. He lived until he was past seventy years of age. One account describes him as dying in his nineties and says he would have lived longer except for asthma! He was buried two miles from House Mountain in Knox County. He is said to have had twelve or thirteen children, the names

McADOO

of the sons being given; namely: John, Jacob, Nicholas (Second) Daniel, David, George Washington, and probably William Gibbs. George Washington Gibbs became a prominent citizen and was the father of Colonel Charles Nicholas Gibbs, who was Secretary of State for Tennessee. Another son of Nicholas, Captain Nicholas, the Second, was killed at the Battle of Tohopka, called the Battle of the Horse Shoe. Another son, John Gibbs, moved from Knox County, Tennessee, to Anderson County. He married Mary Ann Howard. They had at least one daughter, Mary Ann Gibbs, who married John McAdoo, the Third, August 16, 1815.

John McAdoo, the Third, whose wife was Mary Ann Gibbs McAdoo or "Polly," as she was called, lived in Anderson County save for two years that they spent in Knoxville. He died at his home near now within Clinton, Tennessee, October 11, 1854, in his sixty-fifth year. His widow, Mary Ann Gibbs or "Polly" McAdoo, survived him twenty years, dying at Clinton July 9, 1874. Both John and his wife are buried in the family cemetery at Clinton.

John McAdoo, the third, and his wife, Mary Ann Gibbs McAdoo, had eight children, five daughters and three sons. The eldest child was Malinda Emeline McAdoo. She was born at the Island Ford of Clinch River, Anderson County, Tennessee, August 8th, 1816. She married Robert Morrow and had a son, William Morrow, who was State Treasurer for Tennessee. He married Elizabeth Saunders Luttrell, (See Luttrell, Armstrong, Lyle and Calhoun Families), and had nine children, namely: James L. Morrow; Frank Murfree Morrow; Lillie Morrow; Emma Morrow; Sallie Hooper Morrow; Libbie Luttrell Morrow; Ada Murfree Morrow; Walter S. Morrow; and Margaret Bell Morrow. James Luttell Morrow married Jane Ewing and their children are Irene Ewing, who married Dr. Essler Hoss (See Sevier Family), Elizabeth Hoss, who married Arthur Timmons, William Morrow, Jane Morrow and Orville Morrow. Frank Murfree Morrow married Celeste Baylord and left one son, William Leigh Morrow, who married Dolly Post. Lillie Morrow married Judge J. M. Anderson and has one daughter, Emma Anderson who married Harold B. Whiteman. Emma Morrow married John B. Atchison and has Thomas Ayres Atchison, Lillie Morrow Atchison and Emma Morrow Atchison. Sallie Hooper Morrow married T. Ludlow Chrystie and has Elizabeth Ludlow Chrystie, Thomas Witter Chrystie, and Frances Nelson Chrystie. Libbie Luttrell Morrow is not married. Ada Murfree Morrow married Daniel F. Carter Reeves and has Joseph S. Reeves and Daniel F. Carter Reeves, Junior. Walter S. Morrow is not married. Margaret Bell Morrow married Clarence B. Simpson and has Isabel Simpson and John Morrow Simpson.

The third child and eldest son of John McAdoo, the Third, and his wife Mary Ann Gibbs McAdoo, was William Gibbs McAdoo. He was born at the Island Ford, April 4th, 1820.

The fifth child of John McAdoo, the Third, and Mary Ann Gibbs McAdoo, was John David McAdoo, born April 4, 1825, who became a brilliant lawyer and moved to Texas, where he attained distinction and where he died. The next child was Elbert Hamilton McAdoo, born September 7, 1827, who served in the same company with Judge McAdoo, in the Mexican war, where he seems to have contracted the disease of which he died at Clinton April 4, 1849, in his twenty-second year.

William Gibbs McAdoo, first, was born at Island Ford, April 4th, 1820, graduated in 1845 at East Tennessee University, now the University of Tennessee, represented Campbell and Anderson Counties in the General Assembly, took part as a first lieutenant in the siege of Vera Cruz, and later commanded the company at the battle of Cerro Gordo.

He became a practicing lawyer in Knoxville in 1850 and becoming a candidate for the office of district attorney-general received the aid of "Parson," afterwards Senator and Governor William G. Brownlow, was elected by the General Assembly and afterwards by the people, and held the office till 1860, making an admirable record.

Adhering to the Confederate cause he removed during the Civil War to Georgia, and entered the Confederate army, serving gallantly. After the war he opened a law office in Milledgeville, and was appointed district attorney, and judge of the twentieth judicial district, held the presidency of the St. Mary's Western Railroad Company, and finally returned to Knoxville, where he became a member of the faculty of the University at which he had been a student, and continued such until failing health compelled him to relinquish his labors. He died in Knoxville and is buried in Gray Cemetery. Judge McAdoo was the author of an Elementary Geology of Tennessee, as well as various other writings, largely journalistic.

William Gibbs McAdoo was twice married, and there were children by each marriage. He married in 1849 for his first wife, Anna Cleopatra Horsley, eldest daughter of William and Catherine Arnold Horsley who had four other children, John, Alfred, Eliza (who married ——— Helm) and Catherine (who married ——— McNutt.) The children of William Gibbs MacAdoo by his first marriage to Anna Cleopatra Horsly were: Catherine MacAdoo (who married Edwin F. Wyley and had Edwin F. Wyley, Junior, married Garnet Noel and had Edwin F. Wyley, Third, and Llewellyn Wyley; May Wyley; Eleanor Wyley, Catherine Wyley; Virginia Wyley, who married Octave Letory and has no children;

McADOO

Ernest Wyley, Robert Wyley, and Noel Wyley); and Emma Mac-Adoo who died unmarried.

After the death of his first wife, William Gibbs McAdoo married Mary Faith Floyd McDonald, (widow of Randolph Gillies McDonald who died at Savannah in 1854.) She was a great-granddaughter of Charles Floyd of the St. Helena Guards of the Revolution, granddaughter of General John Floyd, who commanded the Georgia troops called out at the outbreak of the Creek War in 1813 and who was afterwards a member of Congress and daughter of Charles Rinaldo Floyd who took part in the Creek Warfare at sixteen years of age, afterwards went to West Point and was later appointed by General Winfield Scott to chief command of the troops who removed the Cherokee Indians in 1838, discharging his duties so admirably as to receive the warm commendation of the hero of Lundy's Lane. She married Judge McAdoo in 1857. There were three sons and four daughters of the marriage. She survived her husband.

The children of William Gibbs MacAdoo by his second wife, Mary Faith Floyd McDonald, (widow of Randolph Gillis McDonald) were Caroline Blackburn McAdoo, who died unmarried; John Floyd Mc-Adoo, who died unmarried; Rosalie Floyd MacAdoo (who married James Saunders O'Neale and has Malcolm Lindsay O'Neale who married Ruby Hawthorne Alanson and has two children, Malcolm Lindsay O'Neale, Second, and Caroline O'Neale; Mary Faith Floyd O'Neale, and Lieutenant James Saunders O'Neale, Junior, married Elizabeth V. Beresford); William Gibbs MacAdoo, Second. A sketch of him follows: Malcolm Ross MacAdoo (who married Maggie Davis and had Mary, married Otis Wilson, Malcolm Ross MacAdoo, Second, and Ann Brooks MacAdoo); Nona Howard MacAdoo (who married George Frank Foster and has no children); Laura S. MacAdoo (who married first Oscar Triggs and married second Pierre Julian Gagey and died and is buried in Paris, leaving one son, Edmond McAdoo Gagey who makes his home with his aunt, Mrs. Rosalie Floyd O'Neale); Charles Lane McAdoo (who died young.)

William Gibbs McAdoo, the second, is the Secretary of the United States Treasury. He was born in 1863 in Georgia while his family was temporarily residing there, and in the midst of the excitement of the War Between the States in which his father was taking an active part on the Southern side. His boyhood life in Georgia was a strenuous one, in the hard times succeeding the war, but he early showed the pluck that has distinguished his career. As a newspaper agent on a small scale he helped to take care of himself. Later he became a student in the University of Tennessee, but did not take a full course. His early professional life in Chattanooga was like that of many struggling young lawyers. At one time he was a partner of John T. Lupton, and at another of the late J. H. Barr. From Chattanooga he went to Knoxville, where he tried to give the people a first-class street railway system, but things went badly, and he left for New York, where for years he engaged in law practice. The inadequate means of transit across the Hudson had long been a serious trouble to the Gothamites. Twice had an attempt been made to establish tunnel communication, but after spending a great amount of money the effort had been abandoned. It was suggested to Mr. McAdoo to take up the task. The confidence thus implied cannot be realized without remembering that he was without any personal resources worth considering in such a matter, and that his training was entirely that of a lawyer and scholar, not at all that of an engineer. His success was brilliant. The two tunnels pushed under the mighty Hudson, and which, though he persistently kept his name off officially, the New Yorkers quite as a matter of course called the "McAdoo" Tubes or Tunnels, the underground railway tracks connected therewith, and the great Terminal Building which might have been called the McAdoo Building had he been a less modest man, the largest office building in the world at the time of its erection, and perhaps even now, if the two connected buildings are considered as one, accommodating about ten thousand people, all represent an expenditure of some sixty million dollars, placed by capitalists in the hands of a compartively young lawyer with no technical training, merely from their faith in his integrity and capacity.

He accepted the office of Secretary of the Treasury under President Woodrow Wilson and his record is a bright page in our Nation's history. Three great Secretaries of the Treasury appear in our annals, Hamilton, who poured life through the sluggish financial veins of our young nation; Chase, who so ably carried the country over the trying period of the War Between the States, McAdoo, who has done so great a work in connection with the reorganization of our whole national monetary system, and under whose administration has come the period of the world war and the responsibility for raising and dispensing billions.

Secretary William Gibbs McAdoo married twice, first Sarah Hazlehurst Fleming in Chattanooga November 18, 1885. (She was a daughter of ——————— Fleming and his wife ——————— Hazlehurst and a niece of Colonel George H. Hazlehurst, of Chattanooga.) By his marriage there were several children, namely:

Sarah Hazlehurst Fleming MacAdoo, Harriet Floyd MacAdoo (who married Charles Taber Martin and has one child, Nona MacAdoo Martin); Francis Huger MacAdoo married Ethel McCormick and has two children, Francis Huger MacAdoo, Second, and Ann Preston McAdoo); Nona Hazlehurst MacAdoo married

McADOO

Prince Frederick de Morenschilte); William Gibbs MacAdoo, Third; Robert Hazlehurst MacAdoo; and Sarah Fleming MacAdoo.

Sarah Fleming McAdoo died in 1910.

May 7, 1914, Secretary McAdoo married Eleanor Randolph Wilson, daughter of President Woodrow Wilson and his first wife, Ellen Axon, in the White House.

The child of William Gibbs MacAdoo, Second, by his second wife, Eleanor Randolph Wilson, is Ellen Wilson MacAdoo.

McGHEE FAMILY

The McGhee family was founded in East Tennessee, by Barcley McGhee, from Pennsylvania. He was of that numerous sturdy Scotch-Irish people, which poured into America during the first half of the eighteenth century, but whether he was a native of Ireland or born in this country is not known. He was born, according to the inscription on his tombstone, in 1759.

The people from whom he came were planted in Ireland from Scotland in the Province of Ulster, probably either in the County of Donegal or Londonderry. Great numbers of the Scotch-Irish settled in Eastern Pennsylvania, chiefly in Lancaster county, from which they emigrated into certain portions of North and South Carolina, and very largely throughout the entire Valley of Virginia, the stream extending further southward through East Tennessee and into Northern Alabama.

Barcley McGhee, born about 1760, married in Lancaster county, Pennsylvania, probably in 1787, Jane McClanahan, (1767) and immediately after the marriage they set out, with some of their kindred for the southwest, stopping probably first, for a very short time, in what is now Sevier county, but very shortly afterwards settling in the present Blount county, in the vicinity of Maryville. Barcley was a planter and merchant, and lived the last years of his life in Maryville, his house now standing on the main street, the property of Charles T. Cates, Senior. He and his wife died in Blount County, he on August 17, 1819, aged almost 60 and she September 8, 1835, aged 68 years, and their graves may yet be seen in New Providence Presbyterian Church burying ground in Maryville.

Barcley McGhee had five children who reached maturity: (1) John, (2) Polly, (3) Betsey, (4) Alexander, and (5) Matthew Wallace. Polly married William Lowry, and lived in or near Athens. But little is known of her family, but she undoubtedly has descendants living in McMinn or Monroe county. Betsey married Thomas Henderson, from Jefferson county, his mother, or grandmother, being a Russell, closely related to, perhaps a sister of, Captain Andrew Russell, who immigrated to Jefferson county, Tennessee, from Augusta county. Virginia, whose very extensive progeny are now scattered nearly half way around the world, a number of them noted for their achievements in civic and military life, and some of the female members being women of unusual beauty and charm.

The only child of Thomas and Betsey McGhee Henderson was Jane, who became the wife of William P. H. McDermott, of Tellico

McGHEE

Plains, Monroe county. Among their children was Penelope, who married Judge J. Burch Cooke, and they are the parents of Thomas Henderson Cooke and Robert Burch Cooke, of Chattanooga, and of Mary, the wife of W. B. Swaney, Esquire, and of Mrs. Penelope Cooke Patty, also of Chattanooga.

Of the foregoing: Thomas Henderson Cooke married Elma Wiehl and has no children. Mary Cooke married William B. Swaney and ad children, Burch Cooke Swaney, who died young, Penelope Swaney who married Marion Hope and has a son, William Green Hope, Mary Elizabeth Swaney who is unmarried, Frances Louise Swaney, who is unmarried, and Elma Roberta Swaney who is unmarried. Penelope Cooke married a Patty and has one son, Burch Cooke Patty who is serving in the United States Army. Robert Burch Cooke married Sarah Divine and has five children, Thomas Henderson Cooke, Junior, Rachel Cooke, Adelaide Cooke, Sarah Cooke and Mary Cooke, all of whom are unmarried.

Alexander McGhee became a physician, and practised the greater part of his life in and near Maryville. He married three times, his first wife being Nancy, the daughter of Judge Thomas Emmerson, one of the Judges of the Tennessee Supreme Court, and the first Mayor of Knoxville. His second wife was Anna Dent Lyle, and his third Ann B. McLin, who after the death of Dr. McGhee, married Colonel Reynolds A. Ramsey, a cousin of Tennessee's distinguished historian, Dr. J. G. M. Ramsey. His descendants live in and about Maryville and Knoxville, two of his great granddaughters being Misses Annie and Elizabeth McGhee, of Knoxville.

Matthew Wallace McGhee, the youngest son, lived near his brother, John, and died unmarried in 1836.

John McGhee, the oldest child of Barcley McGhee, was born October 15, 1788, in the present Sevier or Blount county, October 15, 1788. He was engaged in mercantile business with his brothers in Maryville for a number of years, but his chief occupation was that of a planter, owning at the time of his death several miles of fine lands along the valley of the Little Tennessee river, up and down from the present station of McGhee. Old Fort Loudon (1756-60), the first station established by the English within the limits of the present State of Tennessee, was upon land afterwards owned by him, on the southwest side of the Little Tennessee river, a short distance above the mouth of the Tellico. Quite a number of the Overhill Cherokee Indian villages were situated upon his lands along the river, when the whites first came to this section of the country, and he had intimate relations of one kind or another with these Indians through the greater part of his life. At the time of the removal of the Cherokees in 1838 from their old haunts to the Indian Territory, west of the Mississippi, he had some part in conducting them to their new home. In 1820, he married Betsey Jones McClung, a daughter of Colonel Charles McClung, first County Court Clerk of Knox County, and a member of the Convention which framed the first constitution of Tennessee, and a granddaughter of General James White, the founder of Knoxville in 1791, and who was likewise a member of the Constitutional Convention. Betsey Jones McClung McGhee died in April, 1829. John McGhee died in June, 1851, and both are buried in the family burying-ground near "Riverside," McGhee, Tennessee. John and Betsy McGhee had five children, two of whom died in infancy. The three to reach maturity were (1) Margaret White McGhee, (2) Barcley McGhee, Second, and (3) Charles McClung McGhee.

(1) Margaret White McGhee was born in 1821, and her mother dying when she was eight years old, she was brought up under the direction of her father, who gave her unusual educational advantages, her education being completed in New England. In 1840, she married Andrew Russell Humes, of Knoxville, a descendant of the Captain Andrew Russell, before refererd to. After marriage, he became a planter upon his wife's estate in Monroe county, but lived-only a short time, dying in 1847. They had four children: Betsey Jones Humes, now the wife of Captain Charles P. Storrs, of Knoxville; Thomas W. Humes, of Knoxville; Margaret Humes, who married her stepbrother, Dr. S. D. G. Niles, of McGhee, Tennessee; and Andrea Russell, now Mrs. John L. Dismukes, of Nashville. Margaret McGhee Humes married, in 1852, for her second husband, J. W. J. Niles, a native of New England, but after his marriage to Mrs. Humes, his home was partly in Tennessee and partly in Mississippi. There were three children by this marriage: Charles McGhee Niles and Joseph Warren Niles, who are farmers near Venore, Tennessee, and Amelia Gervais, now the wife of George H. Rogers, of Birmingham, Alabama.

(2) Barcley McGhee, Second, born 1823, spent his life as a planter in Monroe county, on the estate inherited from his father, near the present station of McGhee. He attended the University of North Carolina for one year, and afterwards married successively two sisters, daughters of Arthur H. Henley, who owned a plantation in Monroe county, on the Little Tennessee river, immediately above the McGhees. The wife of Arthur H. Henley was Anna Evelina Moore, daughter of Alexander Spotswood Moore and his wife Elizabeth Aylett, of the Eastern part of Virginia. Alexander Spotswood Moore was son of Bernard Moore of "Chelsea," King William county, Virginia, and his wife Ann Katherine Spotswood, a daughter of General Alexander Spotswood, one of the ablest and most picturesque colonial Governors of Virginia, 1710-1722. The home of General Spotswood was at

McGHEE

Germanna, on the Rapidan river, in Eastern Virginia, near which he established the first iron blast furnace in the Southern Colonies, by reason of which he was sometimes called the "Tubal Cain of Virginia." There is some account of this Moore family in Browning's "Americans of Royal Descent." Barcley McGhee's first wife was Elizabeth Moore Henley, by whom he had but one child, a daughter named for her mother, who became the second wife of J. L. Johnston, of Loudon, Tennessee. Among their children are Hugh M. Johnston, who married Mace Russell and has two daughters, Lynn Russell Johnston and Elizabeth Evans Johnston, of Knoxville, Samuel M. Johnston, merchant of Knoxville, and Thomas H. Johnston, whose wife was Nona G. McDermott. They have Hugh Samuel Johnston and Louise Johnston. Barcley McGhee's second wife was Mary Keller Henley, by whom he had, among others, Margaret White McGhee, now the widow of Charles C. Jones, of Monroe county, John Barcley McGhee, living near Vonore, in Monroe county, and Lavinia Moore McGhee, wife of the Honorable Joshua Rhett Jones, a native of South Carolina, living now at Sunline, on the Little Tennessee river.

(3) Charles McClung McGhee was born, January 23, 1818, near the present station of McGhee, Tennessee, and died at his residence in Knoxville, May, 1907. He graduated at the East Tennessee University in 1846, and became a planter in Monroe county until the War Between the States, when he became a resident of Knoxville, and subsequently made his home in New York. He was a banker; Vice-President of the East Tennessee, Virginia and Georgia Railroad; President of the Knoxville and Ohio Railroad, and President of the Memphis and Charleston Railroad; took an active part in the development of the coal and iron interests of East Tennessee, and was a promoter of manufacturing in Knoxville; was a member of the House of Representatives in the Tennessee Thirty-seventh General Assembly; and founded the Lawson McGhee Library in Knoxville as a memorial to a deceased daughter. He married successively two sisters, daughters of Hugh A. M. White, af Knoxville, grandson of General James White, the founder of Knoxville. The first wife was Isabella McNutt White, who lived less than a year after her marriage. His second wife was Cornelia Humes White, whom he married in 1857. They had five daughters: (1) Margaret White McGhee, (2) May Lawson McGhee, (3) Anne McGhee, (4) Bettie Humes McGhee, and (5) Eleanor Wilson McGhee.

(1) Margaret White McGhee was married to George W. Baxter, a son of the late Judge John Baxter, of the United States Federal Court. He was a graduate of West Point; Lieutenant of Cavalry; saw service among the Indians in the West for several years; resigned and engaged in cattle raising in Wyoming, living at Cheyenne; was

appointed Territorial Governor of Wyoming by President Cleveland in 1886; and afterwards lived for a number of years in Denver, Colorado. He and his wife now make their home in New York. Mrs. Baxter, while she made her home in Knoxville, took an active interest in the Daughters of the American Revolution, and held the office of Regent for Tennessee. Their oldest daughter is Cornelia McGhee, whose first husband was Hugh Tevis, of San Francisco. They made a wedding journey to Japan, and Mr. Tevis died in Yokohoma, in less than two months after the marriage, leaving her a widow in a strange land. She returned with his body to California, and lived for a time at Monterey, in a beautiful home Mr. Tevis had built by the sea just before his marriage, and there her son, Hugh Tevis was born in 1902; Cornelia subsequently made her home in Paris, where she became the wife of Evelyn Toulmin, an Englishman, Paris Manager of Lloyd's Bank of London. The second daughter of George White Baxter and Margaret White McGhee Baxter was Margaret Lawson White. She married Albert Volney Foster, of Chicago, and is the mother of twin sons. The third daughter is Katharine Anne, the wife of Russell Burrage, of Boston. The fourth of Governor and Mrs. Baxter's children is Charles McGhee Baxter who married Marcella Virginia Andrews, daughter of Mr. Matthew Andrews, of Cleveland, Ohio. They make their home in New York. The youngest child is Eleanor Baxter, married Perry Beadleston.

(2 Mary Lawson McGhee, the second daughter of Charles McClung McGhee, married David Shelby Williams, of Nashville, and she and her little daughter of the same name died in less than two years after the marriage. It was as a memorial to her that her father founded the Lawson McGhee Library in Knoxville.

(3) Anne McGhee, the third daughter of Charles McClung McGhee, married her cousin, Calvin M. McClung, of Knoxville, and had two daughters: Eliza Mills McClung, now the wife of William Cary Ross, of Knoxville, and Lawson McClung, now the wife of Thomas G. Melish, a manufacturer of Cincinnati.

Mrs. William Cary Ross is one of the beautiful young leaders of Knoxville society and is as lovely in her life and character as in her face. Mrs. Mellish is a talented young matron.

(4) Bettie Humes McGhee, fourth daughter, married Colonel Laurence D. Tyson, at the time of his marriage a Lieutenant in the United States Army, but now Brigadier General in the United States Army. He is a native of Pitt County, North Carolina; graduated at West Point; became a Lieutenant of Infantry; and saw service among the Indians for several years in the West; was detailed as Instructor of Military Science at the University of Tennessee; studied law while at the University, and was admitted to the Bar; resigned from the Army in

McGHEE

1896; at the beginning of the Spanish-American War was appointed Colonel of the Sixth U. S. Volunteer Infantry and recruited that Regiment in East Tennessee; took it to Porto Rico, and on its return was mustered out at Savannah in 1899; was Member of the Tennessee House of Representatives and its Speaker 1903-1905; he is now a leading manufacturer in Knoxville. Mrs. Tyson is a member of the Bonnie Kate Chapter of the D. A. R. and take an interest in all matters pertaining to the betterment of her city and in promoting its beauty. Colonel and Mrs. Tyson have one son, Charles McGhee, a manufacturer of Knoxville, now in the Aviation Service; he married Betty Carson; and one daughter, Isabella Tyson, who married Lieutenant Kenneth Newcomer Gilpin.

McMILLAN

The McMillan family is of Scotch origin and famous in Scotland for many centuries. The name is Gaelic and was originally Mhavilavin. In Scotland the McMillans were seated in Perth, Argyleshire, Iverness, Arran and Galloway.

The famous Martyr's Monument at Ayr, which was erected in memory of the seven Scotsmen who suffered martyrdom December 27, 1666, for their adherence to the Word of God and Scotland's Covenant, bears the name of Alexander McMillan, second of the seven. Since that date there has always been an Alexander McMillan, or several of them in every generation and the name has been handed down in a direct line to the men who bear it now.

When the McMillans migrated to Ireland they settled in Ulster and from counties in that Province moved to America. They have been noted for piety, sturdiness of character, consistent Presbyterianism and love of education and advancement for themselves and their families. One of their sons, William McMillan, was one of the first graduates of William and Mary College.

Alexander McMillan was born in County Derry, Ireland, August 12, 1749. He emigrated from Ireland to America in 1775 and upon landing at Boston offered himself immediately to the Service of the Colonies. Dr. J. G. M. Ramsey, the noted historian of Tennessee, says of him, "Alexander McMillan on landing at Boston in 1775 immediately joined the Army of the Rebels, starting on the hazardous expedition against Quebec (1776). This was the first service he performed in the cause of American freedom and this was before the Declaration of Independence. His last military service rendered to that glorious cause, was in the hard-fought, but most decisive battle of the Revolutionary War, ending in the defeat and death of Ferguson, and the capture of his whole Army, October 7, 1780. (King's Mountain)."

During his Revolutionary service, probably in the Quebec Expedition, Alexander McMillan had his fingers frozen while holding his gun on picket duty, so that they came off at the first joint. He refused to accept a pension, however, saying, with characteristic decision, that he "did not need it, having ample means of his own."

Alexander McMillan left Ireland to join the McMillan relatives who had preceded him and were settled in Virginia. His service in

McMILLAN

the Quebec campaign delayed his arrival in Virginia, but only for a few years and before the close of the Revolution he did join these relatives in Augusta County (Washington County) Virginia, and there married his first cousin, Margaret McMillan, in 1778.

Alexander and Margaret McMillan moved to Tennessee soon after their marriage and he was probably settled in the eastern part of the state (which was then a part of North Carolina), shortly after the Battle of King's Mountain, in which he was a participant, but his name is given as one of the soldiers in that batle from Washington County, Virginia.

Alexander McMillan, not content with an excellent record in the Revolution, volunteered again and fought with General Jackson in 1812 at New Orleans, though he was already past military age, being then sixty-three years old. His descendants, therefore, are eligible to the Society of 1812, as well as the Societies of the Revolution. Returning to his home in East Tennessee he lived quietly upon his home place, near McMillan's Station, and there died in 1837. His grave is at the Philip Sherrod farm, near the Old Caledonia church, and is marked with his name and age. His wife predeceased him by a year and is buried beside him. In his will he left a half bushel of coined silver to each of his children, except James and John, cutting them off with the proverbial shilling—one dollar each.

Margaret McMillan, who married her first cousin, Alexander McMillan, in Augusta County, Virginia, in 1778, was born April 2, 1762. She was the daughter of William McMillan, brother to Alexander's father, and his wife, Mary Leeper McMillan. Mary Leeper was the daughter of James Leeper and his wife, Margaret Leeper. James Leeper was one of the earliest settlers in Augusta County, Virginia. He had lands surveyed (deed No. 31) May 13, 1838. He died in 1763, as his wife, Margaret Leeper, qualified as administratrix of his estate, June 21, 1763. October 23, 1765 Margaret Leeper. recorded settlement of the estate. A marriage record of Augusta County for September 4, 1731, is for Andrew Leeper, (the bride's name is not given in any of these early records in Augusta County). This Andrew Leeper is probably a son of James and Margaret Leeper and a brother of Mary, who married William McMillan, as she named a son Andrew and the name thereafter continues in the McMillan family.

The marriage of an Edward McMillan is recorded May 16, 1759.

Mary Leeper married William McMillan about 1759. Their first son, William McMillan, Second, was born 1760. William and Mary Leeper McMillan were zealous patriots and Christians. They raised their eldest son, William McMillan, Second, to be a Presbyterian minister. They sent him to college early in life with that end in view and he was one of first graduates of William and Mary College. William McMillan, First, served in the Battle of King's Mountain (Sumner.)

Sumner says the first land surveyed on the Holston and Clinch Rivers, of which any record was preserved was by William McMillan, March 1, 1774, 200 acres on South Fork.

William McMillan, First, died in 1810. I have no record of the death of Mary Leeper McMillan.

William and Mary Leeper McMillan had nine children, namely:
William McMillan, Second.
Margaret McMillan, married Alexander McMillan.
Andrew McMillan.
Francis McMillan.
James McMillan.
Mary McMillan, married James Bell.
Nancy McMillan, married Robert Davis.
Janet McMillan, married Andrew Willoughby.
Elizabeth McMillan married James Fulkerson.

Of the foregoing:

Francis McMillan survived others of his family and was living November 30, 1835, in Barren County, Kentucky, when he wrote to the Masons of Cincinnati assuring them of his interest and co-operation in the monument which they were then about to erect to William McMillan, Second.

James McMillan moved to Ohio with his brother, William, married, and had a family, among other children William. He lived for some years in Covington, Kentucky.

Margaret McMillan will be found in the continuation of this article. as she married Alexander McMillan.

Nancy McMillan married Robert Davis and had James Leeper Davis who married his cousin, Evelyn McMillan; Mary Davis who married ———— Eason; Margaret Davis who married ———— and Robert Earl Davis; James Leeper Davis, who married his cousin, Maxwell; John Davis; William Davis; Frank Davis; Sarah Davis; and Robert Earl Davis. James Leeper Davis, who married his cousin, Evelyn McMillan, had ten children, namely: John Davis (who married, firstly, Lizzie Clapp had Theo and Walter Davis and married secondly Sally Payne and had Elizabeth Davis); Nancy Davis (who married William M. Gray); Almeda Davis; Alice Davis (who married Matt Roberts); Margaret Davis; Robert Davis; James Davis; Rebecca E. Davis; Amelia Evelyn Davis; and James Leeper Davis, Second (who married and has seven children).

William McMilliam, Second, first child of William and Mary Leeper McMillan, born Washington County, 1760, became the most famous of the family. He graduated from William and Mary College. Though raised to be a minister he decided upon the legal profession and studied law. He was admitted to the bar. He moved to Fort Washington, which is now Cincinnati, in 1787. He was elected to several local offices and was elected to the first legislative assembly in the Northwest Territory. He was elected to the Sixth Congress to fill the vacancy caused by the resignation of William Henry Harrison and served from November 24, 1800, to March 3, 1801, declining re-election. He was elected United States District Attorney for Ohio, but died before he assumed the duties of this position.

He accumulated a good deal of real estate and a street in Cincinnati, McMillan Street, bears his name to this day.

He was a man of great intellect and integrity and many testimonials remain to his character. He married but had no children. He was a devoted Mason and left in his will property to the Masons upon a part of which the Masonic Temple in Cincinnati now stands. Thirty years after his death the Masons erected a monument to his memory and published a pamphlet giving his history.

He died in Cincinnati in June, 1804, leaving in his will his estate to his nieces and nephews, with special bequest of property to the Masons.

Three brothers who were cousins to Alexander McMillan, came to America, either with him or about the same time. From them are descended the Whortleberry Springs McMillan Family. Their names were Thomas McMillan, Charles McMillan and "Irish Alexander McMillan."

The following letter was written to Irish Alexander McMillan from Ireland in 1792, and is interesting as it shows various relationships and connects the American Family with those left at home, shows that McMillan and McMullen were interchangeable and also gives interesting light upon taxes, values and educational facilities at that time. The original of this letter belongs to R. A. J. Armstrong, son of Nancy McMillan, daughter of John McMillan, son of Alexander McMillan, for whom certain messages in the letter are intended.

Ireland County of Cavan, July 20, 1792.

Dear Uncle: I embrace this opportunity of writing once more to you to inform you of my health we are all well at present, thanks be to God for his mercies. My mother is dead about eighteen months ago of a fever. I have four children only alive and six dead. Uncle John McMullen had a sore brash of sickness shortly but is recovered and well at present, his wife is also living. He has two sons at home, Andrew and John. His eldest son, William and youngest daughter, Elizabeth left Ireland last May with expectations to see you. His brother, Andrew McMillan and my brother, John White, is resolved, God willing, to go to America next Spring and intend not to make much delay until they see you, hoping they will find you and your family in good health. I received your letter of October, 1791. Uncle John McMullen received one also which gives a good deal happiness to hear of the welfare of you and family. Inform Alexander McMillan that his father is yet alive though very frail, his brother and family is well. Our lands are out of lease and we have taken it again for twelve shillings per acre. I hold about eighteen acres. I commonly pay about six shillings every year of Roads, two shillings of hearth money and as much more won't pay all other taxes. Oat meal is about ten shillings per cwt., potatoes four shillings per barrel vs. thirty-two stone. Beef and pork about twenty-five shillings per cwt. Butter about three pounds per cwt. Linnen has been high this season, eleven hundred of yard wide linnen will be from sixteen to eighteen pence per yard, wool seventeen shillings per stone. The three children my mother had by her last husband is married, the eldest son lives with me, he has no trade. I would prepare for going with my brother John and Cousin Andrew only the landlord will not allow his tenants to sell their place and I have a boy about fifteen years old which has been this three or four years at Latin and Greek, and I suppose it is cheaper to College a boy in Scotland than in America as the College is kept up by the King here. When a boy is fitted for the college he most commonly goes four seasons to Scotland and if a boy is not extravagant he can after being prepared have each winter learning for about 20 lbs. Sterling. I would be glad to hear from you for advice as I have let you know something concerning the cost that attends it here as you can be a better Judge than I as you have had the experience there, whether I shall have him colleged before he goes over or not or if there is much call for young clergymen there or not or what way they are kept up. Your brother, Brice (or Brien) McMullen was alive but frail in May.

Uncle John was there and his wife, his children is all married. Your sister, Margit, is alive and well, her husband, John Bowze, is dead, she has only two children living. Write as soon as possible and fail not. You may direct it to Doctor

McMILLAN

Wright for the person you directed to is dead, as the post boy knows us, and then the (word letter omitted) will not go astray as we commonly see the post once a week. You advised in your last letter to fetch linnen whether is it better to fetch it green or bleached, you may send word. No more at present. But I hope you will remember me to cousins in general. I have a sincere wish for prosperity for you all.

WILLIAM WHITE.

It has long been a tradition in the family that about the year 1790 that a letter was recived from Ireland notifying the connection that a young lady cousin was leaving Ireland in May for New York to join the family in Tennessee and containing a request that she be met. This is evidently the Elizabeth, youngest daughter of "Uncle John McMillan," referred to in the letter. Alexander McMillan left for New York in a covered oxcart containing food and forage and drove through to meet the young cousins and returned with them to Tennessee in time to sow his fall crop of wheat.

By this letter the father of our Alexander McMillan was still living, though "frail," July 20, 1792, and a brother and family still in Ireland were well. Alexander McMillan was born in County Derry and the letter is written from County Cavan.

Henning's Statutes of Virginia, Vol. VII, Pages 202 to 204, shows that in 1758 Alexander McMillan and others received pay for being in the Militia of Albemarle County for protection of the inhabitants on the frontiers. This shows that an Alexander McMillan (or McMullen, the spelling varies) was in the Valley, (Albemarle is the next County East of Augusta and the settlers might easily go from one to the other) in 1758. This Alexander McMillan might have been a brother to William McMillan, First, who was settled in Virginia in 1759 and married Mary Leeper close to that date, or this Alexander McMillan might have been father to William McMillan, who married Mary Leeper, and grandfather to Alexander McMillan who married Margaret McMillan. They were undoubtedly close kinsman.

In this connection, John McMillan Brooks, of Knoxville, wrote in 1896 to Mrs. Boyd, of Knoxville, a letter in which he says that his ancestors, Alexander McMillan and John Brooks came over from Ireland together, settling first in Pennsylvania (as so many of the Irish emigrants did) and later moving to Augusta County, Virginia, and that his records show that John Brooks came over in 1760.

NOTABLE SOUTHERN FAMILIES

THE CHILDREN OF ALEXANDER McMILLAN AND MARGARET McMILLAN.

I.—Polly McMillan, born 1779.
II.—John McMillan, born December 25, 1781.
III.—William McMillan.
IV.—Sally McMillan.
V.—Alexander McMillan, Second.
VI.— Betsey McMillan.
VII.—James McMillan.
VIII.—Andrew McMillan.
IX—.— ——————— McMillan, a daughter, probably died young.
X.— ——————— McMillan, a daughter, probably died young.

I.—POLLY McMILLAN.

Polly McMillan, eldest child of Alexander and Margaret McMillan, was born 1789. She married John Carpenter. Alexander McMillan's Family Bible is now in possession of her descendant, Mary Carpenter. Polly McMillan Carpenter died in 1858.

I.—JOHN McMILLAN.

John McMillan, eldest son of Alexander and Margaret McMillan was born December 25, 1781. He married February 7, 1805, Jane Meek, daughter of John Meek and his wife, Jane McCutcheon Meek, who had moved from Augusta County, Virginia, to Tennessee, in 1790, having been married in Augusta County, June 15, 1770. Jane McCutcheon lived in Rockbridge, Augusta County, Virginia, before she married John Meek and was the daughter of John McCutcheon. He is said to have been in the Battle of King's Mountain. The McCutcheons had been settled in Augusta since 1745. Revolutionary Records give three McCutcheons in the war, John, William and Samuel McCutcheon (possibly sons of John McCutcheon) were all three in the Battle of King's Mountain.

John McCutcheon, the father of the family and the emigrant from Ireland was settled in 1745 at Middlebrook on the headwaters of Middle River in Augusta County, Virginia.

The family record is that "John McCutcheon, the emigrant from Ulster Province, Ireland, was settled in 1745 in Middlebrook, on the headwaters of Middle River in Augusta County." However, by the Virginia records, a Robert McCutcheon is the first of the name who entered lands (1746.) Samuel McCutcheon made a deed in 1746.

McMILLAN

John McCutcheon in 1747 and 1748, James McCutcheon in 1751. These were doubtless all emigrants and possibly all related.

John McCutcheon, who made the deed in 1747 and 1748, is evidently our direct ancestor and the family historian who set down 1746 as the date of his being settled in Middlebrook was evidently close to the truth. He probably did not secure his lands until the next year or so. Possibly he is the son of the first recorded Robert McCutcheon and only took out lands in his own name a year or so after settling with his father.

John McCutcheon had a daughter, Jane McCutcheon, who married John Meek, June 15, 1770. They remained in Augusta County for twenty years and in 1790 removed to Tennessee where they died and are buried. John Meek served in the Revolution and was in the Battle of King's Mountain.

We have the full list of the children of John Meek and his wife, Jane McCutcheon Meek, namely: Thomas Meek, (born March 2, 1772); Margaret Meek (born March 1774); Robert Meek, (born August 5, 1776); Agnes Meek, (born March 5, 1779); Jane Meek (born June 12, 1782, married John McMillan, 1805; died 1875); John Meek (born August 17, 1785); Joseph Meek (born June 21, 1787, or 1788); Rebecca Meek (born May, 1790); Elizabeth Meek (born January, 1793); Rachel Meek (born September, 1795, married ——————— Black); and Sarah Meek (born January 23, 1801, married Andrew Crawford).

John McCutcheon signed a call to Reverend Charles Cummings to preach, as one of the heads of families in the settlement on the Holston (Virginia.) Also William McMillan signed this call.

Waddell's Annals of Augusta County gives this paragraph concerning his son, John McCutcheon, who was born August 13, 1750.

"John McCutcheon served three months in 1777 or 1778 against the Indians, under Captain Andrew Lockridge, Lieutenant Andrew Kincaid and Ensign James Gay and was stationed at Clover Lick (Pocahontas County). He was called out again in June, 1779, by the alarm about an assault by Indians on Donnelly's Fort, Greenbried, and was stationed with others under John Wackub at Warm Springs to protect that place."

The Meek family was also an old one of Augusta County, Virginia. John Meek, (grandfather of the aforementioned John Meek, who married Jane McCutcheon), the first of the name of whom we have positive record, was living on Little River in "Calf Pastures," Augusta County, Virginia, in 1750, with his son, Thomas Meek. John Meck died in 1761. Their son, Thomas Meek was married to Agnes ———————. Thomas Meek was in the Battle of King's Mountain. He died in 1786 or 1787, as his will was proved in 1788. His children were Daniel Meek (who married Elizabeth Allen); Samuel Meek (who married Elizabeth ———); Elizabeth Meek (who married James Peak); John Meek (who married Jane McCutcheon); and Mary Meek (who married John Vachub or Wachub).

The widow of Thomas Meek, Agnes ——— Meek, died in September, 1794, and her eldest son, Daniel Meek, administered the estate. Either Daniel Meek or his brother, Samuel Meek named daughter, Agnes, for their mother and she married Alexander Forgey September 3, 1786. John Meek, who married Jane McCutcheon, also named a daughter Agnes for his mother.

THE CHILDREN OF JOHN McMILLAN AND JANE MEEK McMILLAN.

(1) Nancy McMillan.
(2) Margaret Almeda McMillan.
(3) Evelyn Jane McMillan.
(4) Elizabeth McMillan.
(5) Gaines McMillan.
(6) John Alexander McMillan.
(7) Sarah Rebecca McMillan.
(8) James McMillan.

(1) Nancy McMillan, daughter of John McMillan and Jane Meek McMillan, was born August 23, 1806. She married March 29, 1825, Addison Wear Armstrong. She died August 28, 1880. Her children were: Elizabeth Armstrong, John McMillan Armstrong, Margaret Evelyn Armstrong, Amelia Armstrong and Robert A. J. Armstrong. For all of these see Armstrong Family.

(2) Margaret Almeda McMillan, daughter of John McMillan and Jane Meek McMillan, was born August 2, 1808. She married in 1828 General Joseph A. Brooks. Her children were: Margaret Brooks (who married Reverend George A. Caldwell and had Joseph Caldwell, married ——— Vance, John Caldwell, married ——— Anderson, George Caldwell, died, a daughter, married ——— Wood, Margaret Caldwell married William MacFarland, Ada Caldwell, Maud Caldwell married John Hager, Estelle Caldwell and Clifford Caldwell); Agnes Brooks (who married first Dr. Harvey Baker and married second Richard Wilson and had Maggie Baker, married Dr. Samuel Boyd, Lillie Baker, married James Meek, and Harvey Baker unmarried); Ann Elizabeth Brooks (who married Samuel Davis and had Maggie Davis, married ——— McAdoo. (See that Family.) Joseph Davis married ———, and Georgia Davis married E. N. Willard); Cynthia Almeda Brooks (who married William B.

McMILLAN

Rogers and had Minnie V. Rogers, married John L. Boyd, John Rogers, married ———— Alma Rogers married Herbert Mabrey, T. Belle Rogers married Dan Lee, and Brooks Rogers, unmarried); John McMillan Brooks (who married first Sophy Park and married second Amelia Ervine McDowell and had James Park Brooks, unmarried, Alma Brooks married ———— Wedon, John McMillan Brooks, Second, unmarried, Robert Porter Brooks married Iris Porter); Ademila Brooks (who married Joseph King and had Roy King, Joseph King and three daughters); Josephine E. Brooks (who married James Churchwell Luttrell, Third, see Luttrell Family for her children); Lizzie Brooks (who married George Prater and had Hattie Prater, married R. L. Peters, Mary Blair Prater and Robert Prater); and Fannie Brooks (who married J. C. Duncan and had Malcolm Duncan, Joseph Duncan, Captain Gordon Duncan and Warren Duncan).

(3) Evelyn Jane McMillan, daughter of John McMillan and Jane Meek McMillan, was born December 29, 1810. She married her cousin James Leeper Davis, a son of Nancy McMillan, of Augusta County, Virginia. Their children were: Nancy Davis (who married W. M. Gray); John McMillan Davis (who married, firstly, Lizzie Clapp and had Walter Davis and Theo Davis, and married, secondly, Sallie Payne, of Richmond, Virginia, and had Elizabeth Davis and Robert Davis); Alice M. Davis (who married Matt Roberts); Rebecca E. Davis (who is not married); Amelia Davis (who died young and unmarried); and James L. Davis, second, (who married Amanda Headrick and had Bettie Davis, Evelyn Davis, Boyd Davis, Alice Davis, Lee Davis, Earl Davis and Wade Davis).

(4) Elizabeth McMillan, daughter of John McMillan and Jane Meek McMillan was born June 12, 1813. She married in 1833 Thomas Thornton. She died in 1896. Her children were Jemima Jane Thornton (who married Sterling Rose and had Elizabeth Rose, Wyley Rose and James Rose); John McMillan Thornton (who married Mary Campbell and had Thomas C. Thornton, married Anne Jett, James W. Thornton, married Isabella Few, and John A. Thornton married first Mary Badge and married second Mary Bacey; Wyley Thornton (who married first Susan Martin and married second Sallie ————, and had Eliza Thornton, Wyley Thornton, Second, and John L. Thornton); and Sarah Thornton (who married Thomas McMillan).

(5) Major Gaines McMillan, eldest son of John McMillan and Jane Meek McMillan was born, May 14, 1815. He married in 1838 Mary Ann Goddard for his first wife, by whom he had several children and married for his second, Alice McMillan, daugh-

ter of James McMillan and Alice Houston, by whom he had no children.

The children of Major Gaines McMillan and his first wife, Mary Ann Goddard McMillan, were: Elizabeth McMillan (who married John M. Meek and had Alexander K. Meek, married Fannie Raymond, John Lamar Meek, married Mary Fleming and has one son, Fleming Meek, Gaines McMillan Meek, married Cora Beckett, Daniel White Meek, Mary E. Meek, unmarried, Eugene Holsinger, Margaret B. Meek, unmarried, Nelly Meek, unmarried and Bertha C. Meek, unmarried); Harriet McMillan (who married Lemuel M. Dick and had Alice H. Dick, married C. C. Spears); Daniel McMillan (who married Margaret Roberts and had Henry G. McMillan, married Louisa Barber, Kate A. McMillan, married Clarence Mulline and Robert H. McMillan, married Phebe Park); Cynthia Alice McMillan (who married William H. Salmon, and had Mary Isabella Salmon, who married Robert M. Williams and has three children); Nancy Josephine McMillan (who married Drury P. Love and had Bruce E. Love, married Matilda Gaines McMillan Love, married ———————— Brace, Fred J. Love married Josephine Carter, Hugh G. Love and Rose Love); Margaret E. McMillan (who married J. N. Mast); Florence Roberta McMillan (who is not married); Anna Gaines McMillan (who maried first, George K. Thompson and married second Howard J. Johnston and had Stewart M. Thompson, in the United States Army, Samuel J. Thompson married Eliza VanNess, Lawrence Thompson married Phyllis Plyley and George K. Thompson, second, married Elizabeth Jones and is in the United States Army); and John William McMillan, (who married Elizabeth Gorman and had William Gorman; Gaines McMillan Gorman, Carolee Gorman, and Anne Goddard Gorman).

(6) John Alexander McMillan, son of John McMillan and Jane Meek McMillan, was born April 25, 1817. He married Elizabeth Epps in 1841. He died in 1862. His children were: Almeda McMillan, Adelia McMillan, Rebecca Isabella McMillan, Edward Epps McMillan, John McMillan, Thomas R. McMillan, Mary McMillan, Robert McMilan, Joseph Gaines McMillan, Nancy McMillan and Elizabeth McMillan.

Of the foregoing:

Almeda McMillan married John McMillan Moulden and had John McMillan Moulden, Second, (who married Libbie Mitchell); Belle Moulden (who married George Caldwell); Nannie Moulden (who married J. K. Johnson); Fred Moulden (who married ——— Luttrell).

Martha Adelia McMillan married William Byerly and had Lizzie Byerly (who married Doctor ——————— Hall); Edd Byerly, Lucy

McMILLAN

Byerly (who married Allen Roberts); McMillan Byerly; Thomas Byerly; James Byerly; Robert Byerly and Annie Byerly (who married ──── Beets).

Rebecca Isabella McMillan married T. J. Thomas.

Mary McMillan married H. George and has Edgar George; Albert George (who married Jessie Lady), and Solomon H. George, Junior.

Edward Epps McMillan married Belle Welker, a daughter of Judge James Welker and had Margaret Belle McMillan (who married Hal Bartlett Mebane, Jr. and Edward McMillan Mebane); Edward John McMillan (married Mamie Hennegar); and Helen McMillan (who married Lucian Briscoe).

John Alexander McMillan, Second, married Ester Brownlee.

Nannie McMillan married William Pickle and had John Pickle; Walter Pickle; Edna Pickle (who married ──── Moore); Callie Pickle (who married ──── Fine); and Thomas Pickle.

Thomas T. McMillan married Mayme Hearner and had John McMillan (who married Margaret Todd); and Lillian McMillan (who married first ──── Lewis and married second ──── Haynes). Elizabeth McMillan married A. M. Treadwell and had: Elizabeth McMillan Treadwell; Nelly Treadwell (who married J. R. Booth); Mary Lois Treadwell; Ester Treadwell and Louis Treadwell. Robert L. McMillan married Adelia Smartt and had: Robert McMillan, Second, Edward McMillan (who married Ethel Mae Skeggs); Allen McMillan (who married Lillian Groner); Bessie McMillan; Mary McMillan and Margaret McMillan.

Joseph Gaines McMillan married Esther Brownlee McMillan, his brother, John McMillan's widow.

(7) Sarah Rebecca McMillan, daughter of John McMillan and Jane Meek McMillan, was born January, 1820. She married Alexander Cary Snoddy and had: John McMillan Snoddy (who was killed while serving in the Confederate Army); Thomas Snoddy (who married Mariah Biddel and had Corra Snoddy, married a Felkner, Rebecca Snoddy married Reverend Charles McGill, JohnSnoddy married Mary Caldwell, Stella Snoddy married John Caldwell, Ora Snoddy married ──── and Nelly Snoddy married Guy Wagland); and William Gaines Snoddy (who married Ida Clentine Blackburn and had two daughters.

(8) James McMillan, son of John McMillan and Jane Meek McMillan, was born ────. He married, in 1845, Cynthia Goddard. His children were: Mary Jane McMillan; Nancy Ianthia McMillan, John McMillan, Ademila McMillan, James D. McMillan, Fannie F. McMillan, Cynthia McMillan, William McMillan, Sarah McMillan, Lucy McMillan and Bettie McMillan.

Of the foregoing:

Mary Jane McMillan married James Madison Luttrell. Their children were Walter Madison Luttrell (who married for his first wife Jennie May Anderson and had Louisa Luttrell and Elnora Luttrell, married Herbert Graf, and married for his second wife A. Mariah Crawford.) James B. Luttrell (who married Rena Good); Laura Elizabeth Luttrell (who is unmarried); Lucy A. Luttrell (who is unmarried); G. Albertine Luttrell (who married Hugh Lyle Vance); Mary Iva Luttrell (who married Otho Atkin and died in 1901); Anne E. Luttrell (who married Edward Silver Maclin); William Eugene Luttrell (who married Mattie Lee Walling); Ella Luttrell (who is unmarried); Beulah Luttrell (who is unmarried); and Kate Luttrell (who married Harvey A. McBath.)

Nancy Ianthia McMillan married Jonathan Sherrod and had: Robert Sherrod; Grace Sherrod (who married ——— Kidder); Howard Sherrod; Dana Sherrod; Edward Sherrod; Elsie Sherrod; Linda Sherrod; Annie Sherrod; May Sherrod, and Frank Sherrod.

John McMillan, married Bettie Epps and had: Maude McMillan; Charles McMillan; Bruce McMillan; and Frank McMillan. Ademila McMillan married Reverend ——— Mills and had: Neva Mills and Brice Mills.

James D. McMillan married Sallie Davis and had: Claude McMillan (who married ——— Alexander).

Fannie Fidelia McMillan married William Patillo.

Cynthia McMillan is not married.

William McMillan married Mary Beal and had: Brice McMillan.

Sarah McMillan is not married.

Lucy McMillan died unmarried.

Bettie McMillan married Adam Blake and had: Wremmie Blake; James Blake (who married Minnie Swan); Charles Blake; Harvey Blake; Luther Blake; Belle Blake (who married James Vance); Robert Blake; John Blake and Ruth Blake (who married ——— Armstrong).

III—WILLIAM McMILLAN.

William McMillan, son of Alexander McMillan, First, and his wife, Margaret McMillan McMillan, was named for his maternal uncle, Congressman William McMillan and for his maternal grandfather, William McMillan, the Emigrant. He married a Davis.

IV.—SALLY McMILLAN.

Sallie McMillan, daughter of Alexander McMillan, First, and his wife, Margaret McMillan McMillan, married first, William Thompson and married secondly, Pomain Lovelace.

V.—ALEXANDER McMILLAN, Second.

Alexander McMillan, Second, son of Alexander McMillan, First, and his wife, Margaret McMillan McMillan; of him I have no record.

VI.—BETSEY McMILLAN.

Betsey McMillan, daughter of Alexander McMillan, First, and his wife, Margaret McMillan McMillan, married ———— Leeper.

VII.—JAMES McMILLAN.

Major James McMillan, son of Alexander and Margaret McMillan McMillan, was born ————. He married Alice Houston, daughter of Robert Houston, and his wife, Margaret Davis, or Dallas. (See Armstrong and Howard Families), and had three children, namely: Alice Houston McMillan (who married her first cousin, Major Gaines McMillan, as his second wife and had no children); James White McMillan (who married Laura Hendrick and had Julia Hardin McMillan, Amelia Alice McMillan, Annie L. McMillan, Mary Lurena McMillan, William Hendrick McMillan, Nannie Missouri McMillan, James White McMillan, Second, Luke Hampton McMillan, Laura Houston McMillan, Frances Louise McMillan and Frank Alexander McMillan; Robert Houston McMillan (who married twice, firstly, Martha Isbell, by whom he had two children and secondly her sister, Missouri Isbell, by whom he had two children. His children by his first wife, Martha Isbell McMillan were: James Benjamin McMillan (who married Cynthia Cunningham and had William Cunningham McMillan, Alice McMillan, Rutelia Isbell McMillan, Mary B. McMillan and Kitty McMillan) and Alice McMillan, who is not married. By his second wife, Missouri Isbell McMillan, his children were: Robert Houston McMillan, Second, (who married Sarah Gray and had Robert Houston McMillan, Third, died young, Allen Gray McMillan aod Catherine McMillan); and Fannie McMillan (who married Jesse F. Wikle, and had Robert McMillan Wikle and Jesse F. Wikle, Second).

Major James McMillan married for his second wife, Mrs. Mariah Armstrong Brooks, by whom he had no children.

VIII.—ANDREW McMILLAN.

Andrew McMillan, son of Alexander McMillan, First, and his wife, Margaret McMillan McMillan, married Mary Littleford and had four children, namely: Margaret McMillan, Mariah McMillan, Alexander McMillan, and a son, John D. McMillan, who died unmarried just as he reached his majority and finished college. Mariah McMillan married Simpson Moffet. Her children were John Moffett, Mary Scott Moffet (who married Robert Crouch), William Moffet and Lula Moffat. Margaret McMillan married John Shields and had eight children: Ella Shields, (who died young), Alexander Shields, of San Francisco; Dr. Lawrence Shields, of Xenia, Ohio, William Shields, of California; Mary C. Shields, Margaret Lea Shields, Lizzie Shields and Samuel Shields. (See Shields Family). Alexander McMillan married Margaret Alexander, daughter of Ebenezer Alexander, a descendant of General James White, and had four children, namely: Alexander McMillan (who married Caroline Sinclair Gillem and has one son, Alexander McMillan); Margaret McMillan (who married Martin John Condon and has two children, Mary Condon, who is not married and Martin John Condon, Second married Shirley Cummings and has two children, Martin John Condon, Third, and Billy Condon); Annette McMillan (who married Herbert W. Hall and has three children: Colonel Alexander McMillan Hall, of the United States Army, who is not married, Margaret Hall, who married Charles P. Amos, and Lucie Hall, who married Jesse Thomas and has two children; Jesse Thomas, Junior, and Annette Hall Thomas); and Mamie McMillan (who married Edward E. Hennegar and had six children: Margaret Hennegar, who died unmarried; Anne Hennegar, who married Matthew Thomas, Mamie Hennegar, who married Edward John McMillan, son of Edward E. McMillan and Belle Welker McMillan, Martin Condon Hennegar, Herbert Hall Hennegar, who married Josephine Kendall and Henry Hennegar.

PHINIZY FAMILY

Ferdinand Phinizy, first of the name, first at least in America, was an Italian gentleman who emigrated to America in the eighteenth century. It is believed that he went first from Italy to France, where he spent some time before embarking for America.

He married Margaret Condow and raised a family of five sons and daughters. He established a home in Georgia and acquired great wealth and made a reputation for honesty and integrity of character which was also a legacy to his family, one of the most powerful in Georgia.

Landing absolutely without fortune but possessed of indomitable will and talent, he left his children the foundation of a fortune which at the death of his grandson, Ferdinand Phinizy, the Second, was the greatest in Georgia, if not in the South.

Ferdinand Phinizy, the First, and Margaret Condow Phinizy had five children:

I. Jacob Phinizy.
II. Marco Phinizy.
III. John Phinizy.
IV. Sarah Phinizy.
V. Elizabeth Phinizy.

I. JACOB PHINIZY.

Jacob Phinizy, son of Ferdinand Phinizy, the First, and Margaret Condow Phinizy was raised at the home which his father had established in Oglethorpe County, Georgia. In Historical Collections of Georgia, published in 1855, his name is given as First Lieutenant of the Richmond Blues, having enlisted at Augusta, Georgia, or at least having reported himself from there.

He married Matilda Stewart, daughter of General John B. Stewart, of Virginia, who settled in Georgia after the War of the Revolution in which he had obtained his title. General Stewart's wife was Mourning Floyd of the famous Floyd family. Her nephew was John B. Floyd, Secretary of War under President Buchanan, and another nephew was John C. Breckinridge, of Kentucky.

Jacob and Matilda Stewart Phinizy had four sons and two daughters, namely:

(1) Ferdinand Phinizy, Second.

Ferdinand Phinizy the First

PHINIZY

(2) Sarah Phinizy.
(3) Margaret Phinizy.
(4) Marco Phinizy.
(5) Jacob Phinizy.
(6) John Phinizy.

Sarah Phinizy married John M. Billups of Columbus, Mississippi, and died there during the War Between the States. Margaret Phinizy, the second daughter, married Colonel T. D. Lockhardt, of Nashville, and died. Marco Phinizy, the second son, lived at his brother's home in Athens, Georgia, until his death. Jacob Phinizy, the third son, entered the Confederate Army, was Captain of the Oglethorpe Rifles, and was killed in the battle of Manassas while leading his men. The Oglethorpe Rifles was a part of the Eighth Georgia which General Beauregard commended for unparalleled bravery. John Phinizy, the fourth son of Jacob Phinizy, and Matilda Stewart Phinizy, married Eliza Sherrod Watkins, oldest daughter of Paul J. Watkins. They had at least five children, the eldest Elizabeth Phinizy, married ————— Pointer; Maud Phinizy is not married, Paul Watkins Phinizy has a son, Early Phinizy, of Huntsville, Alabama, James Watts Phinizy and Margaret Floyd Phinizy who married ————— Strong.

FERDINAND PHINIZY, SECOND.

(1) Ferdinand Phinizy, the Second, eldest son and child of Jacob and Matilda Stewart Phinizy, was born at Bowling Green, Oglethorpe County, Georgia, in the home of his father and grandfather on January twentieth, 1819. Shortly after attaining his majority he removed to Augusta, Georgia, and entered business. He married, February twenty-second, 1849, Harriet Hayes Bowdre, only child of Hayes Bowdre, a citizen of Augusta. She bore eight children, seven sons and a daughter, namely, Ferdinand Bowdre Phinizy, Stewart Phinizy, Leonard Phinizy, Louise King Phinizy, Jacob Phinizy, Marion Phinizy, Daniel Phinizy, Billups Phinizy, and Harry Hayes Phinizy. After the death of Harriet Hayes Bowdre Phinizy, Ferdinand Phinizy married for his second wife, Anne S. Barrett, the second daughter of Thomas Barrett and Savannah Glasscock Barrett, of Augusta. The three children of the second marriage were Savannah Glasscock Phinizy, who died young, Barrett Phinizy and Charles Henry Phinizy.

Ferdinand Bowdre Phinizy married Miss Mary Lou Yancey, of Athens, Georgia. They had children: Bowdre and Harriet. After the death of Ferdinand Bowdre Phinizy she married her late husband's cousin, Charles Phinizy, and by this marriage had one daughter.

Stewart Phinizy married Miss Marion Coles, of Columbia, South Carolina. (There were seven children of this marriage, namely: Ferdinand Phinizy, Third, who married Mary Porter; Eliza Pickens Phinizy, who never married; Coles Phinizy, who married Mary Harrison; Marie S. Phinizy, who married J. M. Hull, Jr.; Lousie C. Phinizy, who married R. C. Neely, Jr.; Isaetta Phinizy, who married Henry B. Garrett; Stewart Phinizy, Jr., who never married).

Jacob Phinizy married for his first wife Miss Vannie E. Gartrell, of Atlanta, and for his second wife Miss Mary Vason, of Augusta, Georgia. (They had no children).

Billups Phinizy married Miss Nellie G. Stovall, of Athens, Georgia, and had five daughters: Anne Barrett Phinizy (who married E. H. Johnson and has Billups Phinizy Johnson and Nell Bolling Johnson); Bolling Stovall Phinizy (who married Hughes Spaulding and has Eleanor Phinizy Spaulding and Hughes Spaulding, Junior); Martha Susan Phinizy (who married Leroy Pratt Percy and has Walker Percy and LeRoy Pratt Percy, junior); Nellie Phinizy (who married Lieutenant Robert Malcolm Fortson); and Louise Calhoun Phinizy.

Marion Phinizy never married.

Harry Hayes Phinizy never married.

Louise King Phinizy married Dr. Abner Wellburn Calhoun, of Atlanta, Georgia, and survives her husband. The four children of this marriage are Dr. Ferdinand Phinizy Calhoun, Susan Wellburn Calhoun, Andrew Wellburn Calhoun, and Harriet Calhoun. (Ferdinand Phinizy Calhoun married Marion Peel and has three children, Ferdinand Phinizy Calhoun, Junior, Lawson Peel Calhoun, and Marion Peel Calhoun; Susan Wellburn Calhoun married Junius S. Oglesby and has no children; Andrew Wellburn Calhoun married Mary Guy Trigg, of Chattanooga, and has three children, James Trigg Calhoun, Abner Wellburn Calhoun and Louise Phinizy Calhoun; Harriet Calhoun married Stuart Witham and has one child, Stuart Witham, Junior.)

Charles Henry Phinizy married Miss Nellie Carter Wright, of Atlanta, Georgia, and has two children, Charles Henry Phinizy, Junior, and William Wright Phinizy.

Barrett Phinizy maried Miss Martha Glover, of Atlanta, and their only child is named Laura Anne Phinizy.

II. MARCO PHINIZY

Marco Phinizy, son of Ferdinand Phinizy, the First, and Margaret Condow Phinizy, married Mrs. Dancy and had a son, John F. Phinizy.

PHINIZY

III. JOHN PHINIZY.

John Phinizy, the son of Ferdinand Phinizy, the First, and Margaret Condow Phinizy, married Martha Creswell. They had nine children, six sons and three daughters:

(1) Robert Marco Phinizy.
(2) John Phinizy, the Second.
(3) William Jacob Phinizy.
(4) Thomas Burdell Phinizy.
(5) James Hamilton Phinizy.
(6) Charles H. Phinizy.
(7) Martha Patton Phinizy.
(8) Mary Eliza Phinizy.
(9) Jane Meek Phinizy.

(1) Robert Marco Phinizy, who married Louisa Hamilton Musgrove, had two daughters, Mary and Lula. Both parents died young and the daughters were raised by their grandfather, John Phinizy, and under the guardianship of their uncle, Charles H. Phinizy. Mary married William Micou, of Alabama, and survives her husband, a sweet and gracious example of the charming "old South" type. She lives in Montgomery, Alabama. She has one daughter, Gussie Lou Micou, who married Allen R. Gilchrist and has four children, Robert Allen Gilchrist, Mary Ellen Gilchrist, Martha Augusta Gilchrist, and Ann Monroe Gilchrist.

Lula Phinizy married James B. Turnley, son of Judge Mathew J. Turnley. She died in 1917. She had three sons and two daughters, namely: Louise Turnley, John Phinizy Turnley, James Musgrove Turnley (who married Nettie Brooks and has two children, Mary Florence Turnley and Lula Wilmar Turnley); William Micou Turnley (who married Lillian Crowe and has one child, Lula Elizabeth Turnley); and Janie Bones Turnley (who married Charles Sedbury and died but has no surviving child.)

(2) John Phinizy, the Second, never married.

(3) William Jacob Phinizy never married.

(4) Thomas Burdell Phinizy married Fannie Hamilton and had four children, two sons and two daughters, namely: James Hamilton Phinizy, the Second, who is not married; John Phinizy who married a Miss Irwin and has three sons, Irwin Phinizy, Thomas Phinizy and Frances Phinizy; Margaret Phinizy who married William K. Miller and has Hamilton Miller and William K. Miller, junior, and another daughter who married a Gary and has two sons and one daughter.

(5) James Hamilton Phinizy never married.

(6) Charles H. Phinizy married his deceased cousin's widow,

NOTABLE SOUTHERN FAMILIES

Mrs. Mary Lou Yancey Phinizy and had one daughter, Harriet Phinizy.

(7) Martha Patton Phinizy married C. M. Kolb and had no children.

(8) Mary Eliza Phinizy married W. S. Roberts and had one son and one daughter: John Roberts, who married but has no children; and Minnie Roberts, who married Frank Bean and has three sons.

(9) Jane Meek Phinizy married twice, firstly, Captain John Samuel Bones (by this marriage there was one son, John Phinizy Bones, who is not married and one daughter. Maria McGran Bones who married W. B. Mitchell, of Charleston, and has two daughters, Dorothy Mitchell and Frances Mitchell), and secondly Captain James Walker.

IV. SARAH PHINIZY.

Sarah Phinizy, daughter of Ferdinand Phinizy, the First, and Margaret Condow Phinizy, married Thomas Burdell. They had three sons and two daughters, namely, Thomas Burdell; Joseph Burdell, who married his cousin, Eliza McGran and Ferdinand Burdell.

V. ELIZA PHINIZY.

Eliza Phinizy, daughter of Ferdinand Phinizy, the First, and Margaret Condow Phinizy, married Thomas McGran and had two daughters, Sarah McGran, who married ——————— Jackson; and Eliza McGran who married her cousin, Joseph Burdell.

POLK FAMILY

The Progeniter of the Polk family is John Pollock, a gentleman of landed property near Glasgow, which he left to join the colony often mentioned in these pages in the North of Ireland. His son was Robert Pollock, who married Magdalen Tasker Porter, the daughter of Colonel Tasker, who was Robert Pollock's commander in Oliver Cromwell's Army and the widow of his friend and fellow officer, Colonel Porter.

When the great Protector passed away and Charles, II. came to the throne, Robert Pollock, like so many adherents of the Protector, decided to emigrate. In 1659 he "took ship" and sailed away from Ireland to the new country. He landed in Maryland and was accompanied by his wife and children. It is about this date that "Polk" was evolved from Pollock, and thereafter all his descendants so write the name. That Robert Pollock died in Maryland and that the use of Polk had become fixed, is evident as his widow signs herself, Magdalen Tasker Polk.

His eldest son, John Polk, married Joanna Knox and had William and Nancy Polk.

William Polk, son of John, son of Robert, married Priscilla Roberts and had six children, namely:

(1) Charles Polk; (2) Susan Polk, (who married an Alexander); (3) John Polk; (4) Ezekial Polk, who married first Miss Wilson and second Mrs. Leanard, widow of Major Leanard, who was Sophia Neely; (5) Thomas Polk; (6) Margaret Polk, who married ———— McRee.

Of these—(1) Charles Polk, son of William Polk and Priscilla Roberts, no record is given; (2) Susan Polk, daughter of William Polk and Priscilla Roberts Polk, of him no record is given; (4) Ezekial Polk, son of William Polk and Priscilla Roberts Polk, was born in Mecklenburg County, North Carolina. He served in the Revolution commanding a company, and was an important member of the colonies. He married twice and had eleven children. His first wife was Miss ———— Wilson, and it is probable that his children, William and Louise Polk, were by this wife. He married second Mrs. Leanard, widow of Major Leanard, of the United States Army. She was before her marriage Sophia Neely. She had eight children by Ezekial Polk.

Ezekial Polk's children were: William Polk, Louisa Polk, Mary Polk, Charles Perry Polk, Benegna Polk, Eugenia Polk, Clarissa

Governor James Knox Polk

Mrs. James Knox Polk

POLK

Polk, Samuel Polk, Matilda Polk, Thomas Polk, and Edwin Polk. There is no authority for giving them in this order of birth, as their names have been found in several different documents.

William Polk, son of Ezekial Polk, probably by his first wife, Miss Mary Wilson, married Elizabeth Dodd and had Clarissa Polk (who married a Taylor), Oliva Polk (who married D. D. Berry); Thomas Polk, Joseph Polk, Caroline Polk, (who married John Wirt); Jackson Polk, Mary Polk (who married ———— Howard); Laura Polk (who married first ———— Manly, and second ———— Taylor.)

Louisa Polk, daughter of Ezekial Polk, married Captain Charles Neely and had two sons, Colonel Rufus Polk Neely and Colonel J. J. Neely, both gallant officers in the Confederate Army. (John H. Wheeler gives this Louisa Polk as having married first ———— McNeily, and second D. D. Collier, but he must have confused her with some other Louisa Polk.

Mary Polk, daughter of Ezekial Polk, married Captain Thomas Jones Hardeman, and left children, namely: Monroe Hordeman, Mary Fentress Hardeman, Leonidas Hardeman, and William Hardeman.

Charles Perry Polk, son of Ezekial Polk, married and had children, namely: Charles E. Polk, Eugenia Polk, Perry Polk, Ann C. Polk, James Knox Polk, (not the President.)

Eugenia Polk, daughter of Ezekial Polk, married William Wood and left a daughter, Benegna Wood, who married and had children.

Clarissa Polk, daughter of Ezekial Polk, married Captain Thomas McNeal and had several children, namely: Jane McNeal (who married ———— Brown); Clara McNeal (who married ———— Fulton); Mary McNeal (who married Mark K. Roberts.)

Eugenia Polk, daughter of Ezekial Polk, married Alexander Nelson and had children, namely: Sarah, Ada, Sophia, Charles, William and Hugh Nelson. Alexander Nelson died in Bolivar, Tennessee, and the widow Eugenia Polk Nelson, resided in Corinth, Mississippi, until her death.

Matilda Polk, daughter of Ezekial Polk, married John Campbell.

Thomas Polk, son of Ezekial Polk, of him no record is given.

Edwin Polk, son of Ezekial Polk, was Speaker of the Tennessee Senate at the time of his death, in 1850. He married Octavia Jones, daughter of General Calvin Jones. Their daughter, Octavia Polk, married T. F. Brooks.

Samuel Polk, son of Ezekial Polk and his first wife, Mary Wilson, married Jane Knox, (a daughter of Captain James Knox of the Revolution. They had ten children, one of whom was James Knox Polk, born November 2, 1795; died June 15, 1849, was President of the United States.

The children of Samuel Polk and Jane Knox Polk were: James Knox Polk; Maria Polk; Marshall T. Polk; Eliza Polk; Franklin Polk; Samuel Polk, second; John Polk; Ophelia Polk; Naomi Polk, and William Polk. Of these Marie Polk (married ———— Walker and had Samuel Walker; J. Knox Walker; Marshall Walker; Andrew Walker; Jane Walker, who married a Burnett; Mary Walker, who married a Pickett; Sarah Walker, who married a Green; James Walker, unmarried, and Annie Walker, who married a Phillips.) Eliza Polk (married a Caldwell, of Richmond, and had two children, Samuel Caldwell and James Caldwell.) Naomi Polk (married a Harris and had four children, Maria Harris, Malvina Harris, Laura Harris, and Amelia Harris.) Ophelia Polk (married a Hayes and had two children, Jenny Hayes and Naomi Hayes.) William Polk (married and had three children, James K. Polk, second, William Polk and Tasker Polk.) Franklin Polk (died without issue.) John Polk (died without issue.) Samuel Polk (died without issue.) Marshall T. Polk (had two children, Eunice and Marshall Tate Polk, second.)

PRESIDENT POLK.

President James Knox Polk was born in North Carolina November 2, 1795. He was the eldest son of Samuel Polk and Jane Knox Polk. When he was eleven years of age, (1806), the family moved to what is now Maury County, Tennessee. He went, however, for his education to the University of North Carolina, where he attained a remarkable record. He graduated there in 1818, was admitted to the Bar in Tennessee in 1820, and was elected to Congress in 1825. In 1835 he was elected Speaker of the House and held this office for five sessions. In 1839 he was elected Governor of Tennessee, which state he served ably and successfully. In 1844 he was elected President of the United States. He married Miss Sarah Childress, but left no children. He died June 14, 1849, and is buried in Nashville. He left no children.

Thomas Polk, son of William Polk and Priscilla Roberts Polk, was born about 1732, and died in Charlotte, North Carolina, in 1793. He was a very prominent man in the colonies. He was Colonel of the County and he represented Mecklenburg in the Colonial Legislature. He was a member of the Assembly in 1771 and in 1775 from Mecklenburg. When the famous Mecklenburg Declaration of Independence was passed he was selected to read it to the people from the steps

POLK

of the house in which the Assembly met. He was appointed by the Provincial Congress in 1775 Colonel of the Second Battalion of Minute Men. He was appointed Brigadier General in 1771. He died in Charlotte in 1793. He married Susan Spratt and had four sons: Ezekial Polk, Charles Polk, William Polk, and James Polk, and a daughter. Of these the daughter married a Brevard. Ezekial Polk was a member of the Convention which passed the famous declaration of May 20, 1775. He served in the Revolution. No record is given of his marriage. Charles Polk married ——————— Alexander, and had a son, Thomas Independence Polk, (because of the date of his birth, May 20), who married Sarah Moore, and had Horace Moore Polk and Charles Polk, Second); of James Polk, the fourth son, no record is given. One son was killed at Cane Creek, and James may have been the one.

WILLIAM POLK.

William Polk, son of General Thomas Polk and Susan Spratt, who is called Colonel William Polk, was also a very prominent man in Revolutionary history. Wheeler gives much space to his biography. He was born July 9, 1758, in Mecklenburg County, as given by his application for a pension, and he died January 14, 1843.

He was a gallant officer of the Revolution. He was a spectator though not a member of the Assembly which at Charlotte in 1775 made the famous Declaration of Independence. He removed from Mecklenburg County to Raleigh late in life, and he died there January 14, 1834. He entered, though only seventeen years of age, the Revolution in April, 1775, as a Second Lieutenant of a Company commanded by Captain Ezekial Polk, who was his uncle, Third Regiment of South Carolina State Troops of Mounted Infantry, Colonel William Thompson commanding. He was badly wounded at Eutaw, or Cane Creek, where his brother was killed. In 1776 he was elected by the Provincial Congress of North Carolina, Major of the Ninth North Carolina Battalion. He served at Brandywine and Germantown, where he was wounded in the cheek. He went into the famous winter quarters at Valley Forge. In 1780 Governor John Rutledge, of South Carolina, appointed him Lieutenant Colonel of the Fourth and then the Third South Carolina. He married, for his first wife, Griselda Gilchrist, (daughter of Judge Thomas Gilchrist and his wife, who was Martha Jones, a daughter of Robin Jones.) They had two children, Thomas Gilchrist Polk, born in Mecklenburg County, North Carolina, February 22, 1790, and William J. Polk. Thomas Gilchrist Polk is called General Polk. He married Eloise Trotter and they had Jane (who married Dr. ——————— Bouchelle); Mary (who was the first wife of George Davis, of Wilmington.) William, Richard, Emily and Thomas Gilchrist Polk, Second; William J. Polk, (son of Colonel William Polk and his first wife, Griselda Gilchrist Polk), is called Doctor William J. Polk. He married his cousin, Mary Lunsford Long (daughter of Lunsford Long, (son of Nicholas Long, who was Commissary General of the North Carolina forces in the Revolution), and his wife, who was Rebecca Edwards Jones Long, who was a daughter of Allen Jones, who was a son of Robin Jones. Dr. William J. Polk and his wife, Mary Lunsford Long Polk, had children, one of whom was General Lucius Eugene Polk, of the Confederate States Army who was born in Salisbury, North Carolina, July 10, 1833.

Colonel William Polk married for his second wife Sarah Hawkins and had children, namely: Bishop Leonidas Polk, Mary (who married George E. Badger); Rufus Knox Polk, Alexander Hamilton Polk, George Washington Polk, Susan Polk, (who married Kenneth Raynor), and Andrew J. Polk, and others.

BISHOP POLK.

Bishop Leonidas Polk was born April 10, 1806, in Mecklenburg County, North Carolina; was a son of William Polk by his second wife, Sarah Hawkins. He entered the United States Military Academy at West Point and graduated there in 1827. He served for several years in the United States army, then feeling a strong inclination to the church, gave up his military life to become a minister in the Episcopal Church. He rose rapidly in his work and at the breaking out of the War Between the States, he was Bishop of Louisiana. The war re-awakened his martial spirit, however, and he offered his sword and his service to the Confederate States. He was commissioned a Major General and served with courage and distinction. He was killed in battle June 14, 1864.

He married in Raleigh, North Carolina, Frances Deveraux and had children, namely: Hamilton Polk, (who married a Miss Buck); Katherine Polk (who married William Gale); Frances Polk (who married P. Skipwith); Sally Polk, (who married a Blake, of South Carolina); Susan Polk (who married Dr. Joseph Jones); Lilly Polk (who married William Huger); William Mecklenburg Polk (who married a Miss Lyon, and Lucia Polk (who married Ed. Chapman.)

William Mecklenburg Polk, the last son of Bishop Leonidas Polk, was born in Ashwood, Maury County, Tennessee, August 15, 1844. He was given the name Mecklenburg in memory of the County where so many of his family lived and for the famous Declaration of Independence of Mecklenburg, with which so many members of his

POLK

family played important parts. He married Ida A. Lyon, of Alabama. He served with gallantry in the Confederate Army. His son is Frank Lyon Polk, of the Department of State. (See Gaines Family).

Miss Daisy Polk recently married a French nobleman and General, Count de Buyer-Mimeure, whose Army title however is General Marie Joseph Louis Robert deBuyer.

In marrying a Frenchman of title she followed the example of her kinswoman Antionette Polk, niece of President Polk, and a heroine of the War Between the States, who married the Marquis de Charette. Her grandson, the present Marquis de Charette, is serving in the French Army.

SEVIER FAMILY

The name Sevier, one of the best known in Tennessee's annals, was originally Xavier.

Marie de Xavier, who was heiress of that name and house in the time of the King of Navarre, was also heiress to her mother's name and titles, Azpilueta, of Spain. Her great rank and fortune made her a matrimonial prize in the Court of Navarre in the last years of the fifteenth century. Don Jon de Jasse was the favored suitor, and, as she was sole heiress to the titles and estates of both her houses, he assumed her name and rank. Of the very large family born to Don Jon and Marie de Xavier, the eldest sons took the Spanish names and titles and the youngest sons the French name and titles, Xavier. Among the younger sons was Francis, born April 7, 1506, famous now as St. Francis de Xavier. He was born, as were his brothers, in the Castle of Xavier, which is still standing, eight leagues from Pampelon. Grown to maturity he entered the priesthood, founded the Order of Jesuits, and was subsequently pronounced a Saint by the Catholic Church and is now the best known member of his family, save John Sevier, First Governor of Tennessee. St. Francis Xavier, born in 1506, was the youngest of his many brothers and sisters.

The son of Antoine of Navarre and his wife is known as Queen Jeanne d'Albert, was Henry of Navarre, afterwards King Henry IV. of France.* The eldest of the sons who assumed the name Xavier, Phillip, married the King's close kinswoman. The younger son by some records, was Valentine Xavier, a name, which like John, has remained in the family until the present time. Valentine and

---

* Centuries later a direct descendant of Don Jon de Xavier even of the same name, though in a slightly changed form, Governor John Sevier of Tennessee was to entertain in a strange land, then unknown or but dimly known, a direct descendant of that royal pair to whom he had been counsellor and friend, like Henry of Navarre, a King of France and bearing the same royal name of Bourbon. When the exiled Princes of Bourbon, one of whom became King of France afterward, came to America in the time of the French Revolution. They were sent by President George Washington on a trip through the new territory which is now Tennessee and were guests in Knoxville of Governor John Sevier in the Governor's mansion which was a crude bit of architecture no doubt to these palace-bred young scions of the royal house of Bourbon.

Phillip both espoused the protestant cause and it is said that upon the very morning of the Massacre of St. Bartholomew, August 24, 1572, that Valentine fled from France, being apprised in some way of danger. 1685, or the year of the Revocation of the Edict of Nantes is given by others as the date that Valentine Xavier fled from France to London, when so many of the Huguenots were practically exiled.

Whatever the date it was evidently a Valentine Xavier who fled from France and took up his residence in London.

Valentine Xavier who escaped from France married in London about the year 1700, but this is obviously not the Valentine who was born about 1507. Valentine Xavier married about 1700, a Miss Mary Smith and had among other children, Valentine Sevier, born 1702 and William Sevier. William and Valentine Sevier, (the name had become Anglicized in the interval between that fleeing from France and the London marriage to Mary Smith) ran away from home and sailed for America, presuably in 1740. Either they ran away some years before sailing for America and spent the intervening time elsewhere or else they came to America much earlier than 1740, for it is improbable that men of thirty-eight and forty would have run away. The family tradition, however, is that "they ran away from home while they were still very young and took ship for America." It is certain that they "took ship" about 1740.

Another family record says they were born in London in 1720 and 1722—William 1720, and Valentine, 1722, and that their father, Valentine Sevier married Mary Smith in London in 1715. Valentine Sevier's record however, has been carefully preserved and he died December 30, 1803, aged one hundred and one years, which clearly establishes his birth, 1702.

Upon landing in Baltimore, Maryland, they each married. William Sevier had a son who married and had a son, William Pierre Sevier who married Lucretia Weller. This William Pierre Sevier, also ran away, which must have became a family habit by this time, and fought in the War of 1812 when he was only a lad. He was taken prisoner and was in the Dartmoor Prison at the time of the Massacre. It is told of him that his friend, Granville Sharpe Townsend was shot dead in the arms of Sevier who subsequently named a son for him.

William Pierre Sevier and his wife Lucretia Weller Sevier had among other children Granville Townsend Sevier, noted above, and Theodore Francis Sevier who married Mary Benton Douglas and had among other children: Frank Sevier (who died unmarried); Colonel Granville Sevier, Second (who is unmarried and serving in the United States Army); O'Neil Sevier; Jessie Sevier (who married J. S. deBelle and has Jessie deBelle); and Louise Sevier (who married Frederick Giddings and has Elizabeth Marshall Giddings, Mary Douglas

Giddings, Helen Marshall Giddings, died young, Louise Sevier Giddings, Rose H. Giddings, and Frederick Giddings, Junior).

Valentine Sevier, Second of the name of record and perhaps fourth or fifth even, married shortly after he landed in Baltimore, a "Baltimore lady" as the quaint old records say, some of them not mentioning her name. She was, however, Joanna Goade, granddaughter of John Goade or Goode, who emigrated by way of Barbadoes in 1650. Valentine and Joanna Goode Sevier moved from Maryland, following the train of emigration to the South, and settled first, in Culpepper County, Virginia, and then in Rockingham (Augusta) County, Virginia, early in the decade between 1740 and 1750, for John Sevier, their eldest son, was born there September 23, 1745.

Valentine Sevier and Joanna Goade Sevier had seven children, namely:

John Sevier.
Valentine Sevier, Third.
Robert Sevier.
Joseph Sevier.
Catherine Sevier.
Polly Sevier.
Abraham Sevier.
There was possibly another daughter.

After the death of Joanna Goade Sevier, Valentine Sevier, Second, emigrated to "the Mountains" in 1772, where his famous son, John Sevier, had preceeded him and thereafter his history and that of his sons is identified with what is now Tennessee.

Valentine Sevier, Second, died in "the Mountains," December 30, 1803, aged one hundred and one years. It is by this statement that we know his birth in London in 1702.

COLONEL VALENTINE SEVIER

Colonel Valentine Sevier, Third, son of the foregoing Valentine, Second and Joanna Goade Sevier, was born in Rockingham County, Virginia, in 1747. He served in the Revolution like other members of his family and was Sergeant at the Battle of Point Pleasant. He commanded a company at Cedar Springs, Musgrove's Mill and King's Mountain. He was Colonel of Militia, first sheriff of Washington County, Tennessee, and Justice of the Peace of Washington County. He had moved from Virginia to Tennessee with other members of his family between the year, 1770 and 1780, and after the Revolution he moved again to Red River where Clarksville, Tennessee, now stands, where he died February 23, 1800. His widow survived him many

SEVIER

years, dying in 1844, when she was one hundred and four years of age, showing that she was born in 1740 and that she was seven years older than her husband, if the record has been properly set down. They had several children. Their sons, Robert Sevier and William Sevier, were killed by Indians at Clarksville, in January, 1792, while on their way to join James Robertson's forces at Nashville. A third son, Valentine Sevier, Fourth in the direct line, was killed also by Indians in January, 1792, but not on the same day or place. In relating the tragic event to his brother, Governor John Sevier, Valentine Sevier writes of his great loss but speaks of other sons, "small ones."

One of these "small ones" was named John Sevier for his distinguished uncle, John Sevier, and he had a son, Ambrose Hundley Sevier. This Ambrose Hundley Sevier was born in Greene County, Tennessee, November 10, 1801, moved to Arkansas and became Senator from that state and Minister to Mexico to negotiate the Treaty of Peace.

Valentine Sevier, Third and his wife ———— Sevier had seven children, five sons and two daughters, namely: Robert Sevier, William Sevier, Valentine Sevier, Fourth, Joseph Sevier, John Sevier, Rebecca Sevier and one other daughter. Robert, Valentine and William Sevier were killed by Indians as related above. Joseph Sevier was also killed by Indians, November 11, 1794. On the same date Rebecca Sevier was scalped by Indians, but probably recovered. John Sevier was the only one of Valentine's sons who escaped massacre by the Indians.

CAPTAIN ROBERT SEVIER

Captain Robert Sevier, son of Valentine Sevier, Second and Joanna Goade Sevier was younger than his brothers, John and Valentine, Third, and was probably born about 1749, in Rockingham County, Virginia. He accompanied his father to the Mountains in 1772. He was in the Battle of King's Mountain, October 7, 1780, and was there mortally wounded. He was thought to have been killed out right, but lived nine days. Captain Robert Sevier married Keziah Robertson, daughter of Charles Robertson, one of the two famous brothers, Charles and James Robertson, and had two sons (I) Major Charles Sevier and (II) Valentine Sevier.

(I) Major Charles Sevier married Elizabeth Witt. He served under General Andrew Jackson and had fourteen children, namely:

(1) Robert Sevier whose family is all dead.
(2) Valentine Sevier married Anna Mourney.
(3) John Quinturf Sevier, who married three times, firstly a Henderson, secondly, a Bisckle, thirdly, Sarah Sangster and had at least

two sons, John Bisckle Sevier and Dr. Charles Henry Sevier who married Cora E. Anderson and had two sons, Charles Anderson Sevier, of Jackson, Tennessee, and Dr. John Henry Sevier, of Brownsville, Tennessee.

(4) ———— Sevier, a daughter of Major Charles Sevier married a Russell and had a son Robert Russell, a soldier in the Mexican War and later in the Confederate Army.

I have not the names of the other ten children of Major Charles Sevier.

II Valentine Sevier, second son of Captain Robert Sevier and his wife, Keziah Robertson Sevier, was clerk of the Court at Greeneville for fifty-two years. He married twice, firstly in 1804, Nancy Dinwiddie, by whom he had twelve children, and secondly ———— Cannon by whom he had two children. His children were:

(1) Jane Sevier, married about the year 1834, James H. Vance of Kingsport, Tennessee, and had Charles Robertson Vance (who married Margaret Nelson and had James Isaac Vance, Joseph Anderson Vance, Charles Robertson Vance, Second, Margaret Jane Vance, and Rebecca M. Vance); Maria C. Vance (who married John R. King, of Leesburg, Virginia); Anna Elizabeth Vance (who died young); Keziah Vance; James N. Vance (who married Fannie Miller); Nannie Vance; Joseph Vance (who married Mattie Fain and had Charles Rutledge Vance); and Johnnie Vance.

(2) Robert Sevier, son of Valentine Sevier and Nancy Dinwiddie Sevier was educated at West Point, served in the United States Army and died in Missouri. He married Ann Hopkins Sibley.

(3) Charles Sevier, son of Valentine Sevier and Nancy Dinwiddie, married Elizabeth Briscoe and died in Mississippi, leaving two children, Thomas Sevier and Nannie Sevier.

(4) David Sevier, son of Valentine Sevier and Nancy Dinwiddie Sevier, was Clerk and Master at Greeneville for many years. He married Annie Netherland, daughter of George W. Netherland.

(5) William Robertson Sevier, son of Valentine Sevier and Nancy Dinwiddie Sevier was a physician. He married firstly Martha Ellen Cunningham, daughter of Dr. Samuel Cunningham, eminent physician and First President of the East Tennessee and Virginia and Georgia Railway, now a part of the Southern System, and married secondly, Lucy Evans.

(6) James Sevier, son of Valentine Sevier and Nancy Dinwiddie Sevier married twice, firstly Jane Simpson and secondly Mrs. Eva Moore Neil.

(7) Edward Sevier married Mary Neilson Garrett and resided in Asheville, North Carolina.

SEVIER

(8) Joseph Sevier, son of Valentine Sevier and Nancy Dinwidide Sevier, married Nannie T. Broyles and lived in West Tennessee. He served in the Confederate Army and was killed near Atlanta, July 22, 1864.

(9) Keziah Sevier daughter of Valentine Sevier and Nancy Dinwiddie Sevier married, George Jones, of Greeneville, Tenn.

(10) Isabel Sevier, daughter of Valentine Sevier and Nancy Dinwiddie Sevier married Frank A. McCorkle and had at least one daughter, Nancy McCorkle, who married Cornelius Coffin, and had at least one daughter, Isabella Coffin, who married Thomas Lanier Williams and has Ella Williams (who is not married and is now serving her country in France); Isabel Williams (who married William Gannaway Brownlow, Second, and has no children); and Cornelius Coffin Williams (who married Edwina Dakin and lives in St. Louis and has Rose Isabella Williams and Thomas Lanier Williams, Second).

(11) Elizabeth Sevier, daughter of Valentine Sevier and Nancy Dinwiddie Sevier, married Reverend John Whitfield Cunningham.

(12) Susan Sevier, daughter of Valentine Sevier and Nancy Dinwiddie Sevier, never married, though she lived to a very great age.

(13) Charles Sevier, son of Valentine Sevier and his second wife,——————— Cannon Sevier married Julia Brown.

(14) Henry Sevier, son of Valentine Sevier and his second wife, ———————Cannon Sevier.

JOSEPH SEVIER, SON OF VALENTINE SEVIER, SECOND.

Joseph Sevier, son of Valentine Sevier, Second. and his wife Joanna Goade Sevier, was born in Rockingham County, Virginia, about 1751. He served in the Battle of King's Mountain. (Draper Page 266.) I have no other record of him. He is frequently confused with his namesake, Governor John Sevier's son, Joseph Sevier, who also served in the Battle of King's Mountain.

ABRAHAM SEVIER, SON OF VALENTINE SEVIER, SECOND.

Abraham Sevier, son of Valentine Sevier, Second and his wife, Joanna Goade Sevier, was born like his brothers in Rockingham County, Virginia, and was probably the youngest, probably born before 1760. He also went with his father "to the Mountains" in 1772. He fought also in the Battle of King's Mountain, the youngest of the five Sevier brothers, John, Valentine, Third, Joseph, Robert and Abraham.

CATHERINE, SEVIER, DAUGHTER OF VALENTINE. SEVIER, SECOND.

Catherine Sevier, daughter of Valentine Sevier, Second, and his wife Joanna Goade Sevier, was born in Rockingham County, Virginia,

POLLY SEVIER, DAUGHTER OF VALENTINE SEVIER, SECOND.

Polly Sevier, daughter of Valentine Sevier, Second, and his wife, Joanna Goade Sevier, was born in Rockingham County, Virginia, married William Matlock.

GOVERNOR JOHN SEVIER.

John Sevier, son of Valentine Sevier, Second, and Joanna Goade Sevier, was born in Rockingham, Virginia, September 23, 1745. He was the oldest child and the most distinguished.

He attended the schools of Rockingham and when he was sixteen finished his scholastic education at the Academy near Fredericksburg. He probably had the usual adventures of youth in a pioneer community and at least one story is told of him that hinted of the romance that seemed to accompany his life unto its end. When he was a lad in Rockingham he fell into a mill race and would have been drowned, but two young ladies rescued him; One of these young ladies subsequently became the wife of Colonel Matthews, afterwards Governor Matthews of Georgia.

Just after he had finished his education at Fredericksburg, and before he was seventeen years old, John Sevier married Sarah Hawkins, daughter of Joseph Hawkins and granddaughter of Samuel Hawkins, who was one of four brothers that came to America in 1665. Sarah Hawkins was probably close to his own age. This was in the fall of 1761, when as a matter of fact he was just past sixteen! A few years after his marriage he was attracted by the stories told of life in the "Mountains" as the new settlement in the future Tennessee was called, though it was supposed at that time to be a part of Virginia and was only afterwards discovered to be North Carolina territory. He made the hazardous trip to the "Mountains" and was still more charmed with the prospect. That visit fired his interest and though he returned to Rockingham County to his wife and children, he never again called it home. He was from then a citizen and a leader of

Governor John Sevier

the new settlement. Sarah Hawkins Sevier, however, never left the old home. There her children were born and there in January or February, 1780, she died. She bore her husband ten children, five sons and five daughters, all of whom lived and left descendants, many of them naming daughters for her so that Sarah is a favorite and frequent name in the family to this day.

John Sevier first settled at Newmarket in what is now Tennessee and became famous almost at once among the Mountain people as a leader and as an Indian fighter. Before he was thirty he was Captain of the State Militia in 1772.

From Newmarket he moved to the Wautauga Settlement. Here when he and a few other bold spirits resented the apparent neglect of North Carolina, they organized the State of Franklin, the Free and Independent State of Franklin! John Sevier was its first and only Governor and Samuel Wear its Clerk. The little State was short lived. He was subsequently the first Governor of the State of Tennessee and when he had served six years and by the constitution was disbarred from another successive term the people waited two years and triumphantly elected him for another six years! He was one of the great Captains of King's Mountain and indeed assembled the men of Wautauga in that first great meeting when a draft had to be employed to see which of them should *not* go to war! Which of them should stay at home to protect the women and children. He had four brothers, Robert, Valentine, Joseph and Abraham Sevier, and two sons, Joseph and James Sevier, at King's Mountain.

It is an interesting fact that seven Seviers served in the Battle of King's Mountain, Governor John Sevier and his four brothers, Valentine (Third), Robert, Joseph and Abraham and his two sons, Joseph and James. No other family can show so many participants though the Isbell Family comes next with its record of six brothers in the Battle, John, Livingston, Thomas, Francis, James (Second) and William Isbell, the last named being but fifteen years of age and the youngest soldier in the Battle. (See Howard Family.)

Next in number is the Shelby family with a father and three sons, Evan Shelby, Senior, Evan Shelby, Junior, Colonel Isaac Shelby and Captain Moses Shelby.

He was in Congress from 1811 until his death in 1815, while he was still serving his country, almost a life time of service and in years more than forty. His descendants are eligible to the Societies of the Revolution, 1812, and King's Mountain.

August 14, 1780 John Sevier married Catherine Sherrill, daughter of Samuel Sherrill, of whom a chronicler says "she could out run, out jump, walk more erect, and ride more gracefully than any other female in all the Mountains round about or on the continent at large."

SEVIER

John Sevier's life is as romantic and thrilling as that of any hero of fiction. Adventure and thrills followed each other in succession. Even his marriage with Bonnie Kate Sherrill was like a chapter from romance. Pursued by Indians she leapt almost from their grasp to the stockade of the Block House into her future husband's arms as he cried to her "Jump, my Bonnie Kate, Jump!"

It is not surprising that Bonnie Kate whom he had saved and christened in a breath should attract him for his second spouse, and Bonnie Kate on more than one occasion saved her husband's life in turn. Once a woman, whom she had befriended, though the wife of a renegade, confessed to Bonnie Kate a plot upon the Governor's life and he was saved, and again, his release or rather his escape from the North Carolina authorities was said to be of Madame Sevier's planning. She was the daughter of Samuel Sherrill who is said to have been in the Battle of King's Mountain and she had a brother, George Sherrill, who is said to have been in the Battle of King's Mountain, and two other brothers, Uriah Sherrill and John Sherrill.

It was during his marriage to Catherine Sevier while he was Governor of Tennessee that he entertained in Knoxville the young French Princes, descendants of his ancestor Don Jon de Xavier's royal friends, the King and Queen of Navarre.

Governor John Sevier was universally beloved. He possessed a magnetism, and a charm. that drew all people to him. Even the Indians who feared him adored him and treated him as a god. He possessed extraordinary beauty and men have said that in a crowd of five thousand he was instantly known by his majestic carriage and deep sparkling blue eyes set in a noble face.

He died near Fort Decatur, Georgia, September 24, 1815, being just one day past the alloted three-score years and ten.

His body was removed many years later to Knoxville and lies now beneath a handsome monument in the Court yard of that city where he dwelt as Governor, almost as King in the new Country.

In all the time that John Sevier served his country he served without pay and even equipped and maintained his companies and regiments. Sometimes he was helped in this by the other pioneers who were well to do, but often the entire expense fell upon him. Only in his last years was he an enlisted member of the United States Army and therefore on the pay roll. During all the other years his service was purely voluntary.

John Sevier had eighteen children and all of them but one left descendants. By the first wife, Sarah Hawkins Sevier, there were ten children; and by the second wife, Catherine Sherrill Sevier, there were eight children.

NOTABLE SOUTHERN FAMILIES

The names were given to Dr. Lyman C. Draper (author of King's Mountain and Its Heroes) in a letter from George Washington Sevier in 1839. This letter is to be found with the valuable Draper Manuscripts of the Historical Library at Madison, Wisconsin.

Catherine Sherrill Sevier seems to have devoted herself to the children of the first wife and to have been very much beloved by them. More than one of them named a daughter for her.

She survived her husband many years, going after his death to Middle Tennessee to live upon the magnificent estate of 57,000 acres with her children and grandchildren around her and in the neighborhood many of her brothers and sisters-in-law. At the age of eighty-two years she went with a favorite son, Samuel Sevier, to Russellville, Alabama, where he had established a home, to spend the remainder of her days though they were not many, for she died in the same year, October 7, 1836, in Russellville and is there buried. She was born 1754.

She had eight children. The name Catherine is a most frequent one throughout the connection.

Children of Governor John Sevier, by his first wife, Sarah Hawkins Sevier:

I Joseph Sevier, married an Indian.
II James Sevier, married Nancy Conway.
III John Sevier, Second, married Sophia Garrette.
IV Betsey Sevier, married Major William H. Clark.
V Nancy Sevier, married Walter King.
VI Rebecca Sevier, married ———Waddell.
VII Sarah Hawkins Sevier, married Judge Benjamin Brown.
VIII Mary Ann Sevier, married Joshua Corlin, perhaps Corland.
IX Valentine Sevier.
X Richard Sevier.

Children of Governor John Sevier, by his second wife, Catherine Sherrill Sevier:

XI Ruth Sevier, married Colonel Joseph Sparks, and Daniel Vertner.
XII Catherine Sevier married Archibald Rhea and ——— Campbell.
XIII George Washington Sevier married Catherine Heatherly Chambers.
XIV Joanna Goade Sevier married Joseph H. Wendel.
XV. Samuel Sevier.
XVI Robert Sevier.
XVII Polly Preston Sevier married William Overstreet, Junior.
XVIII Eliza Conway Sevier married Major William McClellan.

SEVIER

I JOSEPH SEVIER

Joseph Sevier, first child of Governor John Sevier and his first wife, Sarah Hawkins Sevier, was born in Rockingham County in 1762, as is shown by the fact that at the Battle of King's Mountain (October 7, 1780) he was just eighteen years old.

Joseph Sevier was with his father, General Sevier, in many of his Indian Battles and Campaigns. At the Battle of King's Mountain he was the last man to cease firing, disobeying the command to cease, crying, "They have killed my father! They have killed my father!"* It was his uncle, Robert Sevier, however, who had fallen and was mortally wounded.

Joseph Sevier married a Cherokee Indian girl, Elizabeth Lowry. Elizabeth Lowry's father was George Lowry, a Scotchman, and her mother was Octlootsa, daughter of the great chief, Oconstota.

Joseph Sevier, when he was only nineteen, was employed by Governor Blount to keep watch on hostile movements. After Joseph Sevier's death at an early age his widow married John Walker, supposed by many to be an Englishman, though Governor Blount calls him a half breed. A son of this marriage was John Walker, Junior, who eloped with Elizabeth Meigs.

Joseph Sevier and Elizabeth Lowry Sevier had at least two daughters, namely:

(1) Margaret Sevier.
(2) Eliza Sevier.

(1) Margaret Sevier, married Gideon Morgan and had Cherokee America Morgan who married Andrew Lewis Rogers and had Connell Rogers, (who married for his first wife Florence Nash and had Ell Nash Rogers and Gertrude Whitman Rogers and married for his second wife, Kate Cunningham and had Marion Sevier Rogers, Lewis Byrne Rogers, Howard Cunningham Rogers and Connell Rogers, Junior); Andrew Lewis Rogers, Junior; Hugh Morgan Rogers, John Otto Rogers; Lucy Rogers; Paul Rogers; and Clifford Rogers.

(2) Eliza Sevier married Templin Ross, of Pennsylvania and had two children, Hannah Ross and Joe Ross. Eliza Sevier Ross and Templin Ross both died of cholera at the time of the emigration in 1836. Their children were cared for by some people in Arkansas.

---

*This story is also told of James Sevier, having evidently happened to one or the other of Governor Sevier's sons.

NOTABLE SOUTHERN FAMILIES

II MAJOR JAMES SEVIER

James Sevier, the second son and second child of Governor John Sevier, by his first wife, Sarah Hawkins Sevier, was born in Augusta County, Virginia, October 25, 1764. He joined his father in "the Mountains" when he was still a lad and was with him in many of the Indian campaigns, accompanying his brother, Joseph Sevier, who was two years his senior. He was not quite sixteen when the Wautauga men assembled for the campaign against Ferguson which resulted in the Battle of King's Mountain. He was too young to be included in the list of men to go or men to stay at home and protect the women and children, but his stepmother, Catherine Sherrill Sevier, interceded with Governor Sevier, saying, "Mr. Sevier, here is another of your sons who wants to go with you." The Governor permitted him to accompany the party and found a horse for him. He was thus one of the two youngest participants in the battle, the other being William Isbell who was only fifteen years old.

Governor Sevier gave to James Sevier the field glasses which General Patrick Ferguson wore in the Battle. His grandson gave them to the Historical Society of Tennessee.

Major Sevier afterwards won his military title by a long and honorable career in the service of the state. He was Clerk of the Court of Washington County, Tennessee, for forty-seven years. He lived near Jonesboro, Tennessee, and died there January 21, 1847.

He married March 25, 1789, Nancy Conway, who was the daughter of Colonel Henry Conway, born 1749, died 1812. Nancy Conway Sevier was born March 22, 1772.

They had eleven children, namely.

(1) Elizabeth Conway Sevier, born July 9, 1790.
(2) Sarah Hundley Sevier, born July 22, 1792.
(3) Maria Antoinette Sevier, born May 12, 1794, died two years later.
(4) Minerva Grainger Sevier, born May 30, 1796.
(5) Pamelia Hawkins Sevier, born March 15, 1798.
(6) Susannah Brown Sevier, born June 25, 1800.
(7) Elbert Franklin Sevier, born September 17, 1802.
(8) Elbridge Gerry Sevier, born March 19, 1805.
(9) Clarissa Carter Sevier, born April 9, 1807.
(10) Louisa Maria Sevier, born December 16, 1811.
(11) Mary Malvina Sevier, born April 4, 1814.

Of the foregoing:

(1) Elizabeth Conway Sevier married James S. Johnston, March 8, 1810.

SEVIER

(2) Sarah Hundley Sevier, second child of Major James Sevier and Nancy Conway Sevier, was born July 22, 1792. She married January 11, 1810, Hugh Douglas Hale (born August 12, 1787, in Farquahr County Virginia). He was a son of Phillip and Catherine Douglas Hale. The children of Hugh Douglas Hale and Sarah Hundley Sevier Hale were:

(1.) James W. Hale
(2) Phillip Perry Hale
(3) Eliza Jane Hale
(4) Catherine Anne Hale
(5) William Dickson Hale
(6) Lemuel Johnson Hale
(7) Sarah Amanda Hale
(8) Laura Evelyn Hale
(9) Hugh Douglas Hale, Second
(10) Franklin Sevier Hale

Of the foregoing:

1. James W. Hale, son of Hugh Douglas Hale and Sarah Hundley Sevier Hale died Sept. 9th, 1842, unmarried. It is told that he was engaged in his young manhood to Miss Taylor, an aunt of Robert L. Taylor, former Governor of Tennessee, and that she was struck by lightning at a Camp Meeting and instantly killed. This is said to have grieved him so deeply that shortly afterward he died.

2. Phillip Perry Hale, son of Hugh Douglas Hale and Sarah Hundley Sevier Hale married Caroline Susan Gullege. Their children were: (1) Sarah Hale, (who married L. B. Snyder and died without issue); (2) Thomas Hale (who died young); (3), Elizabeth Hale (who died young); (4), Franklin Sevier Hale (who died young); (5) Laura Hale (who married Lieutenant Hundley Maloney and died without issue); (6) Fred Douglas Hale (who married first Theodosia Bell and had: Fred P. Hale, Frances Hale, Harriet Susan Hale, John Weller Hale, Josephine Hale and Annie Lee Hale, and married second, Mary Neal and had: Ruth Sevier Hale, Annie Lee Hale, and Elizabeth Hale; and married third Minnie Edwards and had; Phillip Hale, Mildred Hale, Hugh Douglas Hale and James Hale). (7) Anna Eliza Hale (who married Frank Gottseilig and had two children: Bertha Gottseilig and Anna Lauria Gottseilig); (8) Joseph Hale (who married Laura Beauchamp and had three children William Hale, Joseph Hale, Second, and Carolina Susan Hale); (9) Hugh Lemuel Hale (who married Emma Wilkinson and had three children: Philip Hale, Douglas Hale and Eugenia Hale); (10) Phillip Thomas Hale (who married Lena Lyle Bolinger and habd six children: Thomas

NOTABLE SOUTHERN FAMILIES

Farris Hale, William Roy Hale, Phillip Theodore Hale, David Ward Hale, Earl Douglas Hale and Franklin Sevier Hale).

(3) Eliza Jane Hale, daughter of Hugh Douglas Hale and Sarah Hundley Sevier Hale, married David Wendel Carter and had eight children: (1) James William Carter (who married Mary Lou Tindal and had children: Mary Weller Carter, Janie Carter and John Tindel Carter); (2) Alfred Moore Carter (who married first Chassie King and had one daughter, Maud Carter, who married Ellis Crymbel and had two sons, Carter Crymbel and Ellis Crymbel, Second. Alfred Moore Carter married for his second wife Nannie Zimmerman whom he had no children); (3) David Wendal Carter, Second (who married Cornelia Keith and has four children, Lieutenant Keith Carter, David Wendel Carter, Third, and Anne Frazier Carter, Lieutenant Douglas Carter): Stanley Carter; Cornelia Carter; Franklin Alexander Carter (who married Annie Laird and has one daughter, Davie); Ella Douglas Carter (who married Dr. Samuel W. Rhea and has two sons, Joseph Carter Rhea (who married Troupe Davis) and James Wendel Rhea who married Helen Haynes and has one son, James Wendel Rhea, Second).

(4) Catherine Anne Hale married Dr. Porter Jarnagin. Their children were: (1) Dr. John Sevier Jarnagin (who married Katie Hubbard and had two children, Estelle Jarnagin who married Blair Naff and Mary Kate Jarnagin who married Walter Harris); Mary Jarnagin (who married David Swaggerty and had one daughter Katie Swaggerty married Lome McSwain); Dr. Joseph Jarnagin (who married Ida Lester and had Nanie Lester who married Clifford Farmer and had four children; Joseph Jarnagin Farmer, Clifford Corbin Farmer, William James Farmer and Catherine Hale Farmer): Carolina Jarnagin (who married Edward Markwalter and had two children, Edward Markwalter, Second, and Rebecca Markwalter); Lester Jarnagin (who married Daisy Cason); Itie Jarnagin (who married Milton Lufborrow and had two children, Caroline Lufborrow and Charmian Lufborrow).

(5) William Dickson Hale, son of Hugh Douglas Hale and Sarah Hundley Sevier Hale, died young.

(6) Lemuel Johnson Hale, son of Hugh Douglas Hale and Sarah Hundley Sevier Hale, married Martha Powell and had children: Mary Hale, Catherine Hale, Sarah Hale and Leila Hale who married Joseph Green.

(7) Sarah Amanda Hale, daughter of Hugh Douglas Hale and Sarah Hundley Sevier Hale, married Charles W. Meek. Their children were James Hale Meek (who married Jennie Hensley and had one son James W. Meek who married Carolina Corinne McWilliams and has one son James W. Meek, Second); Daniel Kenny Meek (who died

young); William Blair Meek (who married Martha Powers and has two daughters, Vesta Sevier Meek, who married Robert Lee Davis and has one child Katherine Davis, and Iva Douglas Meek who is unmarried); Florine Cornelia Meek (who married James P. Evans and has one son Hubert Evans who married Clara ——————, and a daughter Lula Evans who married William James for her first husband and for her second husband married Dr. Paul Gheering and died at the birth of a daughter): Ida Sevier Meek (who married Jacob Orville Lotspeich and had children Claude Meek Lotspeich, who married Helen Gibbons and had three children: Henry Gibbons Lotspeich, Margaret Sevier Lotspeich and Edgar Hale Lotspeich; Roy Douglas Lotspeich, who married Ethel Weir and had children: Katherine Mildred Lotspeich, Jacob Orville Lotspeich, Second, Helen Lotspeich, Douglas Weir Lotspeich; Edgar Sevier Lotspeich married Ruth Moore and had children: Caroline Lotspeich, Alberta Lotspeich, Edgar Sevier Lotspeich and Robert Orvill Lotspeich); Ella Douglas Meek married Charles E. Lothrop and has two children, Ida Meek Lothrop and Douglas B. Lothrop who married Ruth Dooley. Charles W. Meek married Adah Jariel, and had two children: Joseph Meek and Sarah Meek. Franklin Hale Meek married Almena McG. Smith and had two children: Charles W. Meek died young and Bathurst Lee Smith. Joseph M. Meek married Alma Burt Hughes and has two children James Hughes Meek and Sarabel Meek.

(8) Laura Evelyn Hale, daughter of Hugh Douglas Hale and Sarah Hundley Sevier Hale, married Thomas E. Gosnell and had children: Lemuel Ward Gosnell (who married Mary Elizabeth Hill and had children: Myroyn Aydlett Gosnell, Katherine Lisserand Hill Gosnell, Clara J. Gosnell and Munsey Ward Gosnell. Katherine Lisserand Gosnell married Dr. Sterling P. Martin and had Sterling P. Martin, Second, and two daughters: Clara J. Gosnell married Dr. Davis and has one child, Lemuel Ward Gosnell married for his second wife, Mrs. Cullie Oglesby); Matthew Gosnell (who died young); and Franklin Gosnell (who is unmarried).

(9) Hugh Douglas Hale, Second, son of Hugh Douglas Hale, first, and Sarah Hundley Sevier Hale, married Sarah Vance, a sister of Governor Zebulon Vance of North Carolina and had three children: Margaret Hale, Sarah Hale and Franklin Hale.

(10) Franklin Sevier Hale, son of Hugh Douglas Hale and Sarah Hundley Sevier Hale, was killed in the battle of Franklin, in the war between the States.

SEVIER

(4) Minerva Grainger Sevier married April 30, 1816, John Nelson, who died 1830.

(5) Pamelia Hawkins Sevier (died 1822) married May 6, 1817, Alexander M. Nelson (who died in 1821.) They had a son, Alexander Nelson, Junior, who was born July 23, 1820.

(6) Susanna Brown Sevier married Richard A. Purdom, November 26, 1818. They had a son, James Alexander Purdom, born November 12, 1819.

(7) Elbert Franklin Sevier married for his first wife, Matilda Powell, August 9, 1832, and had Elbert Powell Sevier (who married and had a son, James Sevier) and a daughter Sarah Sevier, who died of cholera with her mother Matilda Powell Sevier, in Knoxville in 1854. Elbert Franklin Sevier married for his second wife, Eliza James, a daughter of Reverend Jesse James, of Chattanooga, and had a son, James Sevier.

(8) Elbridge Gerry Sevier, married November 13, 1827, Mary Caroline Brown, born February 27, 1810, daughter of Thomas Brown and Mary McElwee Brown. They had: Thomas Brown Sevier; Henry Clay Sevier (who married Mary J. Tipton and had one son, Dr. Sevier, who lives in Kansas City); Rowena Jane Sevier (who married H. W. von Aldehoff and has a son, John Sevier Aldehoff, who makes his home in Dallas, Texas). James Sevier, (who was known as Judge, lived in Kingston, Tennessee, and never married); Elbert Franklin Sevier, second, (who lived in Chattanooga, married Bettie Taylor and had Taylor Sevier, unmarried; Edith Sevier, died young; Ethel Sevier, died young; Hazel Sevier, died young; and Evelyn Sevier, who married Gray Gentry and has one son, Fenton Allen Gentry, Junior); John Elbridge Sevier; Charles Bascom Sevier (who married Alice Zedder, lives in Harriman, Tennessee, and has one daughter, Mary Catherine Sevier; who married Thomas T. Reimer). Samuel Conway Sevier, who lives in Kingston, Tennessee, and is unmarried), and Mary Sevier (who died unmarried).

(9) Clarissa Carter Sevier married John Jones, May 7, 1822, and had at least one son, who had a son, Thomas E. Jones, of Knoxville, and he has a son, Derrell E. Jones.

(10) Louisa Maria Sevier married James H. Jones, October 16, 1827.

Five children are entered in the Bible, evidently born to the above couples, but with no statement as to which couple are the parents. They are:

Ann Eliza Jones, born July 5, 1829.
William Elbert Franklin Jones.
Sevier James Elbridge Jones, born February 20, 1823.
Sarah Ann Jones, born January, 1825.
James Sevier Jones, born September, 1830.

Though by the dates of birth, Sevier James Elbridge Jones and Sarah Ann Jones are children of Clarissa Carter Sevier Jones and her husband, John Jones.

(11) Mary Malvina Sevier married James Stuart, July 2, 1829. They had a daughter, Mary Stuart, who married John Howard, of Knoxville.

III JOHN SEVIER, JUNIOR.

Major John Sevier was the third child and third son of Governor John Sevier and his first wife Sarah Hawkins Sevier. He was born June 20, 1766, in New Market Virginia, and was given his father's full name. After his mother's death in 1780, he joined his father in the new home in the Mountains where a few months later his father married Catherine Sherrill for his second wife.

John Sevier, Junior, accompanied his father on several of his Indian campaigns, though he was too young to go into the Battle of King's Mountain. He was elected Reading and Engrossing Clerk of the first Convention of the State of Tennessee.

He married Sophia Garette and had at least two daughters, namely:

(1) Anna Maria Sevier.
(2) Louise Rebecca Sevier.

(1) Anna Sevier married Henry Hoss, of Jonesboro, Tennessee. They had six children: Dora Hoss; Elijah Embree Hoss; Archibald Hoss; Sophie Hoss; John Isaac Hoss and Mattie Hoss.

Of these:

Dora Hoss married Samuel J. Kirkpatrick and had ten children: namely, Minnie Kirkpatrick (who married Charles Kirkland and had five children: Isabel Kirkland, Winifred Kirkland, Jessie Kirkland, Mollie Kirkland and William Kirkland); Hugh Henry Kirkpatrick (who married Anna Belle Murphey and has two children, Mildred Kirkpatrick, who married Max Maloney, also a descendant of John Sevier through James Sevier and has a little daughter, Anna Belle Maloney, and Hugh Henry Kirkpatrick, Junior); Paul White Kirkpatrick (who married Vesta Pennington and has one child Mary Har-

SEVIER

ris Kirkpatrick); Samuel Sevier Kirkpatrick (who married Anna Marie Panhurst and has no children, Jessie Eugenia Kirkpatrick (who married John Henry Bowman and has two children, William Bowman and John Henry Bowman, Junior, who are unmarried); Archibald Hoss Kirkpatrick (who married Bessie Cruikshanks and had four children: Anna Kirkpatrick, William Kirkpatrick, Dorothy Kirkpatrick and Bessie Kirkpatrick who are unmarried); Anna Kirkpatrick (who died unmarried); William Reeves Kirkpatrick (who died unmarried); Mary Kirkpatrick (who died young); and Charles Prescott Kirkpatrick (who married Essie Annie Schuessler and is now a Lieutenant in the United States Army in France).

Elijah Embree Hoss, son of Anna Sevier Hoss and Henry Hoss, was born in Washington County, Tennessee, April 14, 1849, and is now Bishop of the Methodist Episcopal Church, South, for Oklahoma. He married Abbie Clark, of Knoxville, and has three children: Mary Hoss (who married John Headman, of Philadelphia, and has two children, a son, John Headman, Junior, and a daughter, Embree Hoss Headman); Dr. Sessler Hoss (who married Irene Morrow, of Nashville; see Luttrell and Armstrong Families, and has no children); and Elijah Embree Hoss, Second (who married Blanche Divine, of Chattanooga, and has one son, Elijah Embree Hoss, Third).

Archibald Hoss married Allie Susong and has three children: Henry Hoss, Anna Hoss and Dorothy Hoss, all of whom are unmarried.

Sophie Hoss married George D. French, of Morristown, and has two children, Dora French and Abbie French (who married ——— Taylor).

John Isaac Hoss died unmarried.

Mattie Hoss married P. H. Prince and lived in Arkansas. She had two children, Anna Prince and William Prince.

(2) Louise Rebecca Sevier, second daughter of John Sevier, Second, and his wife, Sophia Garrette Sevier, married Byrd Brown and had at least one daughter, Louise Sevier Brown, who married Shelby M. Deaderick, see Deaderick Family, and had a son, Wallace Deaderick.

IV ELIZABETH (BETSEY) SEVIER.

Elizabeth or Betsey Sevier, daughter of Governor John Sevier and his first wife Sarah Hawkins Sevier, was born in Rockingham County, Virginia, about 1768. She married Major William H. Clark, a veteran of King's Mountain and a distinguished soldier. They had several children, namely: Sarah Hawkins Clark, named for the mother and a favorite sister, Elizabeth Clark, John Clark and perhaps Ruth Clark.

Possibly Elizabeth Sevier Clark died shortly after the birth of her daughter, Sarah Hawkins Clark as that child was raised in the home of her grandfather, Governor John Sevier and his second wife, Catherine Sherrill Sevier, and when she became of marriageable age she was married from the Governor's mansion in Knoxville. I have no record of the order of birth of the Clark children, but possibly Sarah Hawkins Clark was the youngest.

(1) Sarah Hawkins Clark was married in Knoxville about 1788 to General James Rutherford Wyly, a grandson of Colonel Benjamin Cleveland of King's Mountain fame. Therefore descendants of this couple have three King's Mountain ancestors. General Wyly was also a distinguished officer in 1812.

General James Rutherford Wyly and Sarah Hawkins Clark Wyly had eight sons and four daughters, namely:

(1) William Clark Wyly.
(2) Oliver Cromwell Wyly.
(3) Benjamin Cleveland Wyly.
(4) John Henry Wyly.
(5) James Rutherford Wyly, Jr.
(6) Robert Wyly.
(7) Walton Wyly.
(8) Augustine Clayton Wyly.
(9) Elizabeth Wyly.
(10) Louisiana Wyly.
(11) Mary Ann Wyly.
(12) Sarah Catherine Wyly.

Of the foregoing:

(1) William Clark Wyly married Amelia Starr and had two children, Robert Wyly, who married and lived out West, and died some years ago, and Eliza Wyly who married William Trammell and died.

(2) Oliver Cromwell Wyly married for his first wife, Lucy Eddins in 1828 and had three daughters and five sons, namely: Newton Cromwell Wyly, born 1829; Benjamin F. Wyly, born 1830; James A. Wyly; Carolyn M. Wyly; Sarah Amelia Wyly; Lula Wyly; Robert A. Wyly; and William Sevier Wyley.

Newton Cromwell Wyly, born 1829, married in 1849, Malinda Townsend and had one son, Homer Virgil Miller Wyly.

Benjamin F. Wyly, born in 1830, married in 1858, Sallie Williams and had three sons, Eugene Wyly, Newton Wyly and ——— Wyly.

SEVIER

James A. Wyly married for his first wife a Miss Williams and had no children and married for his second wife Miss Verner and had a son and a daughter.

Carolyn M. Wyly married Henry Alexander Fuller and had three sons, Oliver Clyde Fuller (who married Kate Fitzhugh Caswell and has Edythe Fuller, Elizabeth Fuller, Inez Fuller, Lytie Fuller, Clyde Fuller, and Robert Fuller); Henry Walter Fuller; Clarence Paul Fuller; and Annie Railey Fuller (deceased).

Sarah Amelia Wyly married Henry Lamar Smith and had two sons: Victor Lamar Smith (who married Carolyn Johnson); and Alexander Wyly Smith (who married Ida Kendrick and has Alexander Wyly Smith, Junior, married Helen Hill Payne and has three children and is a Captain in the United States Army; Kendrick Smith in the United States Aviation Corps; and Ester Smith).

Lula Wyly married ——————— and had a daughter, who married Judge Carter, of Asheville, North Carolina.

Robert A. Wyly married ——— Hatchett and has six sons.

William Sevier Wyly married ——— Hatchett, a sister of his brother, Robert Wyley's wife, and had two sons of whom only one is now living.

Oliver Cromwell Wyly married for his second wife, Adeline Byrd, a daughter of Colonel Thomas Byrd and had four children, two sons and two daughters.

Oliver Cromwell Wyly married for his third wife ——————— and had ten children, all but one of whom are now living in Texas.

(3) Benjamin Cleveland Wyly, son of James Rutherford Wyly and Sarah Hawkins Clark Wyly, married firstly Ann McGhee and had one son, John McGhee Wyly, who married Amelia Forney and had four children: Annie McGhee Wyly (who married David Lowe and has a daughter Annie Wyly Lowe, married Walker Willis); Benjamin F. Wyly (who married Ellie Peck and has three children, Lottie Wyly, Catherine Wyly, married———————, and Forney Wyly); Sadie Swope Wyly (who married F. M. Billings and has Wyly Billings and F. M. Billings, Jr.); and Henry Forney Wyly (who married Sallie Dunlap and has two children, Henry Forney Wyly, Jr., and Sallie Dunlap Wyly).

Benjamin Cleveland Wyly married for his second wife Eliza Snow and had Samuel Snow Wyly; Frank Wyly (a daughter) who married Tom Garlington; Ella Wyly married ——— Brothers; Ida Wyly, married Joe Clay King, and Jennie M. Wyly married William Murray Davidson.

(6) Robert Wyly died unmarried.

(7) Walton Wyly married Mary Johnson and had no children.

(8) Augustine Clayton Wyly married Josephine Hamilton and

had Madeline Wyly, who is not married, Nell Wyly, who married Montagu Gammon and Thomas Hamilton Wyly.

(9) Elizabeth Wyly married Thomas Sparks.

(10) Louisiana Wyly married ——— Byrd.

(11) Mary Ann Wyly married Judge William Henderson Underwood and had Helen Underwood (who married M. A. Nevin and had William Henry Nevin, deceased; Ida Clifton Nevin (who married William A. Patton and is deceased); Thomas O'Connor Nevin, deceased; Sarah Hawkins Nevin, deceased; James Banks Nevin (who married first Alice Wells and married second Mary Bryan); Mary Mitchell Nevin (who married Randolph Wright); Wyatt Holmes Nevin, deceased); Annie Lou Underwood (who married Captain C. Rowell and had William Sinclair Rowell; Neal Rowell, deceased; Mary Wyly Rowell; Martha Cheatham Rowell, deceased; Florence Underwood Rowell, deceased, Elizabeth Clifton Rowell, deceased; and Annie Lou Rowell, deceased); Florence Wyly Underwood (who married E. M. Eastman and has Zoe Eastman, married Charles Robin Pitner, John Eastman married Laura Hume, Helen Eastman, unmarried, and Guy Eastman married Emma Hume); Mary Cordelia Underwood (who married D. D. Plumb and had Rosa Milledge Plumb married J. H. O'Neill); Ida Underwood (who married George H. Snyder and had Wyly Snyder, George Snyder and Clifford Snyder); Wilhelmina Underwood (who married John H. Pitt and has no children); Rosa Underwood (who married C. R. Clark and has one son, Charles Richard Clark, Jr.); John James Underwood (who died young); Charles Walton Underwood (who married Martha Moore and has John Underwood, Charles Walton Underwood, Jr., William H. Underwood, Robert Wyly Underwood, Valentine Xavier Underwood; Mary Underwood, married William Anderson and Evelyn Underwood, married Ralph Tanner.)

(12) Sarah Catherine Wyly married William A. Rogers and has Zoe Rogers, who married W. C. Mansfield and Alah Rogers who married ——— Daniel.

John Clark is by accounts that some members of the family have sent in, the son of Elizabeth Sevier Clark and Major William H. Clark. He married and at least one daughter, Kittie Clark, whom other descendants of Elizabeth Sevier always called "Cousin Kittie."

Mrs. Florence Underwood Eastman, a descendant of Elizabeth Sevier, writes that a sister of Sarah Hawkins Clark, who was named Ruth Clark, married Allen Elston.

Elizabeth Clark, daughter of Elizabeth Sevier and Major William H. Clark, married John Elston (born July 20, 1789, died November 11, 1845.)

They had one child, John Clark Elston, born July 4, 1822, died

SEVIER

March, 1896, married January 21, 1847, Selina Jones and had one daughter, Roxie Carolina Elston, born August 14, 1849, married November 25, 1868, Clark Snow, and had seven children, namely: Kate Corinne Snow (who married Thomas Daniel Jackson and has a daughter Joyce Elston Jackson); Ada Elston Snow (who married C. C. Morgan and has two sons, Marechal Clark Morgan and Norman Snow Morgan); Ruth Snow (who married Samuel Hallman and has no children); Julius Fane Snow (who died young); Maxie Snow (who is not married); Norman Lee Snow (who is not married); Mary Winnifred Snow (who married James N. Griffith and has one child, James Snow Griffith).

V. NANCY SEVIER.

Nancy Sevier, daughter of Governor John Sevier and his first wife Sarah Hawkins Sevier, was born in Virginia. She married Walter King and was still living in 1818. She left children.

VI. REBECCA SEVIER.

Rebecca Sevier, the daughter of Governor John Sevier and his first wife, Sarah Hawkins Sevier, was born in Virginia. She married a Waddell and left children. She evidently died before 1818 as her name is not included in the list of the Governor's children in the court record regarding sale of lands belonging to the heirs of John Sevier.

V. SARAH HAWKINS SEVIER.

Sarah Hawkins Sevier, daughter of Governor John Sevier and his first wife, Sarah Hawkins Sevier, was born in Rockingham County, Virginia, in July, 1770. She received her mother's full name. She married Judge Benjamin Brown and was probably a widow in 1818, when the children of Governor Sevier are cited, as the other daughters are mentioned with their husbands, and she is mentioned alone.

She left children.

VIII. MARY ANN SEVIER.

Mary Ann Sevier, daughter of Governor John Sevier and his first wife, Sarah Hawkins Sevier, was born in Virginia in 1771 or 1772. She married Joshua Corlin or Corland. She was still living in 1818. She left children.

NOTABLE SOUTHERN FAMILIES

IX. VALENTINE SEVIER.

Valentine Sevier, the son of Governor John Sevier and his first wife, Sarah Hawkins Sevier was born in Virginia about 1773. I have been unable to gather any information about him, other than that he was living in 1818, that he married and left descendants.

X. RICHARD SEVIER.

Richard Sevier, son of Governor John Sevier and his first wife, Sarah Hawkins Sevier, was born in Virginia in 1775. I have been unable to gather any information concerning him except that he was living in 1818 and that he married and left descendants.

XI. RUTH SEVIER.

Ruth Sevier, the daughter of Governor John Sevier and his second wife, Catherine Sherrill Sevier, was their first child. She was born 1781 at Plum Grove, John Sevier's residence on the Nollichucky. She was a typical frontier girl of the day, she was remarkable for her strong characteristics and intelligence. She learned the Indian people and their language and was of great assistance to her father on numberless occasions. Governor Sevier at one time kept several Cherokee Indians in his home for three years and from them Ruth acquired fluent Cherokee. She married Colonel Richard Sparks, who in his childhood had been stolen by the Indians and later released. He was the intimate friend and playmate of Tecumseh and his brother, the Prophet, and was given the name of Shawtunte. When he was sixteen he was released and made his way to the Holston Settlement where his mother recognized him by a birthmark. Governor Sevier befriended him and secured him a commission in the army where his knowledge of Indian life and language was of tremendous value. Ruth Sevier taught him to read and write and married him. After his death she married for her second husband Colonel Daniel Vertner and died in 1834. She is the only one of Governor Sevier's children who left no children.

XII. CATHERINE SEVIER.

Catherine Sevier, the daughter of Governor John Sevier and his second wife, Catherine Sherrill Sevier, was born probably in 1782. She married twice, firstly, Archibald Rhea, and secondly a Campbell.

She was living in 1818 and was then the wife of Archibald Rhea. Later she married ——— Campbell. She left children.

XIII. GEORGE WASHINGTON SEVIER.

George Washington Sevier, first son of Governor John Sevier by his second wife, Catherine Sherrill Sevier, was the thirteenth child of the Governor. He was born about 1783. He was Circuit Court Clerk of Overton County, Tennessee. (His mother had removed to that County with her family after the death of Governor Sevier). He was Ensign of the Second Infantry, March 26, 1804, Second Lieutenant, August 22, 1805, First Lieutenant, May 31, 1807, Captain of Rifle Company, May 3, 1808, Lieutenant Colonel, July 6, 1812, Colonel, January 24, 1814. He was still living in 1839, as in that year Dr. Lyman C. Draper went to see him and he gave to Dr. Draper the names of the eighteen Sevier children upon which this article is based.

He married Catherine Weatherly Chambers, by whom he had eleven children, namely:

(1) George Washington Sevier, Second.
(2) Catherine A. Sevier.
(3) William C. Sevier, never married.
(4) Thomas K. Sevier, never married.
(5) Cornelia V. Sevier.
(6) John Vertrees Sevier, never married.
(7) Eliza M. Sevier.
(8) Marion F. Sevier, never married.
(9) Laura J. Sevier.
(10) Putnam M. Sevier, never married.
(11) Henry Clay Sevier, never married.

Of the foregoing:

(1) Dr. George Washington Sevier, Second, married Sarah Knox, of Nashville, niece of Mrs. Andrew Jackson, who was raised at the Hermitage by President and Mrs. Jackson. They had six children, namely: George Washington Sevier, Third, William Sevier, Andrew Jackson Sevier, Mary Catherine Sevier, Eliza Donelson Sevier and Jennie Vertner Sevier. Andrew Jackson Sevier married Columbia Dobys and they had seven children: Columbia Sevier (who married Willard H. Utz, of Louisiana); Andrew Jackson Sevier, Second (who married Mary Day, of Vicksburg); Annie Sevier (who married J. S. Agee, of Alabama); Jennie Vertner Sevier (who married T. F. Young, of Vicksburg); Mary Katherine Sevier (who married W. J. Ward, of Arkansas); and Ada Elizabeth Sevier who married A. C. Williamson, of Arkansas); one daughter, Sarah

Knox, died unmarried many years ago. Mary Catherine Sevier married Robert Dunbar, leaving two children, Robert Dunbar, Second and Nannie Bells Dunbar, both living in Missouri. Jennie Vertner Sevier married George Clarke for her first husband and for her second husband married Adolphus Harris, of Virginia. They had one daughter, Sarah Knox Harris, who married Captain George Sager, of Port Gibson, Mississippi. Eliza Donelson Sevier married W. T. Jeffries, of Port Gibson, Mississippi, and left two children, Mary Sevier Jeffries and Evan Shelby Jeffries. Mrs. Jeffries and Mrs. Utz are the only living children of Dr. George W. Sevier and his wife, who was Sarah Knox, and are among the oldest descendants of Governor John Sevier, and the nearest to him in point of relation, being great-granddaughters. They also represents other early Tennessee families in her relation to the Jackson, Shelby, Knox, and Donelson families.

(2) Catherine Sherrill Sevier, bore her grandmother's full name. She married Albigence Waldo Putnam, a grandson of General Israel Putnam. They had two children: Julia (who married William O'Niel Perkins, lived in Nashville for many years and had no children) and Waldo Washington Putnam (who married Eliza Jane Smith and had three daughters: Emma, Agnes and Caroline. Misses Emma and Agnes Putnam are not married. Miss Caroline Putnam married Robert Morrison, of Chattanooga, and had four children, Kenneth Morrison, who died young, Lieutenant Harold Morrison, who is serving with the Army in France, Louise Morrison, who married Roy L. Baker and has one child, Roy L. Baker, Jr., and Putnam Morrison, who married Elizabeth Venneble and has five daughters: Elizabeth, Agnes, Mary, Esther and Ruth.)

(3) William C. Sevier, never married.
(4) Thomas K. Sevier, never married.
(5) Cornelia V. Sevier.
(6) John Vertrees Sevier, never married.
(7) Eliza M. Sevier married John F. Donald.
(8) Marion F. Sevier, never married.
(9) Laura J. Sevier married Henry L. Norvell and had Joseph A. Norvell (who married Mary Slinkard and had Louise Norvell and Nita Norvell, of Colorado, neither of whom is married); Cornelia Sevier Norvell (who married Albert B. Payne and had Albert B. Payne, Second, never married; Ida Payne, married Minor Scovel, Amy Payne, married Charles Rose, and Douglas Payne married Annie Alexander); Aduella B. Norvell (who never married); Sarah Woods Norvell (who married N. W. Leonard); Moselle Norvell (who married Frank Porterfield Elliott, and is now living in Nashville. Her children are Laura Norvell Elliott and Elizabeth Porterfield Elliott).

(10) Putnam M. Sevier never married.

SEVIER

(11) Henry Clay Sevier married twice, first Mary Clark and second Mary Nash.

XIV. JOANNA GOADE SEVIER.

Joanna Goade Sevier, daughter of Governor John Sevier and his second wife, Catherine Sherrill Sevier, was born in East Tennessee. She married Joseph H. Wendle. She was living in 1818.

XV. SAMUEL SEVIER.

Samuel Sevier, son of Governor John Sevier, and his second wife, Catherine Sherrill Sevier, was born in East Tennessee. He was probably named for Governor Sevier's intimate friend, Colonel Samuel Wear who named a son, born about the same time, John, for Governor Sevier. Samuel Sevier became a physician. He probably died before 1818, as his name is not included in the list of heirs when property was sold in Knox County.

Samuel Sevier married ——— and had a son, Dr. Daniel Vertner Sevier, named evidently for Ruth Sevier's husband, Daniel Vertner. Dr. Daniel Vertner Sevier had a son, Dr. Daniel Vertner Sevier, Jr., who has in his possession a very beautiful minature painted by Peale of John Sevier for his second wife, Catherine, and given by her to her son, Samuel, and inherited by Dr. Sevier.

XVI. ROBERT SEVIER.

Robert Sevier, the son of Governor John Sevier and his second wife, Catherine Sherrill Sevier, was born in East Tennessee. He was living in 1818. He left children, but I have not the names of his wife or children.

XVII. POLLY SEVIER.

Polly Preston Sevier, daughter of Governor John Sevier and his second wife, Catherine Sherrill Sevier, married William Overstreet, Jr., September 18, 1806. She was living in 1818 and she left children.

XVIII. ELIZA CONWAY SEVIER.

Eliza Conway Sevier, daughter of Governor John Sevier and his second wife, Catherine Sherrill Sevier, was born in East Tennessee about 1790. She married Major William McClellan of the United States Army, August 9th, 1810, and had five children, namely:

(1) John McClellan.
(2) Ann McClellan.
(3) Catherine McClellan.
(4) Mary Jane McClellan.
(5) Lida McClellan.

Of the foregoing:

John McClellan married a Miss Gregg and lived in Texas. He had no children.

Ann McClellan married Judge Brown and had children. She lived in Marshall, Texas.

Catherine McClellan married ———— Pickett and lived in Van Buren, Arkansas. She had children.

Mary Jane McClellan married Captain Gabriel Rains, United States Army, afterwards General Gabriel Rains, Confederate States Army. He was a son of General Gabriel Rains. Captain Rains was a distinguished officer of the Army and a graduate of West Point. Immediately upon the breaking out of the War Between the States he resigned from the United States Army and offered his service to the Confederacy and became a Brigadier General. General Gabriel Rains and Mary Jane McClellan Rains had six children, namely: Stella Rains (who died unmarried); Leila Rains (who married first ————Randall and had a son, Charles Rains Randall, died unmarried, and married secondly, Judge William Smythe, of Augusta, and has four children, Jane Harris Smythe, died young, Bonita Smythe, married Lee Hankinson and has four children, Stella Smythe, married John Sherman, of Augusta, and has two children, and Josephine Smythe, married James Welborn Camak, died, leaving one child, a son); Sevier McClellan Rains (who was killed in the West in an engagement with Indians. He was an officer in the United States Army and was unmarried); Catherine McClellan Rains (who married twice, firstly, Colonel Paul of the United States Army, by whom she has one child, Rosalie Paul, and, secondly, Colonel Paddock, United States Army, by whom she has no children); Gabrielle Rains (who married Kirby Tupper, of Charleston, South Carolina, and has two children, Gabrielle Williams Tupper and Sevier Rains Tupper, a Captain in the United States Army); and Fannie May Rains (who married Colonel Walter Chatfield of the United States Army.)

Lida McClellan married John Gregg, a planter in Texas and had three children, Willie Gregg, (who was killed in Battle in the War Between the States); Alla Gregg (who died unmarried and Nola Gregg (who married ———— Nelson).

SEVIER

FROM THE BORDEN GENEALOGY.

The Borden Genealogy, written by Hattie Borden Wells, gives John Borden*, son of John and Mary Borden, and great-grandson of Benjamin Borden, to whom Gov. Gooch, of Virginia, granted Borden's Manor, as having married Catherine Sevier, daughter of Governor John Sevier, about the year 1824.

This is manifestly not Governor John Sevier's daughter, as the date is too late and also as his daughter, Catherine, is fully accounted for in her marriage first to Archibald Rhea and second to ———— Campbell.

The Catherine Sevier who married John Borden, about 1824, might have been a granddaughter of John Sevier and in that case she was the daughter undoubtedly of one of the three sons by the second wife whose name was Catherine Sherrill, as an son would have been more likely to name a child for Catherine Sherrill than a stepson would. As the eldest son of Catherine Sherrill, George Washington Sevier had a daughter, Catherine, who is fully accounted for, this Catherine who married a Borden must have been the daughter of Robert Sevier or Samuel Sevier. I think she was the daughter of Samuel Sevier.

This is the record from the Borden Genealogy.

Catherine Sevier, who married John Borden had six children, namely: (1) Elizabeth Borden; (2) Euphemia Borden; (3) William Joseph Borden; (4) Mary Catherine Borden; (5) Andrew Campbell Borden; and, (6) Joel E. Borden.

Of the foregoing:

Elizabeth Borden was born November 5, 1825. She died September 5, 1851.

Euphemia Borden was born January 4, 1828. She died September 16, 1866.

William Joseph Borden was born in Benton County, Alabama, May 14, 1830. He married Emma Gabriel Gosson, of New Orelans,

---

(*John Borden married twice, the first time Catherine Matlock and the second time, Catherine Sevier, probably married both times into the Sevier family. Catherine Matlock was the daughter of William Matlock. Governor John Sevier had a sister, Catherine, and a sister, Polly. Polly Sevier married William Matlock and as these people lived in the same neighborhood it is more than probable that Catherine Matlock, who married John Borden, was a granddaughter of Polly Sevier, who married William Matlock, and that John Borden's second wife was her cousin, Catherine Sevier, a granddaughter of Governor John Sevier.)

and had Edwin Gosson Borden (who married Caroline Moonch and has Frederick William Borden, Henry Forney Borden, Emma Claudine Borden, and Harriet May Borden);

Willis C. Borden (married ——— Treadway, of Newman, Georgia); Malbert Troupe Borden (married Mildred A. Harris and has Christine Borden); Pelham Borden (married ——— Harper); Ann Borden (married ——— Frey); Ermine B. Borden (married ——— Martin); Joseph Borden (died young); Francis Borden (died young); Benjamin Borden.

Mary Catherine Borden, married ——— Bacon.

Andrew Campbell Borden married first Frances Knighten and married second Frances Bufford, and had Lydia Catherine Borden (died young); Henry Allen Borden (who married Martha Buckingham and had Adelaide Louise Borden, Alberta Lake Borden and Henry Grady Borden); Nancy Lorena Borden (who died young); Lula Ellen Borden (who died young); Charles Lewis Borden; Dora Louise Borden (who married J. M. B. Trammell and has Chesley Trammell); Euphemia Tate Borden; and John Pickens Borden.

Joel E. Borden, married ——————— and has Patrick Donnelly Borden.

SHIELDS

In the third or fourth century there were five kings of as many divisions of Ireland, the King of Munster being O'Brien. Later, and down to about 1200, the O'Briens were head kings of the whole country.

The younger son of this third century O'Brien traveled throughout Europe for twenty years, and then returned to claim his patrimony.

On account of his debonair manners, picked up at the Courts of the Continent, he was dubbed "Siadhal," which means "The Gracious," and because there were so many O'Briens, he adopted the more modernized Irish form of the old word and called himself and his children "Shiel". In Latin the name is Sedulius. We find a great many people of this name prominent both in ecclesiastical and literary history. One of them wrote the first of a series of treatises on Ethics that all the Christian Princes were required to study.

One was attached to the Court of Charlemagne. One was prominent in the Papal family of early times. One introduced Rhyme into Latin poetry and is called the Christian Virgil to this day. He wrote "Carmen Paschale". He had a good biography from the pen of Hellman, published in German in Munich in 1905. Six of them are mentioned by the Four Masters between the years 785 and 855.

A history of the Shields family is found in Rooney's Aristocracy at the time of the Reformation 400 years ago. A copy of this was known to be in America in Bishop Phalen's library, but after his death his books were scattered.

One branch of the family moved to the North of Ireland, Ulster. This family became Protestant and changed its name slightly. It became Shields. It may be that it Anglicised the name "Shiel" because the English were the promoters of the Reformation, and the oppressors of the Catholic Irish.

There was an inter-marriage with the Norman family of Scyld which means "Shield" in English. This Scyld family was in early days the reigning family in Denmark. Whatever the reason, the new name was taken up. The Shiel, O'Shiel, Shiell, etc., are probably all related to the old family that stayed in Munster. Cashel, in Tipperary, is the seat of the old O'Brien Castle and Capitol.

The Irish family records and historical data are the best in existence in any country. This arises from the peculiar land tenure law. The Irish are the direct descendants of the Phoenecians who invented the alphabet and the science of mathematics; but were driven out by the Greeks. They had a custom of appointing a sort of Parliament of Scholars who once each year checked up the facts of current history, and particularly the genealogical records. Thus we have a mine of information, much of it published. This is largely in the annals of the Four Masters.

The Shields of Ulster were all closely connected, without doubt, and seem to have kept the bond of blood even after emigration to America. The four emigrants who are best known and who are ancestors of the Southern families may be designated for convenience:

James Shields, of Rockingham County, Virginia, (probably an emigrant.)

John Shields, of the Mayflower.

———————Shields, who married a Nesbit.

William Shields, of Armagh, Ireland.

JAMES SHIELDS, OF ROCKINGHAM

James Shields, probably an emigrant, died in Rockingham County, Virginia, in 1749. His son, Robert, was a Revolutionary officer. He had twelve children, eleven sons and one daughter. They moved to Sevier County, Tennessee, about 1785.

The daughter married a Tipton, enemy of John Sevier, who was partner of Daniel Boone. Their son was General and United States Senator John Tipton, of Indiana, founder of Indianapolis, Logansport and Columbus. He married his cousin, daughter of one of his mother's brothers, John Shields, the official scout and gunsmith of the Lewis-Clarke Expedition to Oregon, 1803-6. There is a biography of him in any good account of that Expedition. His wife was a White, sister of Hugh Lawson White who ran for President against Jackson and Adams in 1828.

JOHN SHIELDS OF THE MAYFLOWER

John Shields, the emigrant, married Margaret Finley, in 1768. They moved from Ireland, or Wales; came in the ship "The Mayflower." When they reached land, a babe was born. They named it "Thankful," as they were glad it was born on land instead of water. That is how the name originated in this branch of the Shields family.

The children of John Shields and Margaret Finley Shields were, Thankful, John James, David, George, William Alexander, Robert Francis and Rebecca. John James Shields married Elizabeth Higginbotham. Their children were, John James, Samuel, Egbert, William, Robert, Sallie and Nancy (twins), Peggy, Mary, Thankful and Polly Ann. John James Shields son of the emigrant was twice married, first to Francis Ann Plunkett, and second to Nancy Plun-

SHIELDS

kett. They were sisters. Samuel was twice married, first to Susan Wakin Wheeler, and second to Maria Sterritt. Egbert was married first to Ellen Brent, second to Ann Bibb. Sallie married James Higginbotham, as his second wife. Nancy married William Smith. Peggy married Willis Plunkett. Mary married James Marr, Thankful married first Lafayette Johnson, second Robert Brooks, and died at "Valley Rest," near Bowling Green, Kentucky. Robert and Polly Ann never married.

John James Shields and his wife moved with their family to Kentucky near Bowling Green in 1836 or 1837 from Nelson County, Virginia. He bought 1,666 and two third acres of land. At his death his land and slaves were equally divided among his children.

THE SHIELDS WHO MARRIED A NESBIT

Another emigrant Shields, a native of Ireland, was twice married. The name of his first wife is unknown. His second wife was a Nesbit. Their children were, John, James, George, David Robert, Isabella and Elizabeth. No record has been kept of any except James. He was born in Ireland in 1762 and came to America when young with his parents. He lived in Mecklenburg County, North Carolina, where he enlisted in the Revolutionary war and is said to have been in the Battles of King's Mountain, Hanging Rock, etc. He afterward moved to Elbert County, Georgia. Later he went to Tennessee, stopping for a while on Harpeth river, south of Nashville, moving afterward to Giles County, where he and a large number of relatives settled at Elk Ridge church, which they erected of logs and which is still standing about two and a half miles east of Lynnville. In Georgia he married a daughter of Captain Samuel Montgomery, of Shippesburg, Pennsylvania, an officer of the Revolution. Her name was Jane Montgomery. Her sister —————Montgomery married a Samuel Shields, said to have been a son of William Shields of Armagh whose family record follows; but this Samuel Shields is given as being married to Margaret Ware. Possibly he married —————Montgomery as his second wife.

Leander Shields, son of the foregoing James Shields, went from Georgia into Tennessee with his relatives. He married his cousin, Ann King, also given as Elizabeth King.

With them went Samuel Shields, descendant of William Shields, the emigrant, from County Armagh, of Ireland, this Samuel Shields being, doubtless, the one who was married to ————— Montgomery and accompaning the family in consequence of that marriage.

Leander Montgomery Shields, who married his cousin, Ann

King, also given as Elizabeth King, (she possibly bore both names) had among other children James Montgomery Shields, who married Eliza Frances Moore. They had a son, Will Mitt Shields, of Columbia, Tennessee. The Kings, Montgomerys, Shields, McDonolds, McKenziers and Alexanders of Middle Tennessee are all closely connected and all identified with the early history of the State.

Leander Shields, son of the foregoing James Shields, went from Georgia into Tennessee with his relatives. He married his cousin, Ann King.

With them went Samuel Shields, descendant of William Shields, the emigrant, from County Armagh, of Ireland.

WILLIAM SHIELDS, OF ARMAGH

William Shields, the emigrant, was born in the County of Armagh in the Kingdom of Ireland on Sunday, July 14, 1728. He embarked on a sloop commanded by Captain Alex Smith, for America on the 26th of February, 1737, being in the ninth year of his age. On the voyage he lost his father and brother, Robert, who were taken by death. After landing he dwelt in Newcastle County six years, then removed to Cecil County, Maryland, where he remained four years. He then, in 1748, removed to Frederick County, Maryland. He married April 25, 1754, Jane Williams, daughter of John Williams, lately of Chester County, Pennsylvania. Jane Williams was born in Lancaster County, August 16th, 1736.

Their children were:

(1) John Shields, born Thursday, March 20, 1755.
(2) James Shields, born Tuesday, June 12, 1757.
(3) Henry Shields, born November 3, 1759.
(4) William Shields, Second, born October 8, 1761.
(5) Samuel Shields, born March 13, 1764.
(6) Agnes Shields, born December 13, 1766.
(7) David Shields, born June 12, 1769.
(8) Barnes Shields, born October 28, 1772.
(9) Mary Shields, born January 2, 1775.
(10) Ebenezer Shields, born December 22, 1778.
(11) Margaret Shields, born October 2, 1783.

Of the foregoing:

(1) John Shields, eldest child of William Shields of Armagh and Jane Williams Shields (born March 20, 1755, died January 23, 1833), married Mary McCollum (born February 18, 1769, died April 20, 1820).

SHIELDS

Their children were:

Nancy Shields (who married Richard DeWitt); Jane Shields (who married George Stuart of Wythe County, Virginia, and had five children, James Harvey Stuart, Mary Stuart, David Marcellus Stuart, John Howard Stuart, and George Stuart, Second); William Shields (of Iowa); Hester Shields (who married James Anderson of Knoxville); Mary Shields (who married Tighlman A. Howard, and had four daughters, Margaret Howard, Ann Eveline Howard Elizabeth Howard and Martha Howard); Eliza Shields, born 1803, died September 21, 1878, (who married her first cousin, Samuel Shields, of Grainger County, Tennessee, born July 5, 1802, died August 17, 1886); John P. Shields, (of Cocke County, Tennessee); and Henry D. Shields (who left one child, Elizabeth Shields).

(2) James Shields, son of William Shields, of Armagh, and Jane Williams Shields. Of him later.

(4) William Shields, the Second, son of William Shields, of Armagh, and Jane William Shields, married Jane Bentley. They lived and died in Frederick County, Maryland. They had seven sons and four daughters, among others John Shields, who married Mary Collins, and had six daughters and four sons, and Eliza Shields, who married her cousin, Samuel Shields, son of James Shields and Jane Gilliland Shields.

(5) Samuel Shields, son of William Shields, of Armagh, and Jane Williams Shields was born March 13, 1764. He married Margaret Ware, of Blount County, Tennessee. They had several children, some of them going to Oregon to reside. One of the daughters married a Killingsworth.

(6) Agnes Shields, daughter of William Shields, of Armagh, and Jane Williams Shields was born December 13, 1766. She married Jacob Gilliland. They had three children, namely: Betsey Gilliland (who married David Browne and settled near Asbury Church in Washington County, Tennessee); William Gilliland (who lives in Washington County, Tennessee), and John Gilliland, who lives in Aberdeen, Mississippi. Jacob Gilliland moved from Maryland to South Carolina. He went back to Baltimore and died there. His wife then moved to Washington County, Tennessee, and married for her second husband, Michael Woods. (A Michael Woods had married Ester Shields.)

(9) Mary Shields, the daughter of William Shields, of Armagh, and Jane Williams Shields was born January 2, 1775. She married John Blair and lived in Frederick County, Maryland, later going to Cleveland, Ohio, to reside. She had a son, William Blair, who married an Evans, of Greene County, Georgia, and settled in Georgia.

(11) Margaret Shields, daughter of William Shields, of Armagh,

and Jane Williams Shields, was born October 2, 1783. She married Evan Evans. They lived and died in Greene County, Tennessee. Their son, William Evans, lived in Indiana, and was an elder in the Presbyterian Church. Their daughter, Hannah Evans, married Newton Magill, of Kentucky.

(2) James Shields, the Second, son of William Shields, of Armagh, and Jane Williams Shields, was born in Frederick County, Maryland, July 12, 1757, and died in Greene County, Tennessee, August 23, 1840. He was a Captain in the War of the Revolution. He married Jane Gilliland, of Chester County, Maryland, who was born October 15, 1764. They were married in Frederick County, Maryland, Tuesday, April 1, 1783, the Reverend Mr. Martin officiating. Jane Gilliland Shields died at the residence of her daughter, Joanna Shields Lea, in Grainger County, Tennessee, December 21, 1849.

James Shields and Jane Gilliland Shields had eleven children.

Jane Gilliland Shields, mother of these eleven sons and daughters, was the daughter of John Gilliland, who was raised in the County of Athlone in Ireland. His wife was from Holland, and was named Hester Romar. They had three sons, Jacob, John and Peter. It will be seen that Jane Gilliland Shields named her first child "Ester, sometimes called Hester," for her own mother, Hester Romar Shields.

Ester Shields, (sometimes written Hester), first child of James Shields and Jane Gilliland Shields, married Michael Woods.

William Shields, son of James Shields and Jane Gilliland Shields, born 1787, is called William Shields, of Missouri. He married firstly Eliza Conway; secondly, a Patterson, and is presumed to have married a third time. A son by his second wife called Jefferson Shields became a Doctor. Another son of William Shields, David Shields, married Rachel Waddle of Washington County, Tennessee, and a son of theirs married Jane Boyd.

Jane Shields, daughter of James Shields, and Jane Gilliland Shields, born March 2, 1789, married Thomas Rankin.

John Shields, son of James Shields and Jane Gilliland Shields, was born 1792. He married Mary Gill. Of him later.

Mary Shields, daughter of James Shields and Jane Gilliland Shields, was born 1795. She married William Graham.

James Shields, Third, son of James Shields and Jane Gilliland Shields, was born 1797. He married Mary Cobb and had six children. Mrs. Sarah J. Taylor is the only living child.

David Shields, son of James Shields and Jane Gilliland Shields, was born 1800. He married Mary Brabson. They had one daughter, Jennie Shields, who married a Mr. Jones, of Macon, Georgia.

Samuel Shields, son of James Shields and Jane Gilliland Shields,

SHIELDS

was born July 5, 1802. He married his first cousin, Eliza Shields, daughter of his father's brother, John Shields, Second, and Jane Bentley Shields, October 28, 1828, in Cocke County, Tennessee, Reverend William Minnis officiating.

Samuel Shields, eighth child of James and Jane Gilliland Shields, died at his home near Blaine, Grainger County, Tennessee, August 17, 1886. His wife, Eliza Shields Shields, died at the home near Blaine, September 21, 1878.

They had a son, John Howard Shields, who was born September 15, 1829, in Sevier County, Tennessee. He married Margaret Amanda McMillan, daughter of Andrew McMillan and Mary Littleford, (See McMillan Family), January 15, 1852. They had eight children, namely: Ella B. Shields, deceased; Lizzie I. Shields, deceased; Samuel Shields, deceased; Mary C. Shields, who resides in Los Angeles; Alexander McMillan Shields, who resides in San Francisco; Margaret Lea Shields, who resides in Los Angeles; William Shields, who resides in Mentone, California, and Lawrence Shields, who is in the Medical Department of the United States Army.

Margaret McMillan Shields died in Cincinnati, Ohio, August 6, 1900. Her husband, John Howard Shelds, died near Jalapa, Mexico, March 17, 1902.

Milton Shields, son of James Shields and Jane Gilliland Shields, was born 1804. He married Priscilla Jones Brabson, of Brabson's Ferry, in Sevier County, Tennessee He had six sons and four daughters. Four sons and two daughters grew to maturity. Of these: John B. Shields married Carrie E. Long and they lived in Jasper, Alabama. Elizabeth Ester Shields married Reverend C. T. Carroll, of Holston Conference. Joanna Shields married Dr. J. F. Haley. David E. Shields married Lula Stubblefield and they live in Morristown, Tennessee. Henry Will Shields married Lizzie Rice and both are dead. Samuel Shields married Lucy Word and both are dead.

Joanna Shields, daughter of James Shields and Jane Gilliland Shields, was born in 1808. She married Harmond G. Lea and her mother's death is recorded as having taken place in her home in Grainger County, Tennessee, December 21, 1849.

Henry Wood Shields, son of James Shields and Jane Gilliland Shields, was born 1810. He married firstly Susan Crosby and married, secondly, Sallie Bible, and had no children by either marriage.

John Shields, the third child and second son among the eleven children of James Shield and Jane Gilliland Shields, was born 1782. He served in the Revolution and died October 2nd, 1829, at the early age of thirty-seven. He married Mary Gill (daughter of Thomas Gill, a native of Yorkshire, England, and his wife, Elizabeth Harrell, daughter of Thomas Harrell). The two children of John and Mary

Mrs. James T. Shields

Judge James T. Shields

SHIELDS

Gill Shields were Elizabeth, who died unmarried, and James T. Shields, was born in Granger County, Tennessee, September, 1824.

JUDGE JOHN T. SHIELDS

Judge James T. Shields, of Clinchdale, near Tate, Tennessee, was a distinguished citizen. He built a beautiful colonial home on his estate, which is kept now in almost exactly the condition in which he left it. His study where he sat surrounded by law books has not been changed in the slightest. Beautiful old engravings worth a fortune now, hang upon the walls probably as he placed them with his own hands, of Lafayette, Jefferson Davis, Andrew Jackson, men who were in public life during Judge Shields' time and who were probably his guests as well as his friends. The old mahogany furniture in the residence as well as in the office is priceless.

Judge James T. Shields was twice married, first to Mary Aurelia One daughter of this marriage, Aurelia, married W. D. Gammon, and died in 1876, leaving three children. Judge Shields married for his second wife, Elizabeth Simpson, of Rogersville, Tennessee.

They had ten sons, namely:

(1) William Simpson Shields.
(2) John Knight Shields.
(3) Robert Gill Shields, who died unmarried at twenty.
(4) James Thomas Shields, Jr., who died unmarried in Texas.
(5) Samuel Guthrie Shields, who died in Washington in 1915.
(6) Joseph Sevier Shields, who died in New York in 1916.
(7) Milton Lea Shields, who died in Greensboro, North Carolina, in 1903.

Three other sons died when very young.

Of the foregoing:

(1) William S. Shields, the oldest son, is a banker and leading citizen of Knoxville. He is largely interested in mercantile and manufacturing interests in that city, and has taken an active part in the political affairs of his distinguished brother, Senator Shields. He married Miss Alice Watkins, of Chattanooga, and their home is one of the handsomest and one of the most hospitable in Knoxville.

(2) John Knight Shields, the second son, is the Senior United States Senator from Tennessee and makes his home at Clinchdale in Grainger County, the beautiful family estate, which he inherited from his father, consisting of a magnificent farm of more than thirty-five hundred acres. In his youth, he decided to follow his father's profession of law, and early in life, he took an active interest in politics. He has been a delegate to two national democratic conventions, was

appointed chancellor of his chancery division and later was elected, without opposition, to the Supreme Court, where he served for thirteen years. He was Chief Justice of the court for the last three years he was on the bench, and was elected from that position to the United States Senate in January, 1913, which position he is now filling with credit to himself and with honor to his state. He first married Miss Mary Fulkerson, of Rogersville, and his second wife was, before her marriage to Senator Shields, Mrs. Jeanette Dodson Cowan, widow of James D. Cowan, of Knoxville.

(4) James T. Shields, Jr., was a leading and successful merchant in Knoxvile until his health failed him. He was never married.

(5) Samuel G. Shields, like his father and brother, Senator Shields, pursued the profession of the law, and was a leading member of the Knoxville bar until his death. He was at one time a special judge of the Supreme Court of Tennessee. He first married Miss Fannie Brown, of Greeneville, and his second wife was Miss Pauline Woodruff, of Knoxville, who survives him.

(6) Joseph Sevier Shields was a wholesale merchant in New York City for eighteen years, where he died in April, 1916. He married Miss Annie Luttrell, daughter of Mr. and Mrs. James Churchwell Luttrell, of Knoxville, a descendant of the Brooks, Armstrong, Wears McWilliams and Calhouns. One daughter, Josephine Shields, survives her father, and is the only grandchild of Judge James T. Shields, by his second wife. Josephine Shields married Leonard Murphey, of Morristown.

(7) Milton L. Shields, who married Miss Rhoda King, of Knoxville, was, for many years, a merchant in Knoxville and Greensboro, North Carolina, at which latter place he died.

The family of General James Shields, a leading Catholic, was of the Northern Ireland family, re-converted to Catholicism. Most of the emigrant Shields families are Protestant. General James Shields was United States Senator from three states and is one of the two men selected by the state of Illinois for the Hall of Fame. He was prominent in the Mexican War; his picture is the central figure in one of the great battle-pictures of the world, Chapultipec, hanging in the Capitol at Washington. He is buried and has a fine monument at Carrolton, Missouri.

STONE FAMILY

The Stone family name, it has been suggested, comes from residence near or in one of the ancient English towns by the name or from similar proximity to one of the great historic stones, Stonehenge, for instance. In any case, it is one of the oldest patronymics. There are many Stones of record, and in America many have reached distinction; at one time in recent years five Governors Stone sat in the executive chair in as many States of the Union, and they were all descended from Colonial Governor William Stone of Maryland.

GOVERNOR WILLIAM STONE

This progenitor of the Southern family, William Stone, was born in England in Northhamptonshire in 1603. He was the nephew of Thomas Stone of that Shire. In 1648 he emigrated from England to Virginia, where he settled on the eastern shore near Hunger's Creek, and was called Captain William Stone. In the same year, 1648, he negotiated the removal of a party of non-conformists like himself from Virginia to Maryland and in August of 1648 he was appointed Deputy Governor of the Colony of Maryland by Lord Baltimore, the lord proprietor and Governor. Sixteen forty-eight proved rather an eventful year for the emigrant. He married, probably in England before his emigration, and had at least two sons of whom we know: namely, John and David.

David, the second son of the emigrant and Colonial Governor, married Elizabeth Jenifer, daughter of Dr. Daniel Jenifer, and had children: Michael Jenifer Stone, John Hoskins Stone (Governor of Maryland), Thomas Stone (signer of the Declaration of Independence), Frederick Stone and Ezekiel Stone.

GOVERNOR JOHN HOSKINS STONE

Of the sons of Governor William Stone, David was the father of John Hoskins Stone, who also became a Governor of Maryland. He was born in Charles County, where the family resided in 1745. He was the son of David Stone, by his wife, Elizabeth Jenifer, daughter of Dr. Daniel Jenifer. He became the eighth Governor of Maryland and served from 1794 to 1797.

In November, 1774, he was one of the committee from Charles County to carry out resolutions of Congress and was one of the Committee of Correspondence for the County. He was a member of the Association of Freemen of Maryland.

January 14th, 1776, he was elected Captain of the First Company of Colonel William Smallwood's First Maryland Regiment. He was wounded in the Battle of Germantown, being disabled in that encounter. He was a member of the Society of Cincinnati. In 1794 he was elected to the office of Governor.

He married a Scotch lady, a Miss Condon, and had at least one daughter, Eliza Stone, who married Nathaniel Pope Causin. Their son, Nathaniel Pope Causin, second, married Eliza Mactier Warfield, and had children.

Michael Jenifer Stone, son of David Stone and Elizabeth Jenifer, was elected to Congress (1789-1791), and was Judge of the Circuit Court of Charles County.

THOMAS STONE, THE SIGNER

Thomas Stone, the Signer of the Declaration of Independence, was the son of David Stone and his wife, Elizabeth Jenifer Stone, and was grandson of the Colonial Governor William Stone. He was born in the County of Charles, Maryland, in 1743. He was elected delegate to the First Continental Congress in 1774, in Philadelphia, and was one of the Signers of the Declaration of Independence. He died in 1787.

He married and had one son, Frederick Stone, and two daughters, Elizabeth and Mildred Stone. Frederick Stone inherited the family taste for politics and was Congressman from Maryland.

Mildred Stone married Dr. John M. Daniel, of Virginia, and was the grandmother of another congressman, Senator Daniel, of Virginia. Elizabeth Stone also married a Daniel, of Virginia, brother of her sister's husband.

Michael Jenifer Stone, son of David Stone and his wife, Elizabeth Jenifer Stone, was born in Charles County, Maryland, in the year 1750. He was also a Congressman, a representative in Congress, 1791. He voted for the location of the National Capitol on the Potomac river. He died in 1812. He had three sons, namely: William, John and Samuel.

Ezekial Stone, fourth son of David Stone and his wife, Elizabeth Jenifer Stone, was born in Maryland in Charles County in 1760. He enlisted in the Revolutionary War, though he was only sixteen years of age, and served until the close of the conflict. He married Jane Wood, of North Carolina, and removed from Maryland to the French Broad River, in Sevier County, then North Carolina, now Tennessee, in 1784. Ezekiel and Jane Wood Stone had children, William, John, Richard,

STONE

Thomas, Mary, Hannah, Rebecca, Elizabeth and Mary. He died in Sequatchie Valley, Tennessee, in 1860, at the advanced age of ninety-nine years and eleven months. A sister of his wife, another Miss Wood, was the mother of General Wade Hampton.

William Stone, son of Ezekiel Stone, was born in Sevier County, when that county was a part of North Carolina. He married Mary Randal, of the Randal family of Maryland; his children were Teresa, Rebecca, Elvira, Louisa, McDonough P. D., John L., Rhoda Jane and Spencer Clack Stone, who married Rachel Couch, whose mother, Elizabeth Boone was a descendant of the Boone family of which Daniel Boone was a member.

William Stone was a Captain in the Creek War, and was elected Brevet-Brigadier General for gallantry at the Battle of the Horse Shoe. He served with General Jackson in the Louisiana campaign, and was present at the Battle of New Orleans. He was elected to Congress in 1836, and was re-elected in 1838. He died in 1853.

For bravery at the Battle of Tippacanoe he was presented with a cane by Congress, which is now in the possession of his grandson, Wm. M. Stone, of Chattanooga, a son of Spencer Clack Stone. William M. Stone married Genevieve Dair of Ohio, and had five children: Ada Genevieve, Effie Maude, William Otto, Milton Dair and Daniel McQuigg.

Thomas Stone, son of Ezekiel Stone and Elizabeth J. Stone settled in the territory of Mississippi, and married there. His son, John M. Stone, was Governor of that state from 1876 to 1882.

Richard Stone, son of Ezekiel Stone, settled in the territory of Missouri. He married and had one son, "Little Ezekiel".

John Stone, another son of Ezekiel Stone, settled on Stone's River, near Murfreesboro, Tennessee, but afterwards removed to Knox County, where he married. He had three sons, viz: Ezekiel, Richard and Oliver.

SOME OTHER TENNESSEE STONES

The first settlers of Washington County, Tennessee, came from adjoining counties of Virginia and North Carolina. Among these early pioneers was William Stone, who settled near Jonesboro. When Captain William Bean organized his Company in 1778, to protect the settlement against the Tories and Indians. William Stone was one of the company. The Court Journal of Washington County shows him to have been Tax Assessor in 1780. He received a grant of land from the State of North Carolina in 1784. After the Revolution, he moved from Washington County and settled on Richland Creek in Grainger County. He was a member of the Court of Grainger County in 1799. This property is still occupied by his descendants.

NOTABLE SOUTHERN FAMILIES

William Stone, born in Virginia, died in Grainger County, Tennessee, married in Virginia.

His children were:

Robert Stone, married Susan Everett.
Dorcas Stone, married Michael Massengale.
Mary Stone, married William Cox.
John Stone, married Susan Henderson.
Susan Stone, never married.

William Stone, married Nancy Highlander December 18, 1810.

Colonel James Smith, of Pennsylvania, explored the Cumberland Country during the sumer of 1766. The following is an extract from his journal:

"I set out about the last of June, 1766, and went in the first place to the Holston River, and from there I travelled westwardly in company with Joshua Horton, Uriah Stone, William Baker and James Smith, who came from near Carlisle, Pennsylvania.

"We explored the country south of Kentucky. We also explored the Cumberland and Tennessee Rivers from Stone's River down to the Ohio. Stone's River is a South branch of the Cumberland and empties into it above Nashville. We gave it this name in our Journal in May, 1767, after one of my fellow travellers, Mr. Uriah Stone, and I am told it retains the same name unto this day."

Uriah Stone was the father of at least two sons, William Stone and Archibald Stone. William Stone settled in Jackson County, Tennessee, where he died in 1820. His will mentions his wife, Ann, sons Uriah and Elijah; daughters Jane Roberts, wife of Edmond Roberts and Ann Smith, a grandson, Asbury Stone, son of Uriah Stone is also mentioned. The executors were Archibald Stone and James Crawford, of Barren County, Kentucky. The will is dated June 24, 1819.

TURNLEY

The origin of the name Turnley is very clearly from the device borne upon the shield, a turn or turned lily and its use dates to remote times, long before surnames were adopted. The family is Norman and its forerunners probably accompanied William the Conqueror.

In England, the Turnley family dates back to a remote period. Prior to 1550 the name is recorded as a family with a coat of arms in the register's office. When the Herald College in London was burned, this, with so many other recorded coats and blazonry, was destroyed. Those interested in the preservation of these family armorial ensigns, took measures to have those of their respective families registered or recorded, and so preserved them. The Turnleys neglected to do this for a great while. The attempt was at last made, and after long search through the British Museum the record was found in Randal Holme's Academy of Armory, published during the reign of Charles the Second. The family record also was found bearing the coat of arms.

The "Turn Cup Lily" as the arms represent, (page 480, vol. I of Fairbairn's Crests of Great Britain and Ireland) is the following: TURNLEY" on a mount. vert. an oak tree ppr. pendent on (sinister side) a shield, gu. charged with a'cross pattee or perseveranda, pl. 75 cr. 2 cross pl. 141 or more clearly rendered: Turnley's coat of arms consist of a green oak tree growing on a mound; pendent on left side a reddened shield charged with a "pattee" cross; that is, a cross in which the *arms* are very narrow at the *inner* ends and broad at the *outer* ends.

In the reign of Queen Elizabeth, three branches of the Turnley family appeared in England. Richard Turnley belonged to the expedition, which, under the Earl of Essex, embarked from Plymouth, against Spain, and resulted in the capture of Cadiz. He was also in another expedition under Essex, for the protection of Ireland from a threatened invasion from Spain. He returned in 1599 to England, where he remained in private life.

Several members of the family held positions of honor and trust in the state during this period.

We do not see anything more of the name until the Civil war under Charles I. of England. During the latter part of this reign, the Turnleys seem to have been divided between Charles and Parliament, some being on the one side and some on the other. At last, when Charles refused to answer the charges of Parliament, the Turnleys are all found on the side of Parliament, and subsequently in the army of Cromwell. John, Francis and Edmund Turnley served in the army of the Commonwealth, John and Francis as Ensigns, Edmund as Cornet in a squadron of cavalry. When Cromwell became Lord Lieutenant, he dispatched reinforcements to the garrisons in Ireland, and among these reinforcements we find the names of John, Francis and Edmund Turnley. They participated in the little battle near Dublin in 1649, and were present at Drogheda in the same autumn. They remained in service in Ireland till 1651, when they all obtained discharges. John, the eldest, remained in Ireland, married there, and had children. His descendants are still to be found in Ireland.

Francis and Edmund Turnley, after the discharge from the army of Ireland, started to return to England, but stopped in Wales. Francis remained there, married and had children. During a portion of the time he lived in Monmouth, where he died in 1690. His two eldest children were sons, whom he named John and Francis. These two are the progenitors of the Turnleys of America.

Edmund Turnley, the youngest of the brothers who left England in the Cromwellian service, married in Wales, afterward returned to England, and stopped in the town of Bath.

About the same time, another branch of the family (cousin to the one above) James Turnley, resided in the town of Gloucester, near the head of the Bristol Channel. He had three sons, viz., Robert, Isaac and Joseph. The record of these appears in 1700. No accurate account can be obtained of their issue nor of their deaths.

The name is still preserved in both English and Irish branches. A Joseph Turnley was Lord Mayor of London.

John Turnley and Francis Turnley, Second, sons of Francis Turnley, the First, and progenitors of the American family, were born in Monmouth, Wales, John in 1660, Francis in 1662. After attaining their majority, they crossed the channel to the port of Bristol, where they worked for themselves, and finally married, one in 1689, the other in 1690. In 1692, having been tempted by the favorable inducements offered by William and Mary, to emigrants to the American Colonies, they together embarked from the port of Bristol for Norfolk, Virginia. John Turnley, the elder, settled in Botetourt County, Virginia; Francis Turnley in Spottsylvania County. They each had children, and named the eldest sons for themselves respectively—John and Francis Turnley. John (the eldest son of John Turnley of Monmouth), was born in Bristol, 1690, and attained his majority in Botetourt County, 1712. Francis Turnley (eldest son of Francis Turnley, of Monmouth), was born also in Bristol in 1691, and attained his majority in Spottsylvania County, 1713. These are

TURNLEY

the heads of the two American families of Turnley. The fathers, John Turnley, First, and Francis Turnley, Second, of Monmouth, were useful citizens in the new country.

John Turnley, of Monmouth, married in Bristol in 1689 and his eldest son, John Turnley, Second, was born in Bristol in 1690.

John Turnley, the First, of Monmouth, died at an advanced age in his home. I have no record of whom he married in 1689, but he had, among other children, John Turnley, the Second, born in Bristol in 1690, who is ancestor of the Tennessee Turnleys.

Francis Turnley, the Second, of Monmouth, died at an advanced age in his home. I have no record of whom he married in 1690, but he left a son, Francis Turnley, the Third, born in Bristol in 1691, who is ancestor of the Virginia Turnleys.

Francis Turnley, the Third, married Grace ——————— in 1725 in Spottsylvania County, Virginia. They had six children, namely:

Francis Turnley, the Fourth, born February 10, 1726 or 7.
Elizabeth Turnley, born December 8, 1728.
William Turnley, born January 25, 1730.
Ann Turnley, born February 28, 1732.
Grace Turnley, born June 9, 1735.
John Turnley, born November 9, 1737.

Francis Turnley, the Fourth, eldest of the foregoing group married Mary ———————, and is said to have been the father of eight children whose names are given in the family records. A list was furnished Parmenas Taylor Turnley by Nelson G. Turnley in 1869, and a duplicate was found in the papers of John Turnley, of Tennessee, showing that such a list was correct and from old records, possibly a family Bible. This is the list as given:

Susan, born October 8, 1740.
Ellender, born December 18, 1744.
Sarah, born July 6, 1751.
Elizabeth, born February 12, 1753.
Anne, born March 23, 1755.
John, born February 7, 1757.
James, born September 7, 1759.
Francis, born December 31, 1763; died December 23, 1838.

Manifestly these children could not all have been the sons of Francis Turnley, the Fourth, who was born in 1726 or 7 as he would have been a child of thirteen or fourteen at the birth of Susan. I conclude that the two elder children, Susan and Ellender, are kinspeople, who grew up in his house or that he married a widow and that

NOTABLE SOUTHERN FAMILIES

Susan and Ellender are her children, and possibly adopted by Francis Turnley. A considerable period of years, seven, elapses between the birth of Ellender and Sarah whom I conclude to be the first child of Francis Turnley, the Fourth.

Francis Turnley, the Fourth, died November 7, 1796. His wife, Mary, his "consort" as the old records give it, died February 27, 1794.

FRANCIS TURNLEY, THE FIFTH

Francis Turnley, the Fifth, was born December 31, 1763, and died December 23, 1838. He married Susan Wall, of Orange County, Virginia, April 3, 1791. They had eight children:

(1) James Turnley, born January 17, 1792; died July 9, 1862.
(2) Elizabeth Turnley, born January 24, 1794; died in Rome, Georgia, in 1879.
(3) Judith Turnley, born January 21, 1796.
(4) John Turnley, born October 22, 1798; died in 1865.
(5) Mary Turnley, born October 12, 1801.
(6) Whitfield Turnley, born September 15, 1804.
(7) Nelson G. Turnley, born August 8, 1810.
(8) Zachariah Turnley, born February 22, 1813.

(1) James Turnley, the eldest son of Francis Turnley the Fifth, and Susan Wall Turnley, was born January 21, 1796. He left Spottsylvania County, Virginia, while still a young man. He married Mahala Cosby, of Powhatan County, Virginia, November 15, 1832. They had five children, namely: William Francis Turnley, born September 23, 1833; John Jefferson Turnley, born March 15, 1835; James Whitfield Turnley, born May 2, 1837; Susan Williams Turnley, born July 4, 1841, and Georgia Eller Turnley, born March 15, 1844. William Francis Turnley, the eldest son, married Virginia Ann Franklin, of Henrico County, Virginia, and had eight children: Mariah Turnley, died young; James Beauregard Turnley, who lived in Chesterfield County, Virginia; Mary Ida Turnley, deceased; Cosby Turnley; Francis Lee Turnley, who lived in Chesterfield County, Virginia; John Turnley, who lived near Swansboro, Virginia; William Webster Turnley, who lived near Swansboro, Virginia; and Rosa Lee Turnley. John Jefferson, second son of James Turnley and Mahala Cosby Turnley married Helen Rowell, but had no children. James Whitfield Turnley, third son of James Turnley and Mahala Cosby Turnley, married Sarah Jennings, of Suffolk County, Virginia, and had five children, namely: Luella W. Turnley, Fitzhugh Lee Turnley, Julius Turnley, James Atford Turnley and George Eller Turnley. Susan Williams Turnley, daughter of

TURNLEY

James Turnley and Mahala Cosby Turnley, married Benjamin Franklin Wrenn, of Surry County, Virginia, July 20, 1858. They had seven children, namely: Atlelier George Wrenn, Mary Mahala Wrenn, Benjamin Wrenn, Jr., Charles Nicholas Wrenn, Luellen Wrenn, Thadeus, Wrenn, Oneder Wrenn. Georgia Eller Turnley, daughter of James Turnley and Mahala Cosby Turnley, married P. H. Wright, November 27, 1859, and had two children, namely: Cornelia Nelson Wright and John Turnley Wright. (Cornelia Nelson Wright married James T. Garrow and had five children: John Loomer Garrow, Georgia Eller Garrow, Annie Gray Garrow, Patrick Henry Garrow and William Francis Garrow). John Turnley Wright married Fannie Jones, of Warwick County, Virginia, but had no children.

James Turnley died July 9, 1862. His wife, Mahala Cosby Turnley, died March 4, 1864.

(2) Elizabeth Turnley, eldest daughter of Francis Turnley, the Fifth, and Susan Wall Turnley, was born January 24, 1794. She married James Heart, of Spottsylvania County, Virginia, and had five children: James Heart, Silas Heart, Lucy Heart and two others who died young. Lucy Heart married Prof. Morphin, of Charlottesville, Virginia. Mrs. Heart died in Rome, Georgia, at the age of seventy-five years in 1869.

(3) Judith Turnley, second daughter of Francis Turnley the Fifth, and Susan Wall Turnley, born January 21, 1796, died at the age of twenty-five years, unmarried.

(4) John Turnley, son of Francis Turnley, the Fifth, and Susan Wall Turnley, born October 22, 1798, married Malinda Cowin, of Spottsylvania, Virginia, in 1821. They had five children, namely: Judith Turnley, born 1823, Martha E. Turnley, born, 1825, James M. Turnley, born September 14, 1833, John Turnley, born 1835 and William Henry Turnley, born 1837. Of these Judith Turnley the eldest daughter married Andrew Williams in 1850, and had three children, Cornelius Williams, died young, Janetta Williams, died young, and Judson Turnley Williams. Judson Turnley Williams married Ida Watkins. Martha Turnley, daughter of John Turnley and Malinda Cowin married Aaron Hall and had children: Eliza Hall, (who married S. J. Turner of St. Louis and had two children); August Beverly Hall; Murry M. Hall (who married Isabelle Barger, of Virginia, and moved to Los Angeles, California. They had three children, two of whom died in infancy. Their remaining child was Eva Hall). James M. Turnley, son of John Turnley and Malinda Cowin Turnley, married Matilda B. Thorn, of Thornton, West Virginia, and had thirteen children: Mary Alice Turnley; Francis Calvert Turnley; Lee Turnley; Charles Turnley; Luther Wright Turnley; Arthur Peabody Turnley; Eunice I. Turnley; Lucy M. Turnley; Samuel

Tilden Turnley; Thomas Hendricks Turnley; Lelia Luella Turnley; Agatha May Turnley and James Wade Hampton Turnley. Of these: Mary Alice Turnley died young. Francis Calvert Turnley died in 1881. Lee Turnley married Alice Fawcett and had two children, Francis Calvert Turnley, Jr. and Bertha M. Turnley. Charles Turnley married Sophronia Montgomery Luther Wright Turnley married Mary Phillips and had two children, Lula Turnley and Mildred Turnley. Arthur Peabody Turnley married Lizzie Shafferman and had one child, Richard Paul Turnley. Eunice I. Turnley died young. Lucy M. Turnley lived in Virginia. Samuel Tilden Turnley married Agnes Smith and had one child, Parmenas Raphael Turnley. Thomas Hendricks Turnley married Minnie Squires and had two children, Irene Turnley and Carol Bryan Turnley. Lelia Turnley is unmarried. Agatha May Turnley died unmarried. James Wade Turnley did not marry. John Turnley, Jr., the second son of John Turnley and Malinda Cowin Turnley was killed in the War Between the States. William Henry Turnley, son of John Turnley and Malinda Cowin Turnley died young and unmarried.

(5) Mary Turnley, daughter of Francis Turnley the Fifth and Susan Wall Turnley was born August 8, 1801. She married Addison Gibson, and had one child who died young.

(6) Whitfield Turnley, son of Francis Turnley, the Fifth and Susan Wall Turnley was born September 15, 1804. He married May Taylor Janway and had four children: Mary Susan Turnley; Martha Ann Turnley; Melissa Agnes Turnley and Luther Watts Turnley. Mary Susan Turnley married ————Clifford and had one daughter (who married John Lunson and had two children, Clifford Lunson and Mary Isabella Lunson). Martha Ann Turnley died young. Melissa Agnes Turnley married David Furloin and had no children. Luther Watts Turnley married———————————and had two children, Ella Turnley and Hettie Turnley.

(7) Nelson G. Turnley, son of Francis Turnley, the Fifth and Susan Wall Turnley was born August 8, 1810. He married Ann Cox.

(8) Zachariah Turnley, son of Francis Turnley, the Fifth and Susan Wall Turnley died young and unmarried.

It seems rather a pity that Francis Turnley, the Fifth in direct direct succession failed to name a son Francis and therefore broke the generations' long line of "Francis Turnley".

John Turnley, Second, of Botetourt County, Virginia, son of John Turnley, First of Monmouth, was left an orphan at the age of eight years, with his brother Francis, who was younger. About 1760, he married Mary Handy, of Botetourt County, Virginia,

TURNLEY

(born 1725) by whom he had two children: George Turnley and Elizabeth Turnley.

John Turnley, Second, served in the Revolution and was honorably discharged in 1779. John Turnley died in 1808 on the Turnley place which he had established with his son, George Turnley, near Mount Pleasant Tennessee. His widow, Mary Handy Turnley, survived him many years and went after his death to make her home with her only daughter, Elizabeth Turnley Graham, wife of George Graham, who lived two miles away. There Mary Handy Turnley died in 1829 at the age of ninety-four years. Her mother, Mrs. Handy, who had also made her home in her declining years with Elizabeth and George Graham died at the age of one hundred and four years.

The two children of John Turnley and Mary Handy Turnley, were:

George Turnley, born August 30, 1762.
Elizabeth Turnley, born 1764.

At the beginning of the Revolution (1776) George Turnley was a robust lad of fourteen years of age, well grown and a good horseman. By 1777 he had learned of the war and the call for soldiers, and learned that pack horses were needed and men to handle them, for the purpose of carrying supplies into out of the way places where wheeled vehicles could not go. George thought this kind of work would suit him exactly, and he got his father's consent to enter the military service and his assignment to the pack-horse transportation. This service continued, in fact, through his entire three years' enlistment, till about 1781, when he got his discharge and returned home to his father in Botetourt County, (not a very great way from the little town of Fincastle), Virginia.

About 1783 George Turnley left Botetourt County, and make his way southeast as far as the headwaters of the French Broad River to see what kind of a country it was, and then return and report to his father and family. This trip occupied him nearly two years, during which he visited the French Broad River, and the Pigeon and Holston Rivers as far as "White's Fort" (that is, the present Knoxville). From there he started back on his course to return. It was on his return that he finally fixed on a permanent home on the French Broad River at a point thirty-five miles above "White's Fort," or Knoxville. There were several settlers then in that region of new territory, notwithstanding the numerous Indians who roamed over the country in a semi-hostile spirit. There was then beginning to crop out a very hostile feeling in the minds of the Indians against the whites, in the fear that they were to be deprived of their hunting grounds.

NOTABLE SOUTHERN FAMILIES

George Turnley continued his return to Botetourt County, Virginia, where he arrived on his twenty-third birthday, or 1785. He related to his father and mother all he had seen of the lovely and inviting new country he had visited. It was not long before John Turnley and his wife made up their minds to migrate to the new Eldorado.

It was not till 1787 that the Turnleys got entirely ready to take up the line of march southward.

Elizabeth Turnley, the second child of John Turnley and Mary Handy Turnley was born 1764, and was their second child. She married in 1783 in Virginia, George Graham, a Scotchman, who was also desirous of moving to the French Broad country with the Turnleys. The Grahams settled on a place not far from the Turnleys' Mount Pleasant home and there George and Elizabeth raised their ten children and extended warmth of hospitality to Elizabeth's mother, Mrs. Mary Handy Turnley in her old age, and grandmother, Mrs. Handy in her extreme old age. Both died in Elizabeth Turnley Graham's home.

George and Elizabeth Turnley Graham had ten children, namely:

(1) Mary Graham.
(2) William Graham.
(3) James Graham.
(4) John Graham.
(5) Priscilla Graham.
(6) Joseph Graham.
(7) George Graham, Second.
(8) David Graham.
(9) Elizabeth Graham.
(10) A son not known.

Of the foregoing:

(1) Mary Graham, daughter of George Graham and Elizabeth Turnley Graham was born in 1748. She married John Sehorn in 1802.

(2) William Graham, son of George Graham and Elizabeth Turnley Graham was born in October 1786. He married Mary Shields (See Shields Family) in 1814 or 1815. They had two children both daughters. Mary Shields Graham died in 1837. William Graham lost his life when his store burned, September 17, 1857.

(3) James Graham, son of George Graham and Elizabeth Turnley Graham was born in 1787. He married Mary McGort, of Jefferson County, Tennessee in 1816. He was still living in 1865.

TURNLEY

(4) John Graham, son of George Graham and Elizabeth Turnley Graham was born 1788. He married Mary Ross of Greene County, Tennessee. She died and he married for his second wife a Miss Farout, of Blount County, Tennessee

(5) Priscilla Graham, daughter of George Graham and Elizabeth Turnley Graham was born 1790. She married John Gentry, of Jefferson County, Tennessee. She lived near her brother, David Graham and had several children

(6) Joseph Graham, son of George Graham and Elizabeth Turnley Graham was born 1792. He married Sarah Hill in 1812, before he was of age. He had several children, sons and daughters. He died March 30, 1862, at his home two miles above Hays Ferry, on the French Broad River.

(7) George Graham, Second, son of George Graham and Elizabeth Turnley Graham was born 1795. He married—— ——.

(8) David Graham, son of George Graham and Elizabeth Turnley Graham was born March 31, 1798. He married Mary G. Lackins, August 11, 1823. She died August 8, 1856, and he married a second wife in February 1857.

David Graham followed the habit of living a long time. He died at the age of eighty years and five months, August 27, 1878, near Dallas, Texas, where he had moved late in life. He had nine sons and daughters, among them, Eliza Graham, William Glenn Graham and Lavinia Arminta Graham.

(9) Elizabeth Graham, daughter of George Graham and his wife, Elizabeth Turnley Graham was born 1802.

(10) The tenth child of George Graham and Elizabeth Turnley Graham was a son, born May 25, 1809. He died unmarried in October 1833.

GEORGE TURNLEY

George Turnley, the first child and only son of John Turnley, the Second and Mary Handy Turnley was born, August 30, 1762. He married Charlotte Cunnyngham in Greene County, Tennessee, a short time after the Turnleys, Grahams and Cunnynghams had removed from the same neighborhood in Virginia to the French Broad Country, now in Tennessee The marriage took place according to the family records, March 3, 1791. The license was procured as was then the custom some weeks earlier as George Turnley had to ride thirty-five miles to the County Seat to obtain it, then a considerable journey, taking into account the condition of the roads, etc.

Charlotte Cunnyngham was the daughter of James and Arabella Cunnyngham natives of Ireland who had emigrated to America some years before with a family of four children, William H. Cunnyngham, James Cunnyngham, Second, George Cunnyngham and Arabella Cunnyngham. A fifth child, Charlotte Cunnyngham, was born shortly after their arrival in Virginia, April 13, 1770, and later their fourth son and sixth child, Jesse Cunnyngham was born.

James Cunnyngham died in Virginia about 1783, leaving a widow and the six children, namely:

William H. Cunnyngham.
James Cunnyngham, Second.
George Cunnyngham.
Arabella Cunnyngham.
Charlotte Cunnyngham.
Jesse Cunnyngham.

The widow Cunnyngham and her children followed the Turnleys to Tennessee and there George Turnley and Charlotte Cunnynham were married March 3, 1791.
Arabella Cunnynham married John Winton.
George Cunnyngham was killed by Indians in 1792.
William H. Cunnyngham married possibly Mary———— as a letter is preserved with her signature, M. Cunnyngham. They had a son, Jesse Cunnyngham, who married Miss Etter, daughter of George Etter, an emigrant from Germany. Jesse Cunnyngham became a Methodist minister of note and named his son William Etter George Cunnyngham who became in his turn a famous Methodist minister and missionary to China. He married a Miss Litchfield, of Virginia, who accompanied him to China, they had a son, Victor Cunnyngham. William Etter George Cunnyngham returned from China and died in Nashville in 1900.

Charlotte Cunnynham, who married George Turnley was the mother of fourteen children. She was small of stature and possessed great endurance. She had dark hair and black eyes and a dark complexion. It is said that when her first child was very small she, though suffering with the sorrow of her brother George Cunnynham's massacre at the hands of the Indians, urged her husband to undertake a journey to the Indian Council. She died in 18— and was sincerely mourned by her large family.

George Cunnynham was killed by the Indians in 1792 following other outrages, and Governor William Blount (See Blount Family) issued a call for a volunteer to go to the Council of the Cherokee Indians, then south of the Big River, the Tennessee, to take messages and try and conciliate them. Already two much messengers had been sent and had never returned, the presumption being that the Indians had destroyed them.

TURNLEY

With the consent of his wife, George Turnley rode to the Governor's headquarters and offered himself for the apparently almost certain sacrifice.

That he lived to return seems almost a miracle. His journal narrating the story has been preserved and it is an interesting historical document.

GEORGE TURNLEY'S DIARY

"The Cherokee Indians had assembled on the south side of the Tennessee River. They were holding a council there and their intentions were known to be hostile, and, helpless as the settlements were, there was much to fear from an open declaration of war. Many of the scattering Indians among us were friendly, but would be hostile as soon as the council declared open war. Several attempts to communicate with the warriors of this council had been made. Two separate couriers has been started with propositions of peace. They were never heard from, and the fact at last forced itself upon the reluctant people that the Indians would hear no terms, and it was suspected that they had murdered the messengers as a token of this determination.

"None but a pioneer in that dangerous time could have any conception of the panic that spread over the settlements.

"There was no possibility of retreat or succor. To fight to the last, and be massacred at the last, was the only prospect. There was little choice in the modes of death. The men did not appear to care for themselves, but for the women and children.

"I was not the oldest nor the wisest man in the settlements; still, as a woodsman of many years, and an experienced trader among the Indians, people looked to me for some expedient in the emergency. One night my father and my brother-in-law (William Cunnyngham) sat with me over our log fire till late. Our talk was of the impending danger and the best way to avert it. I did not give my opinion; but early next morning I rode over to the camp and proposed to start as messenger, myself, depending upon my knowledge of the Indian character, and the Indian tongue, to aid me in persuading them to accept the terms of friendship and concilation offered by the governor. The offer was accepted, of course. In this extremity any chance would have been seized upon by the terrified people.

"Equipped with blanket and gun, and a knapsack filled with dry venison and corn bread, I mounted my pony and set out alone for the Cherokee country. The distance was about two hundred miles. The route lay from my place to the Clinch River, thence to the Tennessee, twenty miles below the present site of Kingston, and thence across the Tennessee and into the Indian settlements. I reached the Tennessee River on the 24th of December. The weather was bitter cold, the river was thick with running ice, there was no human habitation near, no fords, and no possible way of crossing apparent but to swim. I concluded to pitch camp for the night. I built a fire, fed my horse upon green cane tops, which grew abundantly upon the river bank, fed myself from my knapsack of dried venison, and made a comfortable night of it, for the backwoodsman never troubles himself with what is ahead.

"In the morning we (my pony and I) breakfasted as we had supped. The ice was thicker than ever, coursing slowly and sullenly down the stream, and seeming to preclude all hope of crossing. Just as I had made up my mind to swim and was casting about for come contrivance for conveying my clothes over dry, two white men rode up like myself equipped for a journey. They had seen my camp fire from a distance, and had sought it, hoping to find company, and possibly, assistance, for they, too, wished to cross the river. We talked the chances over; they could not swim, and would not attempt it.

"A happy thought at length suggested itself—we might make a raft. Here our hatchets were called into service, and by the next day we had constructed a raft strong enough to carry all our luggage and the two men, but it would not carry a third man.

"The luggage, consisting of our saddles, knapsacks, and the greater part of my wearing clothes, were transferred to the raft. One of the new comers pushed the raft with a pole, working and cutting a way through the thick ice, while the other held their two horses, which swam by the side. The raft was carried a great way down— a full mile and ahalf—but finally reached the opposite bank in safety. Of course it would have been impossible to return the raft for me, and I had made up my mind to send all my traps and belongings on the raft, excepting my underclothing, and then swim the river by the side of my trusty little horse. The two men most strenuously objected to my attempting such a hazardous venture, but they finally reluctantly assented, when I assured them I knew better than they did what my horse and I could do. Transferring all my traps to the raft, excepting my undershirt and drawers, the men went on board, and while one of them, with my assistance, pushed the raft from the land out into the current, the other man held the bridle reins of the two horses, while I, with a bundle of brush switches, made the two horses plunge into the icy flowing river and they were soon out in the current going down stream, of course, but also making some headway across the river.

"I waited by my camp-fire till I saw the raft had reached the other shore, and till I saw the benumbed men start a fire in the drift pile of dry wood we had seen on the opposite shore. I then plunged in with my horse. I swam on the lower side of the horse, with my left hand holding to his mane near his withers. My horse swam splendidly, and carried me along much faster than the raft had crossed over. On reaching the shore near where the fire was, the two men came to my assistance, and assisted me and my horse to dry land. There was a roaring fire of dead, dry trees and brush, and the men were faithful in their attentions to myself and my horse.

"We spent the night there by our cheerful fireside, and the following morning, after breakfast, we separated, each to pursue his own course through the wilderness. Only yesterday unknown to each other, through the labors and dangers of the day and night, companions and brothers; and today again strangers for ever.

"I took my way to the Cherokee village, yet three days distant, alone. On my arrival I delivered my message and dispatches, but was not admitted to the council. An interpreter received my communications, and I was led at once to an Indian hut, and placed under guard of three strong warriors—later under the care of some squaws.

"They pretended they could not understand a word I said, although I spoke pretty good Cherokee. I was well acquainted with Indian ways, and from the manner of the guards and of the few squaws that came about my place of confinement, I understood that there was an excitement in the council.

"At night I was placed under charge of a couple of old squaws, doubtless as a temptation to escape. Three days passed; the suspense was intolerable, for the delay was unquestionable evidence of their hostile intent, and my poor little life was of very slight importance to them, whatever it might be to me. My tact, skill and power of persuasion were of no avail, since they refused to hear me. I made up my mind for the worst, when, at the end of three days, I saw two warriors coming to my hut. They looked sullen and angry, while in their laconic way they told me, in Cherokee, their Chief wished to see me and they had come to conduct me to him. I believe the certainty of being conducted to the stake would not so have appalled me. There was something in the dim uncertainty more terrible to a brave man than actual and inevitable death.

"I walked to the council lodge with my attendants, two behind and two before, while one walked by my side. The Chief received me with the impassive gravity peculiar to the Cherokee tribe.

" 'Pale face,' he said in pretty good English, 'you want peace; your Great Chief promises many things, but we are afraid he will not do what he promises. We want peace, too, but when we would have peace, the white man will have war; he shoots our game, though he promises that he will not; go home and tell the white Chief that we will not kill his squaws, nor his little ones, but his warriors must keep away from our hunting grounds. The red man is angry, and will kill you if he finds you on our grounds. We will send a warrior with you to take you safe through to the Big River.' (The Tennessee River.)

"With all my knowledge of Indian character, I could not tell whether this was friendly or hostile. The words were fair enough, but the manner was far from reassuring, and did not become more so in the appearance of the warrior who was to be my guide.

"I firmly believed, on quitting the lodge, that I had been destined by the council to death, and that my guide was to be my murderer; still, even that was better than the stake, and it left me a chance of escape. The Chief also gave me a paper to deliver to my Chief, the Governor.

"One Indian was not a match for me then, and I could have held a pretty fair hand with two or three. The Tennessee River was then considered the boundary of the Cherokee country. It was a three days' ride, as I had come; the guide, however, took a shorter trail, and we reached in less than two. I never for a moment believed in the sincerity of the Indian Chief, and the watch that I kept up throughout the journey to the Big River is painful to think of. Not a motion or glance of the Indian escaped me. The last night we encamped on the bank of the river, and I felt this to be the crisis. Here it was my guide must leave me or execute his designs, whatever they might be, but it is always dangerous to manifest distrust to an Indian.

"After our supper, we lay down, wrapped in our blankets, to sleep, but I did not sleep, though I feigned it. I counted the breathing of the Indian through the long night, believing that at any moment he might make a spring for my life, and I was ready for him. Finally, at daybreak, the leaves rustled, the Indian moved, rose, saddled his horse, and prepared for his journey back. He then came to where I lay. After satisfying himself I was asleep, he softly pulled the blanket from over me. On his approach I stole a glance, enough to assure me he had no weapon in his hand. I lay perfectly still while he disengaged the blanket and walked away with it.

"He mounted his pony and was gone. This proved that his intentions were not to murder me. You may ask why did I not rise up and defend myself at his first approach? I could have done so; my gun was ready and under my head, but there was just one chance among many that the Indian did not seek my life. To defend myself by violence was to make him my mortal foe if I should fail to kill him, and in any case to make certain the war which we were so anxious to avert. So I deemed it best to wait and commit no hostile act, except in defense of my life. My policy proved to be the correct one.

"I was left alone with my good pony to pursue my way to the settlements. This time I kept the south bank of the river till I reached a good ford that I knew of. My friends at home had long given me up to the unknown fate of my predecessors, and my return was a surprise scarcely short of a miracle.

"This trip was the means of effecting a treaty with the Cherokee tribe, which secured peace for many years, and, in fact, a permanent peace for that section ever after with all the Cherokee tribe.

"I always regarded the Cherokee Indians as among the noblest of the Indians of this continent."

Signed in diary, GEORGE TURNLEY

George Turnley died September 1848.

George Turnley and Charlotte Cunnyngham Turnley had fourteen chldren:

(1) John Cunnyngham Turnley.
(2) Mary Turnley.
(3) Elizabeth Jane Turnley.
(4) James Alexander Turnley.
(5) Polly Turnley,
(6) William Henderson Turnley.
(7) A child that died in infancy.
(8) Rachel Turnley.
(9) Hugh Lorenzo Turnley.
(10) Matthew Jacob Turnley.
(11) George Washington Turnley.
(12) Greenberry Madison Turnley.
(13) Andrew Jackson Turnley.
(14) Julia Ann Turnley.

(1) John Cunnyngham Turnley, son of George Turnley and Charlotte Cunnyngham Turnley was born February 27, 1792. His birth just preceded the massacre by the Indians of his uncle, George Cunnyngham.

In 1812, being but twenty years of age, when war with Great Britain was declared, he walked to Nashville, a distance of one hundred miles, volunteered in the United States Infantry and was mustered into Captain John Kennedy's Company, which was afterwards attached to the First Regiment of Tennessee Volunteers.

October 9, 1917, he married Mahala Taylor, a daughter of Colonel Parmenas Taylor, who was among the first settlers of East Tennessee. Mahala Taylor Turnley died in 1844 and in 1855

NOTABLE SOUTHERN FAMILIES

John Cunnyngham Turnley married his second wife, Mrs. Dorcas Hayes, widow of James Hayes, but by his second wife he had no children.

John C. Turnley espoused the cause of the South in the conflict of 1861, but was too old for active service.

The children of John Cunnyngham Turnley and Mahala Taylor Turnley were:

Amanda Malvina Turnley, born August 3, 1818, married James Washington Mahoney and had nine children, and married secondly ————Mitchell, and had one child. Oscar Livingston Mahoney (who married Virginia Rosson and had no children); Caroline Elizabeth Mahoney (who married William Hubbard and had seven sons, who died young, Amanda Wilson, married George McDonald, James Brooks Wilson, married and had several sons, Oscar Mahoney Wilson, and David Martin Wilson married and had several sons); John Cunnyngham Mahoney, died unmarried; Parmenas Taylor Mahoney, died unmarried; Augustus Harris Mahoney died young; Amanda Malvina Mahoney; Mary Augusta Mahoney, died young, Cinderella Elvira Mahoney (who married Gibson E. Blackburn, of Little Rock and had three children, two daughters and a son. The son and one daughter married, the other daughter entered a convent); Amanda Taylor Mahoney-Mitchell's tenth child and first by her second husband was Emma Mahala Mitchell.

Caroline Matilda Turnley, daughter of John Cunnyngham Turnley and Mahala Taylor Turnley died young.

Parmenas Taylor Turnley, son of John Cunnyngham Turnley and Mahala Taylor Turnley became one of the most distinguished of the name. He entered West Point and graduated in the class of 1846. He was ordered at once to report to General Zachary Taylor on the Rio Grande. Colonel Parmenas Taylor Turnley after long and faithful service in the Mexican War and in the Army after the close of the war was retired from active service. He married Mary R. Rutter, of Chicago, and had five children: Emma G. Turnley (who married Milton C. Lightner and had Milton Turnley Lightner who married Josephine Prall and has nc children); Ernest Seymore Turnley, died young; and Ethel Turnley (who married her cousin, George R. Nichols, Jr, and has two children; Ernest Turnley Nichols and Mary Ethel Nichols).

To the patient investigation of the late Colonel Parmenas Taylor Turnley, the collection of the Turnley data is due, as this record was much of it secured from his histories of the family. Colonel Turnley died in 1914 the oldest veteran of the Mexican War and the oldest graduate of West Point, and lamented by all who knew him.

TURNLEY

Elvira Ann Turnley, daughter of John Cunnyngham Turnley and Mahala Taylor Turnley married Martin Carpenter and had one child, Alice Mahala Carpenter.

Elizabeth Charlotte Turnley, daughter of John Cunnyngham Turnley and Mahala Taylor Turnley married Jesse R. Evans and had five children: Mahala Caroline Evans (who married Dr. George W. Monroe and had no children); Elvira Miranda Evans, died young; Lilbourne George Evans, died young; Mary Evans (who married George R. Nichols and had three children, Ernestine Nichols, Edith Grace Nichols and George R. Nichols, Jr., who married his cousin Ethel Turnley); and Elizabeth Evans (who married John S. Hoge and had one son, Frank Evans Hoge).

Lilbourne G. Turnley, son of John Cunnyngham Turnley and Mahala Taylor Turnley married Blendina Rumsey and had no children.

Mary Jane Turnley, daughter of John Cunnyngham Turnley and Mahala Taylor Turnley married George R. Moore and had six children, a son and a daughter who died in infancy; Lilbourne G. Moore; Mary L. Moore (who married Shelby McCall); Ida G. Moore (who married first Harry P. Murray and married secondly, Henry C. Riggs, but had no children).

Miranda Elmira Turnley, daughter of John Cunnyngham Turnley and Mahala Turnley died young.

Cinderella Livingston Turnley, daughter of John Cunnyngham Turnley and Mahala Taylor Turnley is living at the late home of her brother, Colonel Parmenas Taylor Turnley at an advanced age. She never married.

(2) Mary Turnley, second child of George Turnley and Charlotte Cunnyngham Turnley died young.

(3) Elizabeth Jane Turnley, third child of George Turnley and Charlotte Cunnyngham Turnley was born April 17, 1794. She died unmarried.

(4) James Alexander Turnley, fourth child of George Turnley and Charlotte Cunnyngham Turnley was born October 25, 1795. He served in the Creek War when but seventeen years of age and was in the Battle of the Horse Shoe. He married Mary Bates, and married for his second wife, Atlanta E. Witcher, by whom he had no children. His ten children by his first wife were: Hugh Lawson White Turnley, died young; Caroline Margaret Turnley (who married George Blackwell); Prior Lee Turnley (who married Mrs. Eliza Lamkin and had four children, only one of whom, a son, reached maturity); James Alexander Turnley, Second, died unmarrie; Julia Ann Burlington Turnley (who married A. J. Powell and had five children: Mollie Powell, Ida Powell, Julia Powell, James Powell,

and Henry Wise Powell); William Henderson Turnley, died young; Mary Bates Turnley (who married E. H. McCall and had three children, William Turnley McCall, Mary Eureka McCall married W. H. Callier and Elijah Lee McCall married Sallie Auxford); Permillia Missouri Turnley (who married her sister Julia's widower, A. J. Powell); Martha Jane Turnley (who married James H. Pittman and had five children, Henry E. Pittman, Gertrude Myra Pittman married Thomas J. Mimms and had six children, Lucile Martha Mimms,, John Henry Mimms, Minnie Lee Mimms, Myra Gertrude Mimms, Grace Marie Mimms, and Bernice Bates Mimms, Freddie R. Pittman, died young, Claudia Bates Pittman, (who married R. C. Brawner and had two children, Claudia Elizabeth Brawner and Mattie Louise Brawner,) and Earl Turnley Pittman; and Laura Elvira Turnley, who died young.

(5) Polly Turnley, the fifth child of George Turnley and Charlotte Cunnyngham Turnley was born December 19, 1797. She married Richard Luttrell (See Luttrell Family). She had seven children:

William Cunnyngham Luttrell married Mary Snow and had Dudley Richard Luttrell (who married Ella Hicks and had five children, among them Maude Luttrell, C. E. Luttrell and Ruth Luttrell who married Sandipher E. Jones); Bessie Luttrell, died young; Annie Priscilla Luttrell, (who married Edward S. Farmer and had five children); Lucinda Snow Luttrell; George William Luttrell married ——————Anderson, Cordelia Caroline Luttrell married George W. Brock, Robert McMillan Luttrell married Dollie Dodd and left one daughter, Katie Garland Luttrell married E. F. Cawthon.

Louisa Jane Luttrell married William Wilson Blaine and had eleven children: James Wilson Blaine, John Howard Blaine, Robert Alexander Blaine, Richard Luttrell Blaine, William Henry Clay Blaine, Russell Franklin Blaine, Mary Elizabeth Blaine, Martha Paralee Blaine, Frances Cordelia Blaine, Florence May Blaine, and Vivienne Sallie Blaine.

John Haynie Luttrell was born May 2, 1821. He married Susan Brock. They had twelve children: William Haynie Luttrell, Martha Jane Luttrell, Sarah Cordelia Luttrell, Margaret Joannah Luttrell, Lilbourne Patty Luttrell, Polly Ann Luttrell, Frances Elizabeth Luttrel, John Wilkerson Luttrell, Harvey Elmore Luttrell, George Washington Luttrell, Louisa Matilda Luttrell, and Susan Elnora Luttrell.

Harvey Wilkerson Luttrell served in the Confederate Army. He married Susan Frances Elston and married secondly, Mrs. Martha E. Doyle by whom he had no children. His eleven children by his first wife were: Corrie Luttrell (who married Charles L. Sowell and had no children), Oscar Fowler Luttrell (who married Mollie Magill Oden and has Oden Luttrell, Oscar Forney Luttrell, and Frank Alexander Luttrell); Elston Luttrell (who married Lucy Barber and had Randolph Luttrell, Corrie Luttrell, Annie Laurie Luttrell, Harvey Luttrell and Alton Luttrell); Chester McAuley Luttrell (who married Gussie Harwell and had Juliet Luttrell, Katie May Luttrell, Elizabeth Lynn Luttrell, and Ethel Luttrell); Bruce Luttrell (who married Lena Crampton and had Sue Elston Luttrell, Ralphine Luttrell, Rush Luttrell, Lucy Grace Luttrell, and Marcie Luttrell); Rush Luttrell and Marcy Luttrell, who died unmarried.

Charlotte Elizabeth Luttrell died unmarried.

Elbert Axley Luttrell married but had no children.

Cordelia Matilda Luttrell married George Washington Crumliss. They had nine children: Vivian, Walter DeWitt Crumbliss (who married Rosanna Weatherford and had eight sons); James Richard Crumbliss, died young; Louisa Magnolia Crumbliss (who married Charles L. Leader and had two children); Hugh Marcus Crumbliss, Oscar Leonidas Crumbliss, (who married Alice May Vandoren and had eight children); Elphalet Fortunatus Crumbliss (who married and had children); Ida Lavade Crumbliss (who married George Wunderlich); Olga Eugenia Crumbliss, died young, and Oliver Martaugh Crumbliss.

(6) William Henderson Turnley, sixth child of George Turnley and Charlotte Cunnyngham Turnley was born January 8, 1800. He became a Methodist minister. He married Sophia Henree and had by her one child, Laura S. Turnley and married for his second wife Martha McCoy by whom he had eight children:

Laura S. Turnley, daughter of William Henderson Turnley by his first wife, Sophia Henree Turnley married Samuel Kibbe and had four children: William Kibbe, Amos Kibbe, Harriett Kibbe, married L. S. Lake, Irene Cynthia Kibbe (also married L. S. Lake, presumably her sister Harriett's widower).

Mary Eliza Turnley, first child of William Henderson Turnley by his second wife, Martha McCoy Turnley married John E. Morris and had five children: William Levy Morris (who married Lelia Sarah Parker and had Helen Corinne T. Morris, John Clyde Morris, Wilheminia Morris, and married for his second wife, Annie McLendon and had Lena Carolyn Morris and Lucile Morris); Rosa Lena Morris (who married Robert Lafayette Reinhart and had Elsie Mary Reinhart, Fred Ray Reinhart, Lucile Reinhart, Robert Morris Reinhart and Elizabeth Reinhart); Lucile Seale Morris (who married William Kidd Duncan and had three children: Ben Morris Duncan, Alma Donald Duncan, William Kidd Duncan, Second; Laura Corinne Morris (who married Ernest Noble Faulk and had a daughter,

NOTABLE SOUTHERN FAMILIES

Mary Faulk); and John Ernest Morris, an officer in the United States Army.

Joseph Walton Turnley, second child of William Henderson Turnley by his second wife, Martha McCoy Turnley died unmarried.

George Alexander Turnley, third child of William Henderson Turnley by his second wife, Martha McCoy died young.

Margaret Frances Turnley, daughter of William Henderson Turnley and his second wife, Martha McCoy Turnley married Harcom Lincecum and had three children, Alma Rosalie Lincecum, Harmon Lincecum and Emily Lincecum.

William Henry Turnley, son of William Henderson Turnley by his second wife, Martha McCoy Turnley married Mary Whatley and and had nine children, William Virgil Turnley, Phineas Victor Turnley, Walter Carrol Turnley, Parmenas Taylor Turnley, Martha Elizabeth Turnley, Melissa Elizabeth Turnley, James Erwin Turnley, Boswell Pearce Turnley, Mary Ellen Turnley.

Alice Turnley, daughter of William Henderson Turnley and his second wife, Martha McCoy Turnley married Albert McCoy and had ten children, Glendora McCoy, James Walton McCoy, Mattie Lou McCoy, Richard Herbert McCoy, Ellen Ione McCoy, William Albert McCoy, Arthur DeWitt McCoy, Mary Frances McCoy, Maud Alice McCoy, Edith McCoy.

Lucy Ellen Turnley, daughter of William Henderson Turnley and his second wife, Martha McCoy Turnley married John Green Walker and had five children, Linus Hugh Walker, John Walton Walker, Moses Turnley Walker, Lucie Alice Walker, and Margaret Ellen Walker.

James McCoy Turnley, son of William Henderson Turnley and his second wife, Martha McCoy Turnley married Sarah A. Whatley and had seven children, Alice Irene Turnley, Martha Ellen Turnley, Joseph Wiley Turnley, George Henry Turnley, Jessie Inez Turnley, James Dickson Turnley, and Newton Calvert Turnley.

(7) The seventh child of George Turnley and Mary Handy Turnley died in infancy.

(8) Rachel Turnley the eighth child of George Turnley and Charlotte Cunnyngham Turnley died in infancy.

(9) Hugh Lorenzo Turnley the ninth child of George Turnley and Charlotte Cunnyngham Turnley was born March 29, 1804. He died young and unmarried.

JUDGE MATTHEW JACOB TURNLEY

(10) Matthew Jacob Turnley, the tenth child of George Turnley and Charlotte Cunnyngham Turnley, was born November 30, 1805.

TURNLEY

He moved to Alabama, became a distinguished lawyer and served the Government at the breaking out of war. Judge Turnley was United States District Attorney for the Northern District of Alabama under the administration of President Buchanan, and when the State of Alabama seceded he sent his resignation to President Buchanan and identified himself with the Southern cause.

After the war Judge Turnley served as Judge for many years in Alabama and had the great distinction of being the only Judge in Alabama whose opinion was never reversed by a higher court. As a great lawyer he was singularly free from the use of diatribes which would make the criminal whom he defended, appear a martyr to social forms or the victim of fanatical prejudices. His mind formed in a large mold, was content to tread the labyrinth of constitutional and common law and from its intricate mazes create a rational defense.

He died March 22, 1889.

He married May 30, 1839, Miriam Isbell, daughter of Benjamin Isbell, of Tennessee, (See Howard Family), and they took their wedding trip to their new home in Alabama on horse back. They had eight children, and in addition raised, though they did not formally adopt, three children of Judge Turnley's deceased sister, Julia Anderson Turnley.

Their children were Martha Julia Turnley, who married John McMillan Armstrong, See Armstrong, McMillan, Lyle and Calhoun Families, and had two children, Turnley F. Armstrong, died unmarried, and Zella Armstrong.

George Isbell Turnley, son of Judge Matthew J. Turnley, and Miriam Isbell Turnley, served in the Confederate Army. He married Willie Woodward and married for his second wife Emma Ross, but has no children.

Mary Ann Turnley, daughter of Judge Matthew J. Turnley and Miriam Isbell Turnley, married John Hughes Reynolds and had six children: Hughes Turnley Reynolds (who married Mary Taylor and has two children, John Hughes Reynolds, Second, and Margaretta Reynolds); William Barton Reynolds, died unmarried; Miriam Reynolds; May Reynolds (who married Raymond Gilmore Scott and had two children, Reynolds Gilmore Scott and May Scott); Ruby Reynolds (who married William F. Ogburn and has one child, Reynolds Ogburn); and John Hughes Reynolds, Junior, died in infancy.

James Benjamin Turnley, son of Judge Matthew J. Turnley, and Miriam Isbell Turnley, married Lula Phinizy, See Phinizy Family, and had five children: Miriam Louisa Turnley, John Phinizy Turnley, Janie B. Turnley (who married Charles Sedberry and left one child that died); James Marco Turnley (who married Nettie Brooks and has two daughters, Florence Turnley and Lula Phinizy Turnley); and

NOTABLE SOUTHERN FAMILIES

William Micou Turnley (who married Sarah Crowe and has one daughter, Lula).

William Franklin Pierce Turnley, son of Judge Matthew Jacob Turnley and Miriam Isbell Turnley, married and left one son, Thomas Turnley.

Thomas Howard Turnley, son of Judge Matthew Turnley and Miriam Isbell Turnley, died unmarried.

Frances A. Turnley, daughter of Judge Matthew J. Turnley and Miriam Isbell Turnley, died in infancy.

Eppie Reynolds Turnley, daughter of Judge Matthew J. Turnley and Miriam Isbell Turnley, married Nathan Calhoun Sayre and has no children.

(11) George Washington Turnley, the eleventh child of George Turnley and Charlotte Cunnyngham Turnley, was born July 7, 1808. He married Mrs. Emily Grant Doyle.

(12) Greenberry Madison Turnley, twelfth child of George Turnley and Charlotte Cunnyngham Turnley, was born May 9, 1910; died unmarried.

(13) Andrew Jackson Turnley, thirteenth child of George Turnley and Charlotte Cunnyngham Turnley, died unmarried.

(14) Julia Ann Charlotte Turnley, the fourteenth child of George and Charlotte Cunnyngham Turnley, was born January 11, 1817. She was the especial charge and interest of her brother, Judge Matthew Jacob Turnley and accompanied him to his new home in Alabama, while she was still a young girl. She there married David Anderson, a native of Scotland. She moved to Texas with her husband and there they both died, leaving four infant children, David Matthew Anderson, Frances Adelaide Anderson, Augustus Anderson and Julia Elizabeth Anderson. Judge Matthew J. Turnley took the long and hazardous trip to Texas and returned with the children, taking them into his own home, one of them, Augustus, had died before the journey began. David Matthew Anderson grew to manhood in his uncle's home, entered the Confederate Army and was mortally wounded at the Battle of Baker's Creek. He had not married.

Frances Adelaide Anderson married Judge S. P. Gaut and had four sons, David Gaut (who died unmarried); Joseph Perry Gaut, (who married Pauline Chambers and has one child, Pauline Gaut); William E. Gaut, (who married Mary Chambers, a sister of his brother's wife, and died leaving one child, Mary Louise Gaut); and Frank P. Gaut (who maried Mary Tillman and has one son, Tillman Gaut).

Julia Elizabeth Anderson married Joseph Callaway and had two children, Sue Lea Callaway and Joseph Jacques Callaway (who married Pauline Williamson and had three children, Elizabeth Callaway, Julia Anderson Callaway, and Pauline Callaway).

VAN DYKE

The Van Dyke family is one of the oldest and most prominent in Tennessee. The genealogy of the family is traced in unbroken line nearly three centuries to Jan Thomasse Van Dyck, II, (son of Thomasse Van Dyck I, of Amsterdam,) who with his two brothers, Hendrick Thomasse and Nicholas Thomasse, came to New Amsterdam in America in 1652. His wife, Tryntje (or Achias) and six children accompanied him, on the good ship Bonta Ke (Spotted Cow). They settled on Long Island. Their children were: Thomas Janse III, born 1646, Antje Janse, born 1642, Anjenietje born 1644, Carl born 1646, Achias born 1648, Jan born 1650, Hendrick born July 2, 1653, in New Amsterdam. In 1687 the three brothers took the oath of allegiance to their adopted country. Their descendants may be found in New York, New Jersey, Delaware, Pennsylvania and Tennessee, numbers of them having risen to prominence.

Thomas Janse Van Dyck III, oldest son of Jan Thomasse and Tryntje Van Dyck married first—Claessen, daughter of Claes Claesen, of Suit of Grarcsend. Their children were: John born about 1667, married Geesje Groot; Groot; Nicholas born August 11, 1670, married first Tryntje Reyneirs, second Fransyntje Hendrickse. Thomas Johnse married second in 1671, Enorretje (Marie) Andrisen. Their children were: Anjeltie born 1672, married Joris Storm; Andrisen baptised August 11, 1675; married Geesje; Abraham born 1680; married Elizabeth Huyck; Isaac baptized September 11, 1681; married Barbara Reyniers. Andriers and Nicholas settled in New Castle, Delaware, previous to 1725.

Claes or Nicholas Thomasse Van Dyck, son of Thomas Janse Van Dyck, born August 11, 1670, married first April 20, 1689, Tryntje Reyniers in Flatbush, Long Island. They had one child, Tryntje, baptised August 24, 1690, in Brooklyn. After her death, he married Fransyntje (Frances) Hendrickse of Flatbush, June 4, 1692. They resided in Brooklyn, April 6, 1724. He sold his farm of 200 acres and removed to Delaware. Their children were: Thomas, baptised April 11, 1693; Geesje born October 4, 1694, baptised November 16, 1694, in Brooklyn; Maria born July 3, 1696; Heuricus died before 1708; Johanna born March 22, 1700; Abraham born January 22, 1702; Antje born July 5, 1704; Nicholas born January 6, 1706, Hendrick born February 10, 1708; baptised April 5, 1708, in Brooklyn, married Marjrietje Teohune and settled in New Jersey on the Loritan River, died before November, 1752; Marjrietje, born January 11, 1711; Daniel, born November 3, 1713. Nicholas Van Dyck died October 27, 1729. Frances Van Dyck, his wife, departed this life ye 25 day of January in the year of our Lord God 1749.

Nicholas Van Dyck, son of the foregoing, was born January 6, 1706, in Brooklyn. He married Rachel Atlee in New Castle, Delaware, May 1, 1724. Their children were John Thomasse, born April 29, 1737; Nicholas, born September 25, 1738; Abraham, born November 6, 1740; Mary, born September 19, 1745; Rachel, born May 25, 1752, died February 15, 1795. Nicholas Van Dyck, Senior, departed this life the 20th day of February in the year of our Lord, 1755.

Nicholas Van Dyck, second son of Nicholas and Rachel Van Dyck, was prominent in the history of his state during the Revolution. He was a member of the Boston Relief Committee in 1774. He was present at the meeting of the Delaware Convention in 1776. He was a field officer in the Delaware militia, rose to the rank of Major in 1799. He was a member of the assembly of Delaware and was Speaker of the House in 1779. He was Governor of Delaware in 1781-3-4-. He married twice. His first wife was Elizabeth Nixon, daughter of Thomas Nixon, of Passy, Dover, Delaware. They had three children: Rachel, born June 28, 1767, died July following; Anne, born August 9, 1768; Nicholas, December 20, 1769; Elizabeth Nixon Van Dyke died January, 1700; Nicholas Van Dyke then married Charlotte Stanley, January 2, 1774. Their children were Susanna, Charelicus, born December 27, 1775; Henry Hendrickson, born January 2, 1777; Mary, born February 6, 1779; Elizabeth Allen, born February 2, 1781; John, born December 22, 1782; Abraham, born January 6, 1784. Governor Nicholas Van Dyke died February 19, 1789, aged fifty years. Abraham Van Dyke, son of Nicholas and Rachel Van Dyke, born November 6, 1730, married Elizabeth. Their children were: Henry; Mary, born December 10, 1774; Rachel, born December 12, 1776, died in 1777; Abraham Van Dyke died March 8, 1777, his wife, died in 1777.

John Thomasse Van Dyck, oldest child of of Nicholas and Rachel Atlee Van Dyke, was born April 29, 1737, in New Castle, Delaware. In 1775, he married Mrs. Letitia Nixon Rogerson, the daughter of Thomas Nixon, of Passy, near Dover. She was a sister of Elizabeth Nixon, who married Nicholas Van Dyke. Thomas Nixon had seven children: Nicholas, Charles, Thomas and Letitia, Elizabeth, Rachel and Anne. Thomas Nixon and his sons were patriots during the Revolution and fought for the independence of their country. Letitia Nixon was married three times. Her first husband was John Rogerson, a planter in the island of Jamaica in the West Indies, by whom

VAN DYKE

she had one daughter, Fedilia, who married William Montgomery, a lawyer in the city of Lancaster, Pennsylvania. Her second husband was John Van Dyke, by whom she had one son, Thomas John Van Dyke, father of Chancellor Thomas Nixon Van Dyke, of Tennessee. John Van Dyke resided in Talbot County, Maryland, for a few years after he married Mrs. Letitia Rogerson. Their son was born at her father's home in Dover in 1777. In 1779, May 13, recorded in the Talbot County Record that John Van Dyke purchased a schooner, Polly, from Alex Gordon. March 7, 1782, he bought three and one-quarter acres of land from John Dickenson. After his death in 1785, his widow moved to Lancaster, Pennsylvania, to make her home with her daughter. There she married Mr. John Coakley, by whom she had one daughter, Letitia Nixon Coakley, who married Richard Smith of Huntingdon, Pennsylvania. Mrs. Letitia Coakley lived in Lancaster until her death in 1819. Here her son, Thomas VanDyke, received his early education. He was then sent to Baltimore, where he studied medicine with his uncle, Daniel Robinson. He obtained his diploma in 1791. The same year he was appointed an ensign in the infantry service of the United States and was soon promoted to a captaincy. In 1798, he was stationed at Belle Canton, near the junction of Tennessee and Little Tennessee Rivers, then in Roane County, Tennessee. Here he married Penelope Smith Campbell, the oldest daughter of Judge David Campbell and his wife, Elizabeth Outlaw, who were then living where Lenoir's Cotton Mill subsequently stood. The Honorable David Campbell was then Judge of the Superior Court of Tennessee, and was afterwards appointed Judge of United States Court for the District of Mississippi. In 1811, Thomas Van Dyke resigned his commission in the army and moved to Washington in Rhea County, where he engaged in the practice of medicine. When war with England was again declared in 1812, he was appointed Surgeon in the United States army and was engaged in two campaigns in the south under General Doughterty against the Indians in 1813 and 1814. December 27, 1814, Dr. Thomas Van Dyke died at Fort Claiborne, Alabama, while in the service of his country. His wife and family then went to live with her mother, Mrs. Campbell, in Washington, Tennessee, Judge Campbell having died a short time previously.

The children of Dr. Thomas Van Dyke and his wife, Penelope Campbell, were: Alexander Outlaw, born 1799; Jefferson Campbell, born January 16, 1801; Thomas Nixon, born January 16, 1803; Mary Hamilton, born 1805; Eliza Rhea, born 1807. Alexander Outlaw Van Dyke entered the United States Navy and died at sea off Carthagena, South America, while with Comodore Porter. He never married. Jefferson Campbell Van Dyke married Miss Eliza Cocke in Tuscaloosa, Alabama, in 1830. He died in 1861, leaving three daughters, who were: Sarah Gille Van Dyke, married Dr. Curry, of Alabama. Their children, a son, who resided in New Orleans, and Mrs. Tena Trippe, of Selma, Alabama; (b) Vandalia Van Dyke, who married Mr. Rhoda Horton, of Alabama, and after his death, she became the wife of Dr. Pegram, of Dayton, Alabama; (c) Caroline Van Dyke married Captain James Ford, of Bastrop, Louisiana; (3) Thomas Nixon Van Dyke married Eliza Ann Deaderick, the second daughter of Dr. William Henry Deaderick and Penelope Hamilton on May 23, 1833. Their children were: (a) Penelope Smith, who married Thomas A. Cleage; (b) William Deaderick married Anna Mary Deaderick; (c) Letitia Smith died aged twelve years; (d) Richard Smith Van Dyke, Lieutenant in Confederate Army, killed in battle near Darksville, Virginia, in 1864, unmarried; (e) John Montgomery Van Dyke, Captain in Confederate Army, killed in battle near Darksville, Virginia, in 1864, unmarried; (f) Frances Levinia Van Dyke never married; (g) Thomas Nixon Van Dyke, Junior, died in Confederate service; (h) Margaret Josephine Van Dyke married Hugh T. Inman, of Atlanta, Georgia; (j) Mary Hamilton Van Dyke married George M. Battey, of Rome, Georgia; (k) Robert Deaderick Van Dyke married Sue C. Gwaltney, of Rome, Georgia. Judge Thomas Nixon Van Dyke was educated in Pennsylvania. He studied law and was admitted to the bar in Huntingdon, appointed an ensign in the infantry Pennsylvania, in 1823. In the fall of 1828, he moved to Alabama, and settled at Tuscaloosa, where he continued his profession. In 1833 he returned to his native state, Tennessee, and settled at Athens, McMinn County. Obtaining a license to practice in all courts of the state, he at once entered on a long and useful career. In 1837, appointed director of a branch of the Bank of Tennessee, and was elected President of a branch of the Bank of Tennessee and was elected President of the Board. He was one of the originators of the Hiawassee Railroad. He was a director and president of the company. In 1854, he was elected Chancellor of the 12th Chancery Division of Tennessee (November 3), at that time comprising eighteen counties. In 1864, Judge Van Dyke was arrested by order of the military authorities of the United States Army and imprisoned as a hostage at Camp Chase, near Columbus, Ohio. His family had also been arrested and sent north of the Ohio River. When he was released, in 1865, he joined his wife at Mineral Point, Wisconsin. In 1866, they returned to Athens and Judge Van Dyke resumed his practice in Tennessee.

Mary Hamilton Van Dyke, born April 7, 1805, was educated at Nolichucky Academy, Jefferson County, Tennessee. With her mother, she moved to Alabama in 1819. After her mother's death, she went to live with her aunt, Mrs. Letitia Nixon Smith, at Huntingdon, Penn-

VAN DYKE

sylvania. There, in 1824, she married General William R. Smith. Later they moved to Mineral Point, Wisconsin. Their children were: Rudolph, Richard, Penelope, Letitia, John.

Eliza Rhea Van Dyke, born September 6, 1807, moved to Alabama with her mother. She married Mr. Scott, of Natchez, Mississippi. They had several children.

Among the living descendants of the Van Dyke family are: Mrs. Hugh T. Inman, Mrs. John Grant, Mrs. Richard Wilmer, Mr. William Grant, Mrs. Hugh Richardson, Mr. Hugh L. Richardson, Mr. Edward Inman, Mrs. George Battey, Mr. George Battey, Junior, Dr. Hugh Battey, Miss Marion Van Dyke, Mrs. George Bonney, Miss Adrenne Bonney, of Atlanta; Mr. R. D. Van Dyke, Mr. William Van Dyke, of Memphis; Mr. J. H. Smith, Mineral Point, Wisconsin; Mrs. Helen Van Dyke, Kentucky; Mr. Theodore Van Dyke, Philadelphia; Dr. Henry Van Dyke, New York; Dr. Paul Van Dyke, of New York; Miss Anna Van Dyke, Mr. T. Nixon Van Dyke, Miss Louise Van Dyke; Mr. T. N. Van Dyke, Mrs. M. B. Ochs, Mr. Van Dyke Ochs, Mr. Adolph Ochs II., Miss Margaret Ochs, Miss Cary Van Dyke, Mrs. Sue C. Johnson, Mrs. W. P. Flower, Jr., A. M. Johnson, Foster Johnson, of Chattanoga; Mrs. S. B. Allen and Miss Penelope Allen, Williamsburg, Va., Mrs. Frank C. Davis, Master John Davies, Miss Sue Davies, of Youngstown, Ohio; Mr. W. D. Cleage, Miss Elizabeth Cleage, Miss Carrie Cleage, of Memphis; Mrs. Thomas A. Cleage, St. Louis, Missouri; Mr. Deaderick Cleage, St. Louis, Missouri; Mr. Richard Cleage, Athens, Tennessee; Mrs. F. C. McCleary, Chicago; Miss Josephine McCleary, Chicago; Mrs. C. P. Dumas, Mobile; Mrs. E. E. Crum, Mobile.

Some of the families whose histories will be contained in
Notable Southern Families, Volume II, are

DONELSON	DAVIS
VANCE	BORDEN
ROBERTSON	HOUSTON
HEISKELL	WHITE
TAYLOR	SHELBY
JOHNSTON	LYON
CARTER	LEA

www.ingramcontent.com/pod-product-compliance
Lightning Source LLC
Chambersburg PA
CBHW031805220426
43662CB00007B/538